React JS

3 Books in 1 - "From Beginner to Pro – Crafting Cutting-Edge Front-End Applications"

Adrian Roberts

Table of Contents

BOOK 1 - React JS: "A Beginner's Guide to Mastering React JS for Front-End Development"

BOOK 2 - React JS: "A Middle-Level Guide to Integrating React JS with Modern Web Technologies"

BOOK 3 - React JS: "A Pro-Level Guide to Next-Gen Front-End Development with React JS"

Introduction

Overview of React JS and its significance in front-end development

React JS, since its introduction by Facebook in 2013, has swiftly become a dominant force in the world of front-end web development. Its prominence is largely due to its innovative approach to building user interfaces, using a component-based architecture that favors a declarative style of UI development. This method simplifies the developer's task and significantly enhances user experience.

Central to React JS's approach is the concept of the Virtual DOM. Traditional front-end frameworks modify the Document Object Model (DOM) directly, but React JS instead employs a lightweight virtual representation of the DOM in memory. When changes occur, React compares the virtual DOM with the actual DOM, updating only what's necessary. This process, known as selective rendering, greatly boosts application performance, a critical advantage for complex, data-heavy websites.

The library's design is built around modular and reusable components. Each component in React encapsulates its structure, logic, and style. This modular nature of components not only aids in keeping code clean and maintainable but fosters scalability in development processes. Components can be developed, tested, and deployed independently, enhancing collaboration among team members and streamlining the development cycle.

React JS's popularity is also bolstered by a robust ecosystem and a supportive community of developers. Being open-source, it has cultivated a dynamic community that contributes to its continuous improvement. The ecosystem is replete with tools and extensions like Redux for state management, React Router for navigation, and many others for various functionalities, empowering developers to craft rich, interactive web applications.

A standout feature of React is its declarative paradigm for UI updates. Developers describe the desired UI state and React efficiently renders the updates, abstracting away the direct DOM manipulations. This focus on the desired end state, rather than the process of achieving it, allows developers to concentrate on the core logic and state of the application, improving development efficiency.

The release of Hooks in React 16.8 was a notable enhancement, providing a more straightforward API for accessing React's features like state and lifecycle, previously confined to class components. Hooks have made these capabilities accessible in functional components, encouraging a more concise and readable codebase. This shift towards functional components aligns with the broader acceptance of functional programming within the JavaScript community, known for its elegance and robustness.

React's flexibility in integration with various backend technologies adds to its appeal. It can be smoothly incorporated with numerous backend frameworks, such as

Node.js, Django, or Ruby on Rails, making it a versatile tool for full-stack development. The principles and patterns of React have also been extended to mobile app development through React Native, further demonstrating its versatility.

From a business standpoint, React JS provides significant advantages. Its efficient development approach, combined with superior application performance, leads to cost-effectiveness and quicker market entry. The library's widespread use has also created a large pool of skilled developers, easing the hiring process for companies. Supported by Facebook's continued investment, React's stability makes it a reliable choice for long-term projects.

In sum, React JS's impact on front-end development is comprehensive. Its methods for efficient DOM handling, its component-based structure, and its declarative approach to UI construction have set new benchmarks in the field. With a rich ecosystem, ongoing community support, and a trajectory of constant innovation, React JS not only influences current technological practices but is well-positioned to shape the future landscape of front-end web development.

Target audience and what to expect from the book

"React JS: A Beginner's Guide to Mastering React JS for Front-End Development" is a meticulously crafted resource, tailored to guide a diverse range of readers through the intricacies of React JS. This section provides an insight into the intended audience of the book and a preview of the enriching experience that awaits them within its pages.

Intended Readership

This book is an essential companion for a variety of learners embarking on their journey into front-end development, particularly with a focus on React JS:

Budding Front-End Developers: Individuals new to the field of front-end development will find this book an essential starting point, offering a gentle introduction to React JS without assuming prior knowledge.

Seasoned Developers Exploring React: For developers proficient in other technologies but new to React, this book acts as a bridge, transferring their existing skills to the React framework.

Computer Science and Related Majors: Students pursuing academic courses in computer science or similar disciplines will find the book a practical supplement to their theoretical studies, offering insights into real-world web development.

Autodidacts in Programming: Those teaching themselves programming will appreciate the structured approach of the book, guiding them methodically through the complexities of React JS.

UI/UX Designers Seeking Technical Insight: Designers aiming to understand the technical execution of their designs will benefit from the book's clear explanations of how UI elements are brought to life in code.

Book Expectations

The book is designed to be more than a typical instructional text; it's a journey through React JS that promises a rich learning experience:

Solid Foundation: Starting with React JS basics, the book ensures readers build a strong understanding of core concepts like JSX, components, state, and props.

Experiential Learning: Theoretical knowledge is reinforced with practical examples and exercises, enabling readers to apply what they learn in real-world contexts.

Development of Complex Applications: Progressing to more advanced topics, the book guides readers through building sophisticated applications, mirroring real-life development challenges.

Adherence to Best Practices: Readers learn industry-standard practices and design patterns essential for crafting efficient, scalable code.

Comprehensive Tooling Overview: An exploration of the React ecosystem's tools and libraries, such as Redux and React Router, equips readers with the knowledge needed in modern web development.

Up-to-Date with Latest Features: Covering the latest in React, including Hooks and the Context API, the book ensures readers are abreast with current developments.

Focus on Performance: Strategies for optimizing React application performance are a key part of the book, preparing readers to build high-performing web applications.

Insights into the Industry: The book offers a glimpse into best practices in the industry and the role of React JS in the job market, helping readers understand current professional trends.

Guidance for Continued Learning: Recognizing the continuous nature of learning, the book concludes with resources for further exploration in React and front-end development.

Community Engagement: Readers are encouraged to connect with the wider React community, fostering collaborative learning and professional networking.

In essence, this book is a comprehensive, hands-on guide that not only imparts knowledge but also aims to inspire and empower readers to excel in the dynamic realm of front-end development using React JS. It promises a complete, engaging learning experience, preparing readers to confidently navigate and succeed in the world of React JS development.

How to use this book effectively

"React JS: A Beginner's Guide to Mastering React JS for Front-End Development" serves as more than just an instructional resource; it is a comprehensive guide designed to facilitate a deep understanding of React JS. To maximize the benefits of this book, readers should adopt a strategic approach to their learning, ensuring an enriching and thorough educational experience.

1. Follow the Structured Path

This book is meticulously organized to progress from basic concepts to more advanced topics. Readers need to adhere to the order of the chapters, as each one builds upon the knowledge established previously. Skipping sections may lead to incomplete understanding, particularly for newcomers to React or programming.

2. Actively Engage with Code Examples

Each theoretical discussion is complemented by practical code examples and exercises. It's crucial to not just read but actively engage with these codes. Typing out and experimenting with the code in a live coding environment reinforces the concepts and nuances of React JS.

3. Complete the Chapter Exercises

Each chapter concludes with exercises, carefully crafted to reinforce and apply the concepts learned. Tackling these exercises independently before checking solutions is an excellent way to solidify understanding and identify areas that may need further study.

4. Enhance with Online Resources

While the book is thorough, additional online resources such as React documentation and community forums can enrich learning. Participation in the React community through various forums and social media platforms can offer valuable insights and keep readers abreast of the latest trends.

5. Embrace Project-Based Learning

Applying learned concepts to personal projects is a key step in the learning process. These projects can range from simple to complex, but the act of building something tangible enhances understanding and provides insight into practical applications.

6. Reflect on Your Learning

Regular reflection on the learned material is important. Summarizing or explaining the concepts to others can help in deeper understanding and retention. This reflective process is integral to internalizing the material.

7. Regularly Revisit Previous Topics

Given React's dynamic nature, regular practice and revisiting past topics are essential. Re-examining previous chapters helps reinforce the foundational principles, ensuring a strong base for advanced learning.

8. Participate in Learning Communities

Joining study groups or online communities can significantly enhance the learning experience. Engaging in discussions, posing questions, and participating in collaborative learning can provide fresh perspectives and a deeper grasp of complex topics.

9. Implement Best Practices

As the book covers best practices in React development, incorporating these into coding exercises and projects is recommended. Practicing these standards from the outset lays a solid foundation for professional growth.

10. Maintain Curiosity and Exploration

The realm of front-end development, especially React, is constantly evolving. Maintaining an exploratory mindset and experimenting with new features or participating in open-source projects keeps skills up-to-date and sharp.

11. Visualize Real-World Implementation

Understanding how the concepts fit into real-world applications is crucial. Envisioning the practical use of React in diverse scenarios, like web and mobile applications or large-scale projects, provides clarity on its effective utilization in professional settings.

12. Gear Up for Professional Opportunities

For those aiming to enter the professional world, this book is an excellent preparation tool. The exercises and projects can be leveraged to enhance portfolios, showcasing capabilities to potential employers.

In essence, to fully benefit from "React JS: A Beginner's Guide to Mastering React JS for Front-End Development," a reader must engage deeply, practice consistently, and remain open to exploration and discovery. This approach not only ensures a thorough understanding of the book's content but also lays a robust foundation for a career in React JS and front-end development.

Chapter One

Getting Started with React JS

Introduction to React JS and its core principles

Since its debut in 2013 by Facebook, React JS has swiftly become a pivotal technology in front-end web development. This JavaScript library is uniquely tailored for crafting user interfaces, especially for single-page applications. React's guiding principles and architecture have substantially altered the landscape of front-end development, offering developers a combination of efficiency, reusability, and an enhanced user experience.

Emphasis on a Declarative Approach

React stands out for its declarative programming model, a departure from the traditional imperative approach. Instead of specifying how to achieve a particular result step by step, developers using React describe the desired state of the UI, and the library manages the DOM updates. This shift simplifies the development process, focusing on the design of the UI state rather than detailed DOM manipulation, making the code more predictable and easier to debug.

Component-Based Structure

Central to React's philosophy is its component-based architecture. A React component is an encapsulated unit that manages its state and rendering, responsible for a segment of the UI. These components are the fundamental building blocks of a React application, and their reusability across different parts of an application or even across projects enhances development efficiency. This modular approach not only aids in managing code but also scales well for larger applications, as components can be individually developed and maintained.

Innovations with Virtual DOM

React's introduction of the Virtual DOM concept marks a significant innovation. The Virtual DOM is a lightweight replica of the actual DOM, and React updates this abstraction first when there are changes in the application's state. Following this, React executes a reconciliation process to update the actual DOM efficiently. This method minimizes direct DOM interactions, which are expensive in terms of performance, resulting in quicker updates.

Unidirectional Data Flow Principle

React adheres to a unidirectional data flow model. Data in a React application moves in one direction: state is passed down as props to child components, and actions are communicated upwards through callbacks. This unidirectional flow ensures more control over the application and simplifies debugging by making it easier to trace data changes and error sources.

Understanding State and Props

Two critical aspects of React are its state and props. The state represents variable data within a component, while props (short for properties) are used to pass data and event handlers to child components. Distinguishing between state and props is vital in React, as it clarifies data flow and component interaction.

Utilizing JSX

JSX, or JavaScript XML, is a syntax extension used in React to describe the UI. Though it resembles HTML, JSX is a syntactic sugar over `React.createElement` function calls, offering a more readable and expressive way to structure UI elements in the code. JSX allows developers to write HTML-style code directly within JavaScript files, seamlessly integrating UI templates with logic.

Component Lifecycle Methods

React components undergo several lifecycle stages, each with specific methods that are invoked at certain points during a component's life in the DOM. These methods provide opportunities to perform actions when a component is created, updated, or destroyed. Grasping these lifecycle methods is crucial for managing side effects, such as data fetching or DOM manipulation.

Introduction of Hooks

With React 16.8 came Hooks, enabling function components to access state and other React features traditionally limited to class components. Hooks offers a more direct way to work with React concepts like state, context, refs, and lifecycle, enabling the creation of more concise and expressive components.

Focus on Performance Optimization

React includes various features for optimizing application performance. Techniques like shouldComponentUpdate, and React.memo for minimizing unnecessary re-renders, and strategies like code-splitting and lazy loading help in reducing initial load times.

Robust Community and Ecosystem

An essential element of React's success is its active community and the extensive ecosystem surrounding it. This includes a range of tools, libraries, and extensions like Redux for state management, React Router for navigation, and development tools like Create React App and Next.js. The community's contributions enhance React's versatility and capabilities in modern web application development.

In summary, React JS has established itself as an essential library for developing user interfaces. Its principles, such as the declarative UI, component-based architecture, Virtual DOM, unidirectional data flow, and the use of JSX, create a solid foundation for building complex, high-performance web applications. Understanding these core concepts is vital for any developer seeking to harness React's capabilities in the realm of front-end development.

Setting up the development environment

Establishing a development environment tailored for React JS is a pivotal first step for any developer diving into this framework. This comprehensive guide outlines the essential components and actions needed to set up an efficient workspace for React JS development, ensuring both ease and productivity in the development process.

1. Installing Node.js and npm

Initiating the setup involves installing Node.js, a JavaScript runtime that enables JavaScript to be run outside of a browser. Node.js comes bundled with npm (Node Package Manager), a crucial tool for managing JavaScript packages. npm acts as a portal to a vast repository of libraries and tools vital for React development.

To install Node.js and npm, visit the Node.js official website, download, and run the installer for your operating system. After installation, you can confirm its success by running `**node −v**` and `**npm −v**` in the command line, which should return the versions installed.

2. Selecting a Suitable Code Editor

The choice of code editor is significant and impacts the ease of coding. Popular editors among React developers include Visual Studio Code (VS Code), Sublime Text, and Atom. These editors offer features like syntax highlighting, intelligent code completion, and built-in terminals.

VS Code is particularly popular in the React community due to its vast array of extensions tailored for React development, including ESLint for code linting, Prettier for formatting, and various React-specific tools for coding efficiency.

3. Initiating a React Project

After setting up Node.js and selecting a code editor, the next step is initiating a new React project. Create React App (CRA) is a widely used tool for this purpose, streamlining the creation of a new React application. To create a new project, execute `npx create-react-app my-app` in your terminal (replacing "my-app" with your project's name). CRA automatically sets up the basic structure of a React application, including necessary configurations and dependencies.

4. Incorporating Version Control with Git

Version control is essential in modern software development. Git, a widely adopted system, helps in tracking and managing changes in the codebase. Starting your React project with Git integration is recommended. Install Git from its official website, then initialize a new repository in your project folder with `git init`.

5. Browser Setup for Development

Using a modern web browser equipped with developer tools is vital for React development. Google Chrome and Mozilla Firefox, with their extensive developer tools, are preferred choices. Enhancements like the React Developer Tools extension can be added to these browsers for in-depth analysis of React components.

6. Integrating Additional Tools and Libraries

React development may involve various additional tools and libraries:

- State Management Tools: For complex applications, libraries like Redux or MobX can be helpful in managing state more effectively.

- CSS Preprocessors: SASS or LESS offer advanced features for CSS management, such as variables and nested syntax.

- Testing Frameworks: Jest, combined with libraries like React Testing Library or Enzyme, forms a robust setup for writing and executing tests.

- API Testing Tools: Tools like Postman or Insomnia are useful for API interaction and testing.

7. Employing Linters and Formatters

For code quality and consistency, especially in collaborative projects, linters and formatters like ESLint and Prettier are indispensable. ESLint assists in identifying and rectifying JavaScript code issues, while Prettier automatically formats code according to predefined rules.

8. Setting up CI/CD Pipelines

Establishing CI/CD (Continuous Integration/Continuous Deployment) pipelines can enhance the development workflow. Services like GitHub Actions, Jenkins, or Travis CI automate testing and deployment, ensuring that every change undergoes automatic checks and is prepared for production.

In summary, the creation of a React JS development environment encompasses the installation of foundational tools like Node.js and npm, the choice of a code editor, the initiation of a React project using tools like Create React App, and the integration of version control using Git. The selection of additional tools, libraries, browsers, and extensions further customizes the environment to meet the specific demands of the project and developer. An appropriately configured development environment not only boosts productivity but also focuses on crafting high-quality React applications.

Creating your first React application

Embarking on the creation of your first React application marks a significant milestone in your front-end development journey. This process encompasses a sequence of pivotal steps, from initializing your project to scripting your inaugural React component. Let's navigate through these fundamental stages, shedding light on the essential practices and concepts for crafting a basic React application.

1. Kickstarting the Project with Create React App

Initiating your React journey begins with the project setup. Utilize Create React App (CRA), a streamlined command-line tool, for this purpose. It simplifies the creation process by executing `npx create-react-app my-first-react-app` in the terminal, replacing "my-first-react-app" with your project's name. This command constructs a new directory, equipping it with all the necessary dependencies, including a development server, Webpack, and Babel for JSX and modern JavaScript processing.

2. Exploring the Project Layout

Post-initialization, delve into the project's directory to understand its structure. Key elements include:

- `public/`: Houses static assets like HTML files and images.

- `src/`: The heart of your React code.

- `src/App.js`: The principal React component, acting as the entry point.

- `src/index.js`: Where the React app is injected into the DOM.

- `package.json`: Lists your project's dependencies and scripts.

3. Launching the Development Server

To bring your application to life, activate the development server using `npm start` within your project's directory. This command opens your application in a browser and features hot reloading to reflect code changes instantly.

4. Crafting Your Initial Component

React's building blocks are components, modular pieces of the UI. Whether it's a simple button or a complex page, everything in React is a component.

Create a new file, say `**MyComponent.js**`, in the `**src/**` folder. This component should be a JavaScript function returning JSX. For instance:

```
import React from 'react';

function MyComponent() {
  return <h1>Hello, React!</h1>;
}

export default MyComponent;
```

This snippet illustrates a basic component displaying a greeting.

5. Integrating Your Component

To incorporate your newly created component, import it into `**App.js**`. Here's how you can render `**MyComponent**` within the App component:

```
import React from 'react';
import MyComponent from './MyComponent';

function App() {
  return (
    <div className="App">
      <MyComponent />
    </div>
  );
}

export default App;
```

6. Decoding JSX

JSX, an integral part of React, enables HTML-like syntax within JavaScript files. It simplifies defining the UI structure, which React internally converts into JavaScript function calls to create the elements.

7. Styling Your Components

To style components, create a CSS file, e.g., `MyComponent.css`, and define your styles. Then, import this CSS file in your component to apply the styles:

```
import './MyComponent.css';
```

8. Managing State in Components

State management is vital in React, tracking data or properties that change over time. Use `this.state` in class components or `useState` in functional components to handle state.

9. Event Handling in React

React facilitates user interaction handling through event handlers. For example, adding a button to your component and managing its `onClick` event can be done as follows:

```
function MyComponent() {
  const handleClick = () => {
    alert('Button clicked!');
  };

  return <button onClick={handleClick}>Click me</button>;
}
```

10. Organizing Your Project

As your application expands, maintaining an organized structure becomes crucial. Establish dedicated directories for components, utilities, and styles. Ensure regular code refactoring and clean up redundant files or code.

11. Preparing and Deploying Your Application

To deploy, execute `npm run build` to generate a `build/` directory containing your app's production build. This build can be hosted on platforms like GitHub Pages, Netlify, or Vercel.

In essence, creating your initial React application involves setting up your development environment, constructing your first components, and grasping React's core principles like JSX, components, state management, and event handling. These initial steps lay the groundwork for your continued exploration and mastery of React development.

Chapter Two

Understanding JSX

Explaining JSX and its role in React

JSX, or JavaScript XML, stands as a critical element in the realm of React, a renowned JavaScript library for crafting user interfaces. Originating from Facebook's development team, JSX presents a syntax that merges JavaScript's functionality with HTML's ease, playing a crucial role in the way developers conceive and construct UI components in React. This detailed exploration aims to shed light on the nature of JSX, its operational mechanics, and its pivotal role in React development.

1. Merging HTML with JavaScript

JSX is a syntactic extension for JavaScript, mirroring the structure and syntax of HTML. In traditional web development practices, JavaScript and HTML are used in tandem – HTML for markup and JavaScript for logic. JSX revolutionizes this approach by allowing the integration of HTML-like code directly within JavaScript files. This blend simplifies the creation of intricate user interfaces, merging the markup and logic of components into a cohesive coding environment.

2. JSX's Function in React

In React's architecture, components serve as the foundational elements of the user interface, with JSX being the language to define these components' layout and structure. It enables developers to describe the UI's appearance in a declarative and easily comprehensible manner. When a React component is rendered, JSX lays out how the UI should materialize based on the component's state and props.

3. The Inner Workings of JSX

JSX may look like standard HTML, but it isn't inherently understood by web browsers. Instead, JSX expressions are transmuted into conventional JavaScript objects. Typically, this conversion is handled by a transpiler like Babel. For instance, a JSX expression such as `<div>Hello World</div>` is converted into `React.createElement('div', null, 'Hello World')`. This process generates a React element, a streamlined representation of a DOM element.

4. Benefits of Employing JSX

JSX's main advantage is its declarative characteristic, enhancing code readability and comprehension. By visually outlining the UI structure, JSX lets developers directly observe and comprehend the interface's hierarchy and composition within the code. This clarity becomes increasingly beneficial in larger, more complex UI projects.

JSX also incorporates JavaScript expressions within `{}`, enabling dynamic content within the UI. This feature facilitates the integration of JavaScript logic, including variables and functions, right within the UI structure.

5. JSX and the Art of Component Composition

React encourages building UIs from small, reusable components, and JSX is integral to this compositional approach. It allows for components to be nested within one another, akin to HTML tags, reflecting the inherent hierarchical nature of UIs and making the composition of components intuitive.

6. Incorporating Custom Components in JSX

Beyond standard HTML elements, JSX seamlessly integrates custom React components. Custom components can be rendered in JSX just like HTML elements. For example, a custom `Button` component can be used in JSX as `<Button />`, streamlining the development workflow by treating standard and custom elements uniformly.

7. Event Management with JSX

React and JSX simplify event handling. In JSX, event handlers are written in camelCase and are assigned as functions, not strings. For instance, an onClick event in JSX would be expressed as `onClick={handleClick}`, where `handleClick` is a function within the component.

8. Conditional Rendering in JSX

JSX adeptly handles conditional rendering, which is used to display different elements based on certain conditions. This is achieved using JavaScript's logical and ternary operators within JSX. An example would be `{isLoggedIn &&

**<LogoutButton />}`**, which only renders the `LogoutButton` if `isLoggedIn` is true.

9. Looping and Mapping in JSX

JSX effectively manages the rendering of lists or collections. Utilizing JavaScript's `map` function within JSX, developers can loop through an array of items, rendering a component for each one. This integration of JavaScript loops within JSX simplifies the rendering of dynamic content.

10. Challenges and Learning Curve

Despite its numerous advantages, JSX does come with a learning curve, especially for those accustomed to the traditional separation of HTML and JavaScript. Moreover, as JSX ultimately compiles down to JavaScript, any errors in JSX can lead to JavaScript errors, necessitating vigilant debugging.

In Summary

In essence, JSX is a transformative element within React, offering a novel approach to UI development. It allows for the integration of HTML-like code within JavaScript, fostering a seamless combination of markup and logic. This synergy not only enhances code readability but also streamlines the process of component composition and development. Mastery of JSX is indispensable for developers working with React, underpinning the library's philosophy and methodology in crafting user interfaces.

Basic syntax and conventions

Understanding the basic syntax and conventions in programming is essential for writing effective and collaborative code. Syntax, the set of rules that defines the valid combinations of symbols in a programming language, is akin to the grammar of the language. It dictates what constitutes a correctly structured program. Conventions, although not enforced by the language's syntax, are widely recognized best practices that enhance code readability and maintainability. This discussion aims to provide insight into these fundamental aspects, underscoring their significance and application in the world of programming.

1. The Critical Role of Syntax and Conventions

Syntax and conventions are cornerstone elements in programming:

- Syntax: This is akin to the foundational grammar rules of programming languages. Adhering to these rules is imperative for the functionality of programs, as syntax errors can lead to program failures.

- Conventions: These encompass coding standards, such as naming conventions, indentation styles, and commenting approaches. Conventions, while not impacting program execution, are vital for code clarity, making it easier for teams to collaborate and maintain code over time.

2. Core Syntax Elements in Programming

Various programming languages may have unique syntax, but some common elements are prevalent across many languages:

- Variables and Data Types: The declaration and assignment of variables, along with understanding fundamental data types like integers, strings, and arrays.

- Control Structures: These are elements like conditional statements (if, else) and looping constructs (for, while), governing the flow of code execution.

- Function and Method Definitions: Creating blocks of reusable code, complete with parameters and return values.

- Object-Oriented Elements: In languages that support object-oriented programming, defining classes and creating objects.

- Syntax-Specific Characters: Languages use specific characters like semicolons, braces, and commas for structuring code.

3. Naming Standards

Effective naming is crucial for clear code:

- CamelCase and PascalCase: Commonly used in variable and function names (`**userAge**`, `**calculateTotal**`) and class names (`**ShoppingCart**`), respectively.

- Descriptive Naming: Choosing names that clearly describe the purpose or function (e.g., `isEmpty`, `retrieveData`).

- Constants Naming: Typically in uppercase with underscores separating words (e.g., `MAX_LIMIT`, `API_ENDPOINT`).

4. Code Formatting

Proper code indentation and formatting play a pivotal role in readability. Consistent use of spaces or tabs for indentation, especially in nested structures, is a standard practice.

5. The Art of Commenting

Comments are integral for explaining complex logic or providing in-line documentation. They should be clear, concise, and relevant, avoiding the over-commenting of self-explanatory code.

6. Error Handling and Code Clarity

Good syntax practice includes comprehensive error handling and prioritizing code clarity. This means using understandable error messages and managing exceptions effectively.

7. Unique Language Conventions

Each programming language can have its specific conventions. Python, for example, focuses on readability with significant indentation. JavaScript has particular practices around asynchronous programming, while Java follows strict conventions regarding class structure and error handling.

8. Conventions in Frameworks and Libraries

Different frameworks and libraries might have their own set of conventions. For instance, React in JavaScript has specific patterns for component creation and state management, and Angular in TypeScript has distinct conventions regarding modules and services.

9. Utilizing Linters and Formatters

Tools like linters and formatters assist in maintaining syntax and conventions, automatically formatting code and highlighting deviations from standard practices.

10. Evolution of Conventions

Staying informed about the evolving conventions in programming is vital. Keeping abreast with the latest best practices involves engaging with community discussions, reviewing updated documentation, and studying code from reputable sources.

In Conclusion

Mastering basic syntax and adhering to coding conventions are fundamental skills for any programmer. Syntax ensures the functional correctness of code, while conventions make code more legible and easier to maintain. As programming languages and technologies evolve, so do these conventions, making ongoing learning and adaptation key to maintaining proficiency in software development.

JSX vs. HTML: Differences and similarities

JSX (JavaScript XML) and HTML (Hypertext Markup Language) are integral components in the domain of web development, each serving a distinct purpose in shaping web content's structure and presentation. While they share visual similarities, particularly in their syntax, JSX and HTML are characterized by notable differences in functionality and usage, especially within the context of React development. This examination aims to dissect the parallels and variances between JSX and HTML, providing clarity on their respective functions and roles in contemporary web development.

1. Parallel Traits of JSX and HTML

JSX and HTML display several resemblances, a deliberate design choice to leverage the familiarity developers have with HTML. These similarities include:

- Tag-Based Framework: Both employ a tag-based structure for defining elements, with tags such as `<div>`, `<span>`, and `<a>` appearing similarly in both JSX and HTML.

- Attribute Utilization: JSX attributes closely mirror those in HTML, enabling developers to set properties and configurations for elements.

- Nested Structure: JSX and HTML both organize elements in a hierarchical manner, establishing parent-child relationships among various elements.

2. Divergences in Syntax and Functionality

Despite these parallels, JSX and HTML diverge significantly in syntax and behavior:

- JavaScript Fusion: JSX is adept at integrating with JavaScript, allowing developers to embed JavaScript expressions within `{}`. This capability for dynamic content rendering is not inherent in standard HTML.

- Property Naming with CamelCase: JSX adopts the camelCase convention for DOM properties and attributes, as opposed to HTML's lowercase approach. For instance, `className` in JSX corresponds to `class` in HTML, and `onClick` in JSX to `onclick` in HTML.

- Expression Rendering: JSX can render complex expressions and display their outcomes, a feature not available in static HTML content.

- Component Inclusion: JSX uniquely facilitates the inclusion of React components within its structure, a feature not shared by HTML.

3. JSX's Foundation in JavaScript

JSX fundamentally extends JavaScript's syntax, processed through JavaScript engines via transpilers like Babel. This processing renders JSX down to JavaScript functions, unlike HTML, which is a markup language interpreted directly by web browsers.

4. HTML's Role as a Markup Language

As the standard language for web documents, HTML structures and lays out web content but does not execute logic or generate dynamic content without JavaScript's assistance.

5. Dynamic Versus Static Characteristics

JSX, especially within React, is geared towards dynamic web applications, enabling interactive UIs that respond to user interactions. In contrast, HTML is traditionally more static, requiring external scripting for dynamic behavior.

6. Event Handling Capabilities

Event handling in JSX is more robust, integrating into the component structure and utilizing camelCase. HTML's event handling is more declarative and often needs additional JavaScript for managing interactions.

7. Rendering Flexibility

JSX offers enhanced flexibility in UI rendering, capable of conditional rendering and dynamically generating elements based on state or props. HTML lacks these native capabilities.

8. Associated Tooling and Ecosystem

JSX's tooling is intricately linked with the React ecosystem, encompassing aspects like state management and component lifecycle. HTML's tooling, however, spans a wider array of web technologies and frameworks.

9. Considerations for Accessibility and SEO

Both JSX and HTML need to align with web accessibility standards, but their implementation methods may vary. React applications using JSX may require additional SEO and accessibility strategies due to their dynamic nature.

In Summary

In essence, JSX and HTML, while sharing a tag-based syntax and a hierarchical approach to organizing web content, exhibit significant differences in their capabilities and applications. JSX's strength lies in its integration with JavaScript, enabling the creation of dynamic and complex UIs within React applications. HTML, the foundational markup language of the web, is essential for defining the basic structure of web pages. For web developers, particularly those working with React, an understanding of the interplay and distinctions between JSX and HTML is crucial. This knowledge is key to effectively leveraging both languages in developing engaging, interactive, and well-structured web applications.

Chapter Three

Components in React

Understanding components and their importance

In the landscape of contemporary web development, particularly within frameworks like React, the concept of components stands as a cornerstone, profoundly influencing how web applications are built and structured. A deep comprehension of components and their pivotal role is indispensable for developers aspiring to excel in crafting efficient, scalable, and maintainable web applications.

1. The Essence of Components

Components in web development are autonomous units responsible for handling specific sections of a web application's user interface. These components are the foundational elements, encapsulating HTML, CSS, and JavaScript. In environments like React, components are typically defined using JSX, blending both markup and logic into a unified entity.

2. Reusability and Modular Design

Components shine in their ability to be reused, curtailing redundant coding. For instance, a button component with particular styling and functionality can be utilized repeatedly across an application, enhancing efficiency and ensuring UI consistency.

3. Encapsulation and Distinct Responsibilities

Components embody encapsulation, keeping their internal state and logic concealed from the rest of the application. This aligns with the principle of separation of concerns, where different application parts independently manage specific functionalities. Such an approach streamlines organization and simplifies debugging and maintenance processes.

4. Facilitating Maintenance

The compartmentalized nature of components greatly aids in application maintenance. Updates or fixes within a component generally have limited impact, reducing the likelihood of unintended consequences elsewhere in the application.

5. Scalability Benefits

As applications expand in complexity, managing a monolithic code structure becomes daunting. Components allow for breaking down complex interfaces into manageable segments, each independently developed, tested, and maintained, aiding in application scalability.

6. Collaborative Development Advantages

Component-based architecture is particularly conducive to team-based development settings. Team members can concurrently work on different components, enhancing efficiency and reducing development time, especially in extensive projects.

7. Managing State and Data

Components often handle their state and can receive data from parent components via props. This setup is crucial for creating dynamic applications with responsive and interactive UIs.

8. Lifecycle Management and Functional Hooks

Frameworks like React endow components with lifecycle methods, enabling specific code execution at various stages of a component's existence. Functional components leverage hooks to utilize state and other features without the need for class-based components.

9. Dynamic UIs through Re-rendering

Components automatically re-render in response to state or prop alterations, a key attribute for developing dynamic interfaces that adapt to real-time user interactions and data changes.

10. Versatility with Custom and Third-Party Components

The flexibility to craft bespoke components or employ third-party library components allows developers to rapidly build applications with both custom and standardized functionalities.

11. SEO and Accessibility Considerations

While focusing on UI and behavior, it's also vital to integrate SEO and accessibility considerations within components, ensuring the creation of inclusive and search-engine-friendly applications.

12. Streamlined Testing

The isolated nature of components simplifies testing, as each can be independently verified, contributing significantly to the overall application's stability and quality.

Summarizing the Importance

To encapsulate, components are a fundamental aspect of modern web development, especially in React-like frameworks. They offer a structured, efficient approach to developing web applications, irrespective of scale. The benefits of modularity, encapsulation, and ease of maintenance make components a preferred method for developers. Grasping the utilization of components is crucial for anyone seeking to develop dynamic, robust, and user-centric web applications. They not only facilitate the development process but also improve collaboration, testing, and maintenance, cementing their essential role in the web development domain.

Class components vs. functional components

In the world of React, a widely-used JavaScript library for creating user interfaces, there are two primary ways to define components: class components and functional components. Each type serves to encapsulate both the logic and presentation of parts of an application, yet they differ in their syntax and functional scope. This discussion aims to dissect class and functional components in React, examining their distinct features, applications, and how they integrate within the React framework.

1. Class Components Overview

Class components in React are based on ES6 classes extending from `**React.Component**`.

- State Management: They are capable of holding and managing state, allowing them to store information that changes over time and necessitates UI updates.

- Lifecycle Methods Access: Class components have access to React's lifecycle methods like `**componentDidMount**`, `**componentDidUpdate**`, and `**componentWillUnmount**`, enabling specific actions at various points in a component's lifecycle.

- Verbose Syntax: They typically have a more elaborate syntax, often including a constructor for state initialization and a `**render**` method that returns JSX.

- Class Component Example:

```
class Welcome extends React.Component {
  constructor(props) {
    super(props);
    this.state = { greeting: 'Hello' };
  }

  render() {
    return <h1>{this.state.greeting}, {this.props.name}</h1>;
  }
}
```

2. Functional Components Characteristics

Functional components are defined using JavaScript functions and have evolved with React's advancements.

- Simplicity in Design: They are usually less verbose and simpler than class components, consisting of functions that return JSX.

- Introduction of Hooks: Hooks, introduced in React 16.8, enable functional components to handle state (`useState`), manage side effects (`useEffect`), and utilize context (`useContext`).

- Absence of 'this' Keyword: These components don't use the `this` keyword, often simplifying their development and maintenance.

- Functional Component Example:

```
function Welcome(props) {
  const [greeting, setGreeting] = useState('Hello');

  return <h1>{greeting}, {props.name}</h1>;
}
```

3. Class vs. Functional Components: A Comparative View

- Syntax and Verbosity: Class components generally involve more extensive syntax than functional components, which are more concise.

- Historical Role of State and Lifecycle: Initially, state management and lifecycle methods were exclusive to class components, but with Hooks, functional components now share these capabilities.

- Performance Perspectives: It's a common belief that functional components are more performant, but the difference is usually minimal.

- Trending Preferences: The React community has been gradually favoring functional components, primarily due to their succinctness and the power of Hooks.

- React's Evolution: React's updates have shown a preference for functional components in new development, although class components remain supported.

4. The Evolution in Component Usage

React's evolution has witnessed a notable shift from class components to functional components, largely driven by the introduction and adoption of Hooks, which equip functional components with abilities previously exclusive to class components.

Summarizing the Distinctions

In summary, both class and functional components are essential in React development. Class components provide a more traditional approach, complete with lifecycle methods and state handling. However, functional components have gained popularity and functionality, especially with Hooks, making them an increasingly preferred choice for developers. The selection between class and functional components often depends on personal or project-specific preferences, though the trend in the React community is leaning more towards functional components for their streamlined syntax and comprehensive capabilities. For React developers, understanding the differences and strengths of each component type is vital, enabling more informed development decisions and efficient coding practices.

Building reusable components

In today's web development landscape, particularly within frameworks such as React, the creation of reusable components is a key strategy. These components are essential for building web applications that are efficient, maintainable, and scalable. Reusable components enable developers to craft consistent user interfaces while reducing code redundancy, thereby boosting productivity and maintaining uniformity across various parts of an application.

1. Concept of Reusable Components

Reusable components are independent, modular units that encapsulate both functionality and aesthetics, designed to be employed repeatedly within an application or across different projects. Their generic and adaptable nature allows them to fit into various contexts and use cases.

2. Advantages of Reusable Components

- Development Efficiency: They cut down on repetitive coding, saving time and effort.

- UI Consistency: Consistent user interfaces are easier to achieve as the same components are reused.

- Streamlined Maintenance: Updating a single instance of a component updates it everywhere, simplifying the maintenance process.

- Enhanced Code Quality: Repeated use and testing of these components typically lead to fewer bugs and higher code quality.

3. Principles for Crafting Reusable Components

- Simplicity and Compatibility: Components should be straightforward and able to work with other components.

- Customizability: They should be configurable via props or settings for easy adaptation.

- Self-sufficiency: Components should ideally be independent and not reliant on external states or data structures.

- Effective State Handling: Consider how state is managed within and across components, possibly using tools like Redux or Context API.

4. Best Practices in Component Development

- Intuitive Naming: Component names should reflect their functionality, aiding in clarity and maintenance.

- Comprehensive Documentation: Well-documented components with clear explanations of their properties and use cases are more easily reusable.

- Reliable Error Handling: Components should handle errors effectively, preventing them from disrupting the overall application.

- Performance Considerations: Optimizing components for performance, including minimizing unnecessary rendering.

- Thorough Testing: Components should undergo extensive testing both individually and within the application context.

5. Building a Component Library

Creating a centralized library of reusable components can be highly beneficial, especially in large-scale applications or across multiple projects.

6. Potential Challenges

- Risk of Over-Generalization: Making components too generic can complicate the code unnecessarily.

- Initial Time Investment: Developing reusable components might require more upfront time compared to creating specific, one-time-use components.

7. Utilizing Third-Party Libraries

In some cases, using existing third-party component libraries can be more efficient than building every component from scratch.

8. Managing Component Styles

Styling can be a complex aspect of reusable components. Approaches like CSS Modules or Styled Components can be effective in managing styles without conflict.

9. Common Reusable Components

Typical reusable components include elements like buttons, input fields, modals, navigation bars, and tables, which usually have standard functionalities and designs.

10. Adapting and Refining Based on Feedback

The design and functionality of reusable components should continually evolve based on user feedback and usage patterns, ensuring they remain effective and relevant.

Summation

In summary, the development of reusable components is a fundamental aspect of modern web application development, especially in component-based frameworks such as React. These components not only make the development process more efficient but also ensure consistency across the user interface. While creating and managing a library of reusable components, developers should be mindful of challenges and continuously refine these components based on practical feedback. For web developers, the skill of creating reusable components is invaluable, contributing significantly to the scalability and robustness of web applications.

Chapter Four

State and Props

Exploring state and props in React

In React, a prominent JavaScript library for user interface development, grasping the concepts of "state" and "props" is crucial. These elements are pivotal in crafting dynamic and interactive web applications, playing distinct roles in how components function and interact within the React environment.

1. The Concept of State in React

State in a React component is essentially an object that contains data or information that might change over the component's life. It is confined to the component itself and is not accessible or modifiable from outside the component.

- Nature of State:

    - Changeable: State is mutable. It can be altered using the `setState` method in class components or the `useState` hook in functional components.

    - Asynchronous Update Nature: React performs state updates asynchronously for efficiency, grouping multiple `setState` calls.

- Encapsulation within Component: State is unique to its component, encapsulating its relevant data.

- Application of State:

  - State is typically employed for data that changes, like user inputs, server responses, or interface statuses (like active/inactive).

  - In class components, state is usually set up in the constructor. In contrast, functional components use the `useState` hook for state declaration.

2. Understanding Props in React

Props, an abbreviation for properties, are the means through which data is passed from parent to child components in React. They are immutable, implying that a child component cannot alter the props it receives.

- Properties of Props:

  - Immutable Nature: Props are read-only and cannot be modified by the receiving component.

  - Facilitating Component Interaction: Props enable different components to communicate, passing data from parent to child.

  - Upholding Functional Integrity: They provide essential data to components for rendering, maintaining the component's functional integrity.

- Utilization of Props:

  - Props are fundamental for transferring data and event handlers to child components.

  - They allow the personalization of child components by the parent.

  - Props contribute to component reusability by making them adaptable and dynamic.

3. Distinguishing State and Props

State and props, while both integral to React components, serve distinct functions:

- Changeability: State is mutable and used for data that evolves within the component. Props, conversely, are immutable and passed to a component.

- Ownership and Source: State is generated and managed within its own component. Props are received by a component, thus not originally part of it.

4. Effective Handling of State and Props

Proper management of state and props is key to building robust React applications:

- Elevating State: When state needs to be shared among components, it's often moved up to their closest shared ancestor. This centralizes the state and simplifies management.

- Maximizing Component Reusability: Designing components for maximum reusability typically involves making them stateless, using props for data passing.

- Minimizing Prop Drilling: Excessive passing down of props through many layers, known as prop drilling, can be circumvented using React Context or state management libraries like Redux.

5. Stateful vs. Stateless Components in React

React components are often categorized based on their relationship with state:

- Stateful Components: Also referred to as "containers," these components handle and manage state, dealing with the logic of the application.

- Stateless Components: Also known as "presentational" components, they focus on rendering the UI, accepting props, and not managing state.

Wrapping Up

In essence, a comprehensive understanding of state and props is a cornerstone of proficiency in React. They enable components to manage, maintain, and exchange data, facilitating complex interactions within applications. State allows for internal data management within components, whereas props enable components to interact and share data across the application. For React developers, skillfully balancing and employing state and props is essential for creating dynamic, efficient, and maintainable web applications. Recognizing and applying the nuances of these two concepts is a vital aspect of effective React development.

State management in class and functional components

State management in React, crucial for creating interactive web applications, differs notably between class and functional components. This key distinction is essential for developers to comprehend as it significantly affects how data is managed and manipulated within React apps.

1. Managing State in Class Components

In class components, state is handled using the this.state property alongside the setState method.

- State Initialization:

    - Typically, state is set up in the component's constructor, where **this.state** is assigned to an initial state object.

    - Example:

```
constructor(props) {
    super(props);
    this.state = { counter: 0 };
}
```

Updating State:

- The `**setState**` method is employed for updating the component's state. It schedules an update and signals React to re-render the component and its children.

- It's asynchronous, hence immediate reading of `**this.state**` post-update might not reflect the new state.

- Example:

```
this.setState({ counter: this.state.counter + 1 });
```

- Lifecycle Methods Integration:

  - Class components have lifecycle methods that are instrumental in state management, particularly for operations involving side effects or external data.

2. State Management in Functional Components

With React 16.8's introduction of Hooks, functional components gained the capability to manage state, a feature once exclusive to class components.

- Utilizing the `**useState**` Hook:

  - `**useState**` adds state to functional components, returning a pair consisting of the current state and a function to update it.

  - Example:

```
const [counter, setCounter] = useState(0);
```

State Update Mechanism:

- The update function from `useState` (e.g., `setCounter`) modifies the state. It's similar to `setState` but doesn't merge old and new state objects.

- Functional updates can be used for dependable state transitions.

- Example:

```
setCounter(prevCounter => prevCounter + 1);
```

- Streamlined Code with Hooks:

  - The `useState` hook typically results in more concise and modular code than the class component equivalent.

3. Comparing State in Class and Functional Components

- Syntax Differences:

  - Class components generally require more elaborate syntax for managing state, whereas functional components use the succinct `useState` hook.

- Lifecycle vs. Hooks:

  - Lifecycle methods in class components are paralleled by hooks like `useEffect` in functional components, offering a more direct approach for handling side effects.

- Initial State Setting:

  - In class components, state initialization happens in the constructor, while in functional components, it's directly in the component body via `**useState**`.

4. Effective State Management Practices

- Maintain Minimal State:

  - State should be kept minimal and only include data that changes and impacts the render.

- Judicious Use of State:

  - State should be used carefully to avoid complexity and performance issues in larger applications. Contexts or external state management tools can be beneficial in complex scenarios.

Conclusion

In essence, grasping how to manage state in both class and functional components is a critical skill for React developers. Class components present a more traditional method of state management with `**setState**` and lifecycle methods. In contrast, functional components offer a streamlined method with the `**useState**` hook. The choice between these approaches depends on the application's specific requirements and the developer's preferences. Properly managing state, irrespective of the component type, is key to developing dynamic, efficient, and maintainable React applications.

Data flow between parent and child components

In the realm of React, a prominent JavaScript library for building interfaces, mastering the flow of data between parent and child components is fundamental. This flow, inherently unidirectional, is a core principle that guides how information is shared across the component hierarchy, moving from parent to child elements. For developers working with React, comprehending this data flow is pivotal, as it influences the structural design of applications and the interaction dynamics between components.

1. The Principle of Unidirectional Data Flow

React enforces a unidirectional data flow pattern, where data travels in a single direction – from parent components to their children. This approach reduces complexity in data handling and enhances the ease of tracking and debugging data-related issues.

2. Data Transmission via Props

Props (short for properties) are the main conduit for data flow in React. Parents pass data down to their children using props, which can encompass a range of data types, from simple strings to complex objects and even functions.

- Data Passing Example Using Props:

```
function ParentComponent() {
    const parentMessage = 'Message from parent';
    return <ChildComponent message={parentMessage} />;
}

function ChildComponent(props) {
    return <h1>{props.message}</h1>;
}
```

Here, the `ParentComponent` sends the `parentMessage` string down to the `ChildComponent` through props.

3. Immutable Nature of Props

Props in React are immutable. Child components cannot alter the props they receive, a design choice that ensures the unidirectional flow of data remains consistent and predictable.

4. Role of State in Data Handling

While props are for passing data down, state is used within components to manage data that changes over time, influencing rendering and behavior. State changes trigger re-renders in React, updating the component's presentation.

- Lifting State Upward: When several components need to access the same data, it's common to lift the state to their nearest common parent. The state resides in the parent, with changes flowing down to the children via props.

5. Reverse Data Flow via Functions as Props

React's unidirectional flow can be complemented with reverse communication from child to parent through functions passed as props. Children can invoke these functions to send data or events back up to their parents.

- Function as Props Illustration:

```
function ParentComponent() {
    const onChildEvent = (childData) => {
        console.log('Received from child:', childData);
    };

    return <ChildComponent notifyParent={onChildEvent} />;
}

function ChildComponent(props) {
    const childData = 'Child's data';
    return <button onClick={() => props.notifyParent(childData)}>Click me</button>;
}
```

In this setup, `ParentComponent` passes a function `onChildEvent` down to `ChildComponent`. When the button in the child is clicked, it triggers the function, relaying data back to the parent.

6. Utilizing Component Composition

Component composition in React offers an alternative approach to managing data flow, especially in complex structures. It involves designing components that can nest other components, providing flexibility and reusability.

7. Employing Context API to Avoid Prop Drilling

To circumvent the challenge of "prop drilling" – passing props through multiple component layers – React introduces the Context API. This tool allows data to be shared directly with deeply nested components, bypassing the need for manual prop propagation through every level.

Summation

In summary, understanding the data flow between parent and child components in React is crucial for structuring and managing applications effectively. This unidirectional flow, facilitated primarily through props, is key to maintaining order and predictability in data management. Components maintain their internal state, with state lifting patterns employed for shared data scenarios. The immutable nature of props, combined with the use of functions as props for reverse communication, ensures a well-organized flow of data. Grasping these concepts and utilizing tools like component composition and the Context API is vital for developers to create well-architected, efficient React applications. Such understanding and application of data flow principles are indispensable in the realm of React development.

Chapter Five

Event Handling in React

Basics of event handling in React

Event handling is a crucial element in building interactive web applications, and in the context of React, it assumes a central role in crafting responsive interfaces. React's methodology for handling various user actions, such as clicks, form submissions, and keyboard events, is integral to its component-based design. For developers utilizing React, a thorough understanding of how to manage events is key to developing dynamic and intuitive interfaces.

1. Fundamentals of Event Handling in React

React's approach to event handling involves a wrapper around the native browser events called SyntheticEvent. This wrapper standardizes event handling across different browsers by normalizing the event object.

2. Implementing Event Handlers in React

In React, event handlers are JavaScript functions triggered in response to user interactions. These functions are typically assigned as props to React elements and follow the camelCase naming convention.

- Event Handler Example:

```
function MyComponent() {
  function handleClick() {
    console.log('Button was clicked');
  }

  return <button onClick={handleClick}>Click Me</button>;
}
```

This snippet illustrates a `handleClick` event handler function assigned to a button's `onClick` event.

3. Binding Methods in Class Components

Event handlers in class components require appropriate binding to the component's instance. This can be achieved through constructor binding or by employing class field syntax.

- Binding in Constructor:

```
class MyComponent extends React.Component {
  constructor(props) {
    super(props);
    this.handleClick = this.handleClick.bind(this);
  }

  handleClick() {
    console.log('Button was clicked');
  }

  render() {
    return <button onClick={this.handleClick}>Click Me</button>;
  }
}
```

- Using Class Field Syntax:

```
class MyComponent extends React.Component {
  handleClick = () => {
    console.log('Button was clicked');
  };

  render() {
    return <button onClick={this.handleClick}>Click Me</button>;
  }
}
```

4. Passing Additional Parameters to Handlers

There are situations where passing extra arguments to event handlers is necessary, achievable via arrow functions or the `bind` method.

- Arrow Function Approach:

```
<button onClick={() => this.handleClick(someId)}>Click Me</button>
```

- Using `bind`:

```
<button onClick={this.handleClick.bind(this, someId)}>Click Me</button>
```

5. React's Event Pooling

React enhances performance through event pooling, where the SyntheticEvent object is reused. This means event properties are not retained asynchronously. To access the event properties later, `event.persist()` should be used.

6. Managing Forms via Controlled Components

React treats form elements like inputs and textareas as controlled components, meaning their state is managed by React, not the DOM.

- Controlled Component Example:

```
class MyForm extends React.Component {
    constructor(props) {
        super(props);
        this.state = { inputValue: '' };

        this.handleChange = this.handleChange.bind(this);
        this.handleSubmit = this.handleSubmit.bind(this);
    }

    handleChange(event) {
        this.setState({ inputValue: event.target.value });
    }

    handleSubmit(event) {
        alert('Submitted value: ' + this.state.inputValue);
        event.preventDefault();
    }

    render() {
        return (
            <form onSubmit={this.handleSubmit}>
                <label>
                    Name:
                    <input type="text" value={this.state.inputValue} onChange={this.handleChange} />
                </label>
                <input type="submit" value="Submit" />
            </form>
        );
    }
}
```

Wrapping Up

In essence, mastering event handling within React is essential for creating user interfaces that are both interactive and user-friendly. Understanding the nuances of setting up and managing event handlers, properly binding them in class components, handling additional arguments, and working with React's event pooling is fundamental. Additionally, employing controlled components for form handling enriches the developer's toolkit, enabling the management of complex user inputs and forms. Proficiency in these areas is critical for developers aiming to craft advanced web applications that provide engaging user experiences.

Binding events in class components

Binding events in React class components is a critical practice in handling user interactions effectively within the application. This process relates to how event handlers are connected to the components, ensuring that the 'this' keyword within these handlers accurately refers to the component instance itself.

1. Importance of Binding in Class Components

In JavaScript classes, 'this' is not automatically bound to the instance of the class. In the context of React class components, this leads to challenges, particularly when 'this' is utilized inside event handlers. Without proper binding, 'this' does not point to the class instance, often resulting in errors, especially when accessing state or class methods.

2. Methods for Event Handler Binding

There are several strategies for binding event handlers in React class components, each with its specific considerations.

- Constructor Binding:

    - A common and recommended approach is to bind event handlers in the component's constructor. This method ensures the handler is bound once, enhancing performance.

- Example:

```
class MyComponent extends React.Component {
    constructor(props) {
        super(props);
        this.state = { isActive: false };
        this.handleClick = this.handleClick.bind(this);
    }

    handleClick() {
        this.setState({ isActive: true });
    }

    render() {
        return <button onClick={this.handleClick}>Click me</button>;
    }
}
```

- Class Fields for Event Handlers:

  - Using class fields to define event handlers inherently binds them to the class instance.

- Example:

```
class MyComponent extends React.Component {
    state = { isActive: false };

    handleClick = () => {
        this.setState({ isActive: true });
    };

    render() {
        return <button onClick={this.handleClick}>Click me</button>;
    }
}
```

- Inline Arrow Functions:

    - Arrow functions in the JSX **render** method can ensure proper binding but may impact performance as they create a new function on every render.

    - Example:

```
class MyComponent extends React.Component {
    state = { isActive: false };

    render() {
        return (
            <button onClick={() => this.setState({ isActive: true })}>
                Click me
            </button>
        );
    }
}
```

3. Handling Arguments in Event Handlers

Passing additional parameters to event handlers in class components can be done through arrow functions or the `bind` method in the JSX callbacks.

- Arrow Function Approach:

```
<button onClick={() => this.handleClick(argument)}>Click me</button>
```

- Binding with Parameters:

```
<button onClick={this.handleClick.bind(this, argument)}>Click me</button>
```

4. Recommended Practices for Binding

- Limit Inline Arrow Functions: While convenient, inline arrow functions can lead to performance issues in larger applications. It's advisable to bind handlers in the constructor or use class fields.

- Avoid Multiple Bindings: Rebinding the same event handler numerous times can lead to unnecessary memory use and potential performance problems.

- Consistency in Binding Techniques: Adopting a consistent approach to event binding across components enhances the code's readability and maintainability.

Summarizing the Concept

In summary, event binding in React class components is essential for managing user events like clicks and form submissions. The method of binding affects both performance and code clarity. Preferred techniques include constructor binding and class field methods, with special attention to how event handlers are bound and how additional arguments are passed to these handlers. Proficiency in these binding strategies is crucial for developing effective, responsive React applications with interactive user interfaces.

Handling events in functional components

Event management in React's functional components is a critical component of crafting dynamic and engaging web applications. Differing from class components, functional components utilize hooks and the principles of closures, offering a more concise and contemporary approach to managing user interactions. It's essential for React developers to grasp this approach to effectively create interactive user interfaces.

1. Fundamental Event Handling in Functional Components

Event handling in functional components is straightforward, with handlers defined as functions within the component. These functions are directly accessible, negating the need for binding 'this'.

- Event Handler Definition:

    - Handlers are functions declared within the functional component.

- Example:

```
function MyComponent() {
    const handleButtonClick = () => {
        console.log('Button was clicked');
    };

    return <button onClick={handleButtonClick}>Click Me</button>;
}
```

2. Utilizing Closures in Event Handlers

Functional components take advantage of JavaScript closures, allowing handlers to access component scope, including state variables and props.

- Closure Access to State and Props:

    - Handlers within a functional component can access state and props due to closures.

    - Example:

```
function MyComponent({ greeting }) {
    const [count, setCount] = useState(0);

    const handleButtonClick = () => {
        console.log(greeting, count);
        setCount(count + 1);
    };

    return <button onClick={handleButtonClick}>Click Me</button>;
}
```

3. Argument Passing in Event Handlers

Arguments can be passed to event handlers in functional components using arrow functions in the JSX.

- **Passing Arguments Example:**

```
function MyComponent() {
    const handleItemSelect = (itemId) => {
        console.log('Selected item:', itemId);
    };

    return (
        <div>
            {items.map(item => (
                <button onClick={() => handleItemSelect(item.id)}>
                    {item.name}
                </button>
            ))}
        </div>
    );
}
```

4. Inline Function Event Handling

Inline functions can be employed for simple event handling within JSX. These functions are recreated during each render, potentially impacting performance.

- Inline Function Handling Example:

```
function MyComponent() {
    const [count, setCount] = useState(0);

    return (
        <button onClick={() => setCount(count + 1)}>
            Increase Count
        </button>
    );
}
```

5. Debounce and Throttle Techniques

To optimize performance for events like scrolling or typing, debounce and throttle techniques are beneficial. These can be incorporated through custom hooks or external libraries.

6. Crafting Custom Hooks for Event Logic

Complex event handling logic can be modularized using custom hooks, enhancing reusability across components.

- Custom Hook for Events Example:

```
function useAdvancedEventHandling() {
    // Complex event handling logic
}

function MyComponent() {
    const eventHandler = useAdvancedEventHandling();
    return <button onClick={eventHandler}>Click Me</button>;
}
```

7. Managing Form Events in Functional Components

Form events are managed in a similar fashion, with controlled components like inputs using the useState hook for state management, and event handlers for form submissions.

- **Form Event Management Example:**

```
function MyFormComponent() {
    const [inputValue, setInputValue] = useState('');

    const handleFormSubmit = (event) => {
        event.preventDefault();
        console.log('Form value:', inputValue);
    };

    return (
        <form onSubmit={handleFormSubmit}>
            <input type="text" value={inputValue} onChange={(e) => setInputValue(e.target.value)} />
            <button type="submit">Submit</button>
        </form>
    );
}
```

Summary

In essence, managing events in React functional components is a streamlined and efficient process, using the power of JavaScript closures and React hooks. Grasping these event handling patterns is crucial for building responsive and interactive applications in React. Effective event management in functional components allows developers to create sophisticated and intuitive user interfaces, significantly enhancing the user experience.

Chapter Six

Lifecycle Methods

Understanding lifecycle methods in React

Grasping lifecycle methods in React is essential for developers working with this widely-used JavaScript framework. These methods are special functions that occur at specific points in a component's life cycle, playing a crucial role in tasks like setting up data fetching operations and managing UI updates in response to data changes.

1. Component Lifecycle Overview in React

A React component undergoes several key stages:

- Mounting Phase: This is when the component is being constructed and integrated into the DOM.

- Updating Phase: This occurs when the component undergoes re-rendering due to changes in its props or state.

- Unmounting Phase: The final stage where the component is removed from the DOM.

2. Lifecycle Methods During Mounting

These methods are invoked in a specific sequence when a component instance is being created and inserted into the DOM:

- constructor(): Called before the component is mounted, it's typically used for two main purposes: setting up the component's internal state and binding event handler methods.

- static getDerivedStateFromProps(): Executed right before the `render` method, both during the initial mount and subsequent updates. It should return an object to update the state or `null` if no changes are needed.

- render(): A required method that specifies the HTML output of a component. It should be a pure function, meaning it does not modify the component's state and returns the same output each time.

- componentDidMount(): Called immediately after the component is mounted, this is where you can perform any necessary setup that requires DOM nodes. It's also ideal for setting up subscriptions, with the caveat to cancel these in `componentWillUnmount()`.

3. Lifecycle Methods During Updates

Updates can occur due to changes in props or state. These methods are invoked in order during a component's re-render:

- static getDerivedStateFromProps(): Called before the `render` method.

- shouldComponentUpdate(nextProps, nextState): Lets you control if re-rendering should happen. It defaults to true.

- render(): Renders the component.

- getSnapshotBeforeUpdate(prevProps,   prevState): Invoked right before the DOM is updated. It allows the capture of information from the DOM prior to potentially changing it.

- componentDidUpdate(prevProps, prevState, snapshot): Executed immediately after the update occurs. Not called on the initial render.

4. Lifecycle Method for Unmounting

This method is invoked when a component is being removed from the DOM:

- componentWillUnmount(): Called right before a component is unmounted and destroyed. This is where you should clean up any subscriptions, event listeners, or any ongoing operations initiated in `componentDidMount`.

5. Error Handling Lifecycle Methods

React 16 introduced new methods to manage errors:

- static getDerivedStateFromError(error): Triggered after an error occurs in a descendant component.

- componentDidCatch(error, info): Called in response to errors during rendering, in a lifecycle method, or within the constructor of any child component.

6. Proper Use of Lifecycle Methods

Knowing when and how to use these lifecycle methods is crucial. Misuse can lead to inefficiencies, while proper use can prevent bugs and ensure smooth UI updates. For example, fetching data should not occur in the `render` method but rather in `componentDidMount` or `componentDidUpdate`.

Concluding Thoughts

Lifecycle methods are integral to managing a React component's behavior from creation to destruction. Effective use of these methods is key to handling side-effects, managing data fetching, and ensuring efficient component updates. Keeping abreast of best practices and updates in lifecycle methods is important for developing well-functioning React applications.

Different lifecycle stages and their usage

In React development, comprehending the distinct lifecycle stages of components and their respective functionalities is key to creating efficient and robust applications. React components undergo several phases: mounting, updating, and unmounting, each offering specific hooks for developers to intervene effectively.

1. Introduction to the Mounting Phase

The mounting phase signifies the initial introduction of a component into the DOM and encompasses several critical methods:

- constructor(): The first lifecycle method in the sequence, the constructor is used for initializing state and binding event handlers. It should be straightforward and free of complex logic.

```
constructor(props) {
    super(props);
    this.state = { /* initial state setup */ };
}
```

- static getDerivedStateFromProps(props, state): Invoked both prior to the initial mount and on subsequent updates, this method allows the component to adjust its internal state in response to prop changes.

- render(): Essential and mandatory, the render method dictates the component's JSX output. It's critical that this method remains pure, with no state modifications.

- componentDidMount(): This post-mounting method is ideal for setting up network requests, event listeners, or establishing subscriptions. Cleanup for these operations should be handled in `**componentWillUnmount**`.

2. The Update Phase

A component enters the update phase when its props or state changes, necessitating a re-render:

- static getDerivedStateFromProps(props, state): Similar to its role in mounting, it's called before rendering when new props or state are received.

- shouldComponentUpdate(nextProps, nextState): This method allows control over the component's update process. By default, it returns true but can be used to prevent unnecessary rendering.

- render(): Re-executes to reflect the updated state or props.

- getSnapshotBeforeUpdate(prevProps, prevState): Executes just before the DOM updates, allowing the capture of current DOM state.

- componentDidUpdate(prevProps, prevState, snapshot): This method is useful for operations post-update, like fetching new data, and should include conditions to avoid unnecessary network requests.

3. Unmounting Phase

The final lifecycle stage is unmounting, where the component is removed from the DOM:

- componentWillUnmount(): Here, developers should perform cleanup tasks such as aborting unfinished network requests, detaching event listeners, or canceling any subscriptions established in `componentDidMount`.

4. Managing Errors with Lifecycle Methods

React 16 introduced methods for catching errors in a component's child tree:

- static getDerivedStateFromError(error): Utilized for rendering a fallback UI post-error.

- componentDidCatch(error, errorInfo): Allows logging of error details.

5. Practical Application of Lifecycle Methods

These methods are instrumental in resource management and guiding component behavior in reaction to data changes. Typical use cases include:

- Setting Up State and Event Handlers: Commonly done in the constructor.

- Data Fetching: Network requests are usually initiated in `componentDidMount` and `componentDidUpdate`.

- Enhancing Performance: Methods like `shouldComponentUpdate` and `getDerivedStateFromProps` help prevent unnecessary re-renders.

- Resource Clean-Up: This is crucial in `componentWillUnmount` to avoid memory leaks.

Conclusion

In essence, lifecycle methods in React components offer significant control over a component's behavior throughout its existence. From initial setup and data fetching to performance optimization and resource cleanup, these methods provide strategic points of intervention. Proper understanding and implementation of these lifecycle methods are vital for building effective, responsive, and well-functioning React applications.

Lifecycle methods in functional components with hooks

With the advent of hooks in React version 16.8, the landscape of handling lifecycle events in functional components underwent a significant transformation. Hooks offer a refreshed, more succinct approach to managing these events, diverging from the traditional lifecycle methods used in class components. This shift is pivotal for developers in modern React development for creating more efficient and intuitive user interfaces.

1. Transition from Lifecycle Methods to Hooks

Previously, class components in React utilized lifecycle methods for managing events throughout a component's life. However, with functional components, hooks now enable similar functionalities without the complexity of classes.

2. Implementing State with `useState`

- State in Functional Components:

    - The `useState` hook is pivotal for adding state to functional components. It provides a state variable and a function to update this state, akin to `this.state` and `this.setState` in class components.

    - Example:

```
const [count, setCount] = useState(0);
```

3. Side Effects with `**useEffect**`

- Managing Side Effects:

  - For side effects, `**useEffect**` functions as a combination of `**componentDidMount**`, `**componentDidUpdate**`, and `**componentWillUnmount**`.

  - Example:

```
useEffect(() => {
    // Side effect logic
    return () => {
        // Cleanup actions
    };
}, [dependencies]);
```

  - It runs after rendering and can be controlled by its dependencies array.

4. Accessing Context via useContext

- Simplifying Context Usage:

  - The `**useContext**` hook offers an uncomplicated way to access React context in functional components.

  - Example:

```
const contextValue = useContext(MyContext);
```

5. Complex State Logic with useReducer

- Advanced State Management:

  - For intricate state logic, `useReducer` is an alternative to `useState`, providing more control over state transitions.

  - Example:

```
const [state, dispatch] = useReducer(reducer, initialState);
```

6. Refs and Mutable Values with `useRef`

- Interacting with DOM Elements:

  - `useRef` is used for interacting with DOM elements and storing mutable values that don't trigger re-renders.

  - Example:

```
const myRef = useRef(initialValue);
```

7. Crafting Custom Hooks

- Creating Reusable Stateful Logic:

  - Custom hooks allow for building reusable stateful logic, combining various hooks for new functionalities.

- Example:

```
function useMyCustomHook() {
    const [state, setState] = useState(initialState);
    // Custom logic
    return [state, customLogicFunction];
}
```

8. Performance Enhancement with `useMemo` and `useCallback`

- Optimizing with Memoization:

  - `useMemo` and `useCallback` provide memoization capabilities to optimize functional components, preventing unnecessary recalculations or renders.

  - They are particularly useful for conserving computational resources by memoizing values and functions, especially when dependencies remain unchanged.

Summarizing the Impact of Hooks

Hooks have redefined the approach to managing lifecycle events and states in React's functional components. They streamline component logic, making it more readable and manageable. Grasping these hooks is crucial for developers to effectively utilize React in creating sophisticated, efficient web applications. As React evolves, staying adept with these advancements is vital for any developer looking to excel in modern web application development.

Chapter Seven

Working with Forms

Building forms in React

Creating forms in React, a common task in web application development, involves collecting and managing user input. React streamlines this process by handling the state of the form, enabling developers to efficiently capture and utilize user data. Mastering form construction and management in React is crucial for developers, as it significantly impacts user interaction and data handling.

1. Controlled Components vs. Uncontrolled Components

React offers two main methodologies for form data management: controlled and uncontrolled components.

- Controlled Components:

    - In a controlled component, the React state serves as the primary repository for form data.

- Example:

```
class FormComponent extends React.Component {
  state = { formData: '' };

  handleInputChange = (event) => {
    this.setState({ formData: event.target.value });
  };

  render() {
    return (
      <input type="text" value={this.state.formData} onChange={this.handleInputChange} />
    );
  }
}
```

- The state is updated with every change, making it easy to track and validate user input.

- Uncontrolled Components:

  - Uncontrolled components utilize refs for accessing form values directly from the DOM, bypassing the component state.

- Example:

```
class FormComponent extends React.Component {
    inputRef = React.createRef();

    handleFormSubmit = (event) => {
        alert('Input Value: ' + this.inputRef.current.value);
        event.preventDefault();
    };

    render() {
        return (
            <form onSubmit={this.handleFormSubmit}>
                <input type="text" ref={this.inputRef} />
                <button type="submit">Submit</button>
            </form>
        );
    }
}
```

- This approach is closer to traditional HTML form handling and can be simpler for managing multiple inputs.

2. Managing Form Interactions

React's form event handlers, such as onChange and onSubmit, are integral to user interaction.

- onChange: Utilized for tracking changes in input fields and often used to update the state.

- onSubmit: Handles the form submission process, where final processing or validation of the form occurs.

3. Implementing Form Validation

Validating user input is essential for ensuring data correctness.

- Client-Side Validation: Involves checking inputs before submission. React's state management facilitates on-the-fly validations or checks before the form is submitted.

- Server-Side Validation: React can also handle validations performed by the server, displaying any error messages returned.

4. Utilizing Third-Party Form Libraries

For more complex forms, libraries like Formik, Redux Form, and React Hook Form offer advanced solutions for managing form state, validation, and submission. These libraries provide enhanced features and abstractions beneficial in sophisticated scenarios.

5. Constructing Multi-Step Forms

Developing multi-step forms, or wizards, is often required. React's component structure allows developers to craft distinct components for each step, managing the overall state at a higher level.

6. Ensuring Form Accessibility

Making forms accessible is critical, involving the proper implementation of labels, error handling, and keyboard navigation. React's JSX syntax aids in integrating these accessibility features.

Summary

In summary, form creation in React provides versatility and control, whether through controlled or uncontrolled components. Comprehending the intricacies of event handling, conducting validations, and leveraging third-party libraries is key to crafting effective, user-friendly forms. Additionally, attention to accessibility and employing React's component architecture for complex forms like multi-step processes further improves usability and functionality. For React developers, being adept in these facets of form building is essential for creating comprehensive, interactive user interfaces.

Handling form submissions

In React development, effectively managing form submissions is essential. This process typically encompasses capturing user input and processing the submit action.

1. Fundamentals of React Form Submission

React's approach to form submissions involves managing input data and executing actions upon form submission.

- Data Capture:

    - Controlled components in React manage form data through state, with input fields being governed by state-updating functions.

    - Uncontrolled components use refs to directly gather data from DOM elements.

- Submit Event Handling:

    - The `onSubmit` event on the form element is crucial, triggering a function that dictates the form submission behavior.

2. Submission in Controlled Components

Controlled components allow for direct state access during form submission.

- Illustration:

```
class ExampleForm extends React.Component {
    state = { data: '' };

    handleInputChange = (event) => {
        this.setState({ data: event.target.value });
    };

    handleSubmit = (event) => {
        event.preventDefault();
        // Processing form data
        console.log(this.state.data);
    };

    render() {
        return (
            <form onSubmit={this.handleSubmit}>
                <input type="text" value={this.state.data} onChange={this.handleInputChange} />
                <button type="submit">Submit</button>
            </form>
        );
    }
}
```

3. Uncontrolled Component Approach

Uncontrolled components utilize refs for accessing form data at the submission point.

94

- Example:

```
class ExampleForm extends React.Component {
  inputReference = React.createRef();

  handleSubmit = (event) => {
    event.preventDefault();
    console.log('Form Value: ', this.inputReference.current.value);
  };

  render() {
    return (
      <form onSubmit={this.handleSubmit}>
        <input type="text" ref={this.inputReference} />
        <button type="submit">Submit</button>
      </form>
    );
  }
}
```

4. Implementing Form Validation

Validation of form data is a critical step, whether done on the client side before submission or on the server side post-submission.

- Client-Side Validation: This includes checks before the data is sent to the server, such as field completeness or email format validation.

- Server-Side Validation: Conducted after data submission, serving as the final gatekeeper before data processing.

5. Asynchronous Form Submissions

Modern web applications often handle form submissions asynchronously, using AJAX to maintain page responsiveness.

95

- AJAX with Fetch or Axios: These tools facilitate HTTP requests to send and receive data from a server asynchronously.

6. Managing UI States During Submission

The user experience is enhanced by managing UI states like loading, success, and error during form submission.

- Loading State: Indicates ongoing data processing.

- Success State: Confirms successful form submission.

- Error State: Notifies users of any submission errors.

Wrapping Up

In React, managing form submissions encompasses understanding controlled and uncontrolled components, effective validation strategies, and handling UI states during submission. Handling forms asynchronously for a dynamic user experience is also a key consideration. Mastery in these areas is crucial for developers in creating robust, user-centric, and secure form interactions in React applications. Forms are integral to many web applications, and proficient handling in React is a valuable skill for developers in this domain.

Form validation techniques

Form validation plays a vital role in web application development, ensuring the accuracy, completeness, and security of user-provided data. Effective validation of form inputs is crucial not only for maintaining data integrity but also for enhancing user experience by preventing the submission of incorrect or malicious data. Different strategies and practices exist for form validation, each tailored to specific needs and use cases.

1. Client-Side and Server-Side Validation

- Client-Side Validation: This takes place within the user's browser before data is sent to the server. It offers immediate feedback to users and reduces server load, though it should not be the sole validation method due to potential security bypasses.

- Server-Side Validation: Conducted on the server after data submission, server-side validation is critical for security and ensuring data integrity, acting as a definitive checkpoint before data processing.

2. JavaScript-Based Validation

JavaScript offers a dynamic approach to client-side validation in frameworks like React, where form data is often managed through component state.

- Regular Expressions for Format Validation: Regex can validate specific data formats, including emails, phone numbers, and passwords.

- Event Handler-Based Validation: Using events like `onChange`, `onBlur`, or `onSubmit` to validate user input during form interactions.

3. HTML5 Validation Techniques

HTML5 introduces native form validation features using input types (`type="email"`, `type="number"`), alongside attributes such as `required`, `minlength`, `maxlength`, and `pattern`.

- Implementing HTML5 Constraints: These provide basic validation without extra JavaScript but may lack comprehensive validation needs and customization options for error messaging and styling.

4. Utilizing CSS Pseudo-Classes

CSS pseudo-classes (`:invalid`, `:valid`, `:required`) can complement HTML5 validation by providing visual cues to the user.

- Styling Based on Validity: Altering the appearance of form fields based on validation state.

5. Framework and Library Solutions

Many JavaScript frameworks and libraries offer solutions for more streamlined form validation.

- React Validation Tools: Libraries like Formik or React Hook Form offer extended form handling capabilities, including validation.

- Schema-Based Validators: Libraries such as Yup or Joi provide structured validation schemas.

6. Custom Validation Routines

For more intricate validation requirements, custom JavaScript functions are employed.

- **Building Modular Validation Functions:** Creating specific functions for various validation checks that can be applied across different forms.

7. Asynchronous Validation for Server Checks

Asynchronous validation is used where server-side verification is necessary, like checking the uniqueness of an email or username.

- **Incorporating AJAX for Dynamic Validation:** Employing AJAX in validation logic to check certain inputs against server-side data.

8. Effective Error Messaging

Properly displaying error messages significantly impacts user experience.

- **Clear and Specific Error Messages:** Providing concise and relevant error information near the associated input field.

- **Accessibility in Error Reporting:** Ensuring that error messages and states are accessible to all users, including those with disabilities.

9. Security Focus in Validation

Validation also encompasses preventing threats like SQL Injection and Cross-Site Scripting (XSS).

- Input Sanitization: Cleaning input data to remove potentially harmful code or scripts.

Wrapping Up

In summary, form validation is a multifaceted aspect of web development, involving a blend of client-side and server-side techniques. Employing a combination of HTML5 features, JavaScript, CSS, and various validation libraries ensures comprehensive validation. Effective validation enhances user interaction, secures the data collection process, and is a crucial skill in web development, necessitating technical savvy and an understanding of user experience and security considerations.

Chapter Eight

Introduction to Hooks

Understanding hooks in React

Grasping the concept of hooks in React is crucial for developers engaged in modern web application development. Introduced in React version 16.8, hooks have revolutionized the way functional components are utilized, allowing for state and other React features to be managed in a more streamlined and efficient manner.

1. Introduction to Hooks in React

Prior to hooks, React's component architecture was split into stateful class components and stateless functional components. Hooks have bridged this divide, enabling functional components to handle state and replicate the capabilities previously exclusive to class components.

2. Key Hooks and Their Usage

- useState:

  - The `useState` hook introduces state management to functional components. It returns a pair consisting of the current state and a function to update it, analogous to `this.state` and `this.setState` in class components.

- Example:

```
const [value, setValue] = useState(0);
```

- useEffect:

    - `useEffect` serves to handle side effects in functional components, akin to `componentDidMount`, `componentDidUpdate`, and `componentWillUnmount` in classes.

    - Example:

```
useEffect(() => {
    // Side effect code and cleanup
}, [dependencies]);
```

    - The effect runs after rendering and the dependencies array determines its re-execution.

- useContext:

    - The `useContext` hook allows for easy access to React context within functional components.

    - Example:

```
const contextValue = useContext(MyContext);
```

3. Hooks for Complex Scenarios

- useReducer:

  - **`useReducer`** is an alternative to **`useState`** for complex state logic, providing a more detailed approach to state transitions.

  - Example:

```
const [state, dispatch] = useReducer(reducerFunction, initialState);
```

- useCallback and useMemo:

  - **`useCallback`** delivers a memoized callback function, aiding in performance by reducing re-renders.

  - **`useMemo`** offers memoized values, suitable for costly computations.

  - Both depend on a set of dependencies for their operation.

- useRef:

  - **`useRef`** is used for direct DOM access and storing mutable values that don't cause re-renders.

  - Example:

```
const domRef = useRef(initialValue);
```

4. Developing Custom Hooks

Custom hooks allow for the extraction and reuse of component logic in a modular function.

- Example of Custom Hook:

```
function useMyHook() {
    const [state, setState] = useState(initialState);
    // Custom Logic
    return [state, customLogic];
}
```

5. Adhering to Hooks Rules

Hooks come with specific usage rules:

- Top-Level Execution: Hooks should be called at the top level of React functions, not inside loops or conditions.

- Use in React Functions Only: They should be invoked within React functional components or custom hooks.

6. Benefits of Utilizing Hooks

- Component Simplification: Hooks allow developers to utilize functional components extensively, reducing the need to understand class-based complexities.

- Reusable Logic: Custom hooks facilitate the sharing of stateful logic across components.

- Enhanced Code Organization: Hooks encourage more organized and maintainable code, grouping related logic within components.

Wrapping Up

In essence, hooks are a transformative addition to React, providing a more functional approach to component development. They simplify state management, enable side effect handling, and allow for logic encapsulation and reuse. Mastery of hooks is now integral to React development, enabling cleaner, more effective code and sophisticated application functionality. As React evolves, staying proficient with hooks and their best practices remains essential for any React developer.

useState and useEffect hooks

In React's ecosystem, the advent of hooks, particularly **useState** and **useEffect**, has been a game-changer in how functional components are developed. These hooks have streamlined the process of managing state and handling side effects, enhancing the capabilities of functional components.

1. `**useState**` Hook: Simplifying State Management

The `**useState**` hook is a cornerstone in React for adding state to functional components, a feature traditionally limited to class components.

- Implementing `**useState**`:

  - This hook allows the declaration of state variables in functional components. It returns a pair: the state variable and a function to update it.

  - Example:

```
const [value, setValue] = useState(0);
```

- Here, `value` is the state variable, while `setValue` is the function for updating the state.

- Advantages:

  - It offers a more intuitive and concise approach to state management compared to the `this.setState` method in class components.

  - `useState` supports dynamic state initialization, useful for operations that require initial heavy lifting.

2. `useEffect` Hook: Handling Side Effects

`useEffect` is designed to execute side effects in functional components, replacing class lifecycle methods.

- Basic Functionality:

  - The hook executes after the initial render and subsequent updates. It accepts a function for the side effect and a dependencies array.

  - Example:

```
useEffect(() => {
    document.title = `Clicked ${value} times`;
}, [value]);
```

  - This effect modifies the document title, depending on the `value` state.

106

- Managing Cleanup:

    - Effects that need cleanup can return a function that handles it. This is particularly useful for subscriptions or event listeners.

    - Example:

```
useEffect(() => {
    const handle = subscribeToSomething(id);
    return () => {
        unsubscribeFromSomething(handle);
    };
}, [id]);
```

- Performance Optimization:

    - The dependencies array controls when the effect reruns, optimizing component performance.

3. Best Practices and Usage Patterns

- Reusable State Logic:

    - Hooks facilitate the sharing of state logic across components, reducing redundancy.

- Conditional Effects:

    - Effects should be controlled using the dependencies array, not within the effect body.

- Focused Concerns:

- Multiple `useEffect` instances can be used within a component for different concerns, aiding in clearer code organization.

4. Potential Challenges and Recommendations

- State Overuse:

  - Excessive state declarations can lead to performance bottlenecks. Consolidating state and using it judiciously is recommended.

- Dependencies Management:

  - Carefully managing the dependencies array in `useEffect` is essential to prevent unintended effect executions.

- Embracing Hooks Philosophy:

  - Rather than mimicking class component patterns, embracing the unique approach of hooks often results in more efficient code.

Wrapping Up

In conclusion, `useState` and `useEffect` represent pivotal elements in React functional components, providing a streamlined way to manage state and side effects. These hooks enhance the readability and maintainability of code, offering a declarative approach to defining component behavior. For React developers, proficiency in these hooks is crucial, as they form the backbone of modern, effective React component development.

Custom hooks for advanced scenarios

In React's development landscape, custom hooks have become a pivotal asset for handling intricate component logic. These user-defined hooks extend the functionality of React's standard hooks, tailoring them to specific, complex use cases. Custom hooks contribute significantly to improving code modularity, reusability, and the clear separation of different functionalities within applications.

1. Essence of Custom Hooks in React

Custom hooks are JavaScript functions that employ React's native hooks to encapsulate distinct, stateful logic, making it reusable across various components. They typically follow the naming pattern starting with 'use', mirroring React's intrinsic hooks.

2. Benefits of Custom Hooks

- Logic Reusability: Custom hooks enable the extraction and repurposing of common logic across numerous components, diminishing code repetition.

- Streamlined Component Design: They help in segregating complex functionalities from components, focusing the latter more on rendering aspects, thereby boosting code clarity and ease of maintenance.

- Portability Across Projects: These hooks can be easily transported and utilized across different projects, fostering a culture of sharing and reusability in the developer community.

3. Crafting Custom Hooks for Elaborate State Handling

Custom hooks can adeptly manage intricate states and interactions that might be unwieldy or inefficient within individual components.

- Use Case Illustration:

    - Developing a hook for intricate form handling or state management in a digital storefront.

    - Such a hook would handle tasks like updating form fields, conducting input validations, managing errors, or overseeing shopping cart items and quantities.

4. Custom Hooks for Efficient Data Fetching

One of the prime applications of custom hooks lies in data fetching and API interaction.

- API Interaction Abstraction:

    - A custom hook can streamline API interactions, managing data retrieval, loading statuses, error handling, and even data caching mechanisms.

    - Example Implementation:

```
function useApiData(url) {
    const [data, setData] = useState(null);
    const [isLoading, setIsLoading] = useState(true);
    const [error, setError] = useState(null);

    useEffect(() => {
        fetch(url)
            .then(response => response.json())
            .then(setData)
            .catch(setError)
            .finally(() => setIsLoading(false));
    }, [url]);

    return { data, isLoading, error };
}
```

5. Custom Hooks for Event Listener and Timer Management

Handling event listeners and timers can be intricate, particularly concerning correct setup and teardown to prevent memory leaks.

- DOM Event Handling:

  - Custom hooks can proficiently manage adding and removing event listeners.

- Managing Timers:

  - They can encapsulate the logic for creating and clearing timers or intervals.

6. Custom Hooks in Animations and Side Effects

Complex animations or intricate side effects in applications can be efficiently managed through custom hooks.

- Animation Control:
    - Hooks can be used to manage the entire lifecycle of animations, including initiation, termination, and handling interruptions.

7. Testing and Debugging Strategies for Custom Hooks

Like any code segment, custom hooks require thorough testing and debugging.

- Unit Testing Approaches:
    - Utilizing tools such as React Testing Library and Jest to ensure the hooks perform as expected.
- Debugging Techniques:
    - Involves scrutinizing the internal state and the effects initiated by the hook.

8. Disseminating Custom Hooks

Once crafted, custom hooks can be disseminated across different projects or shared within the developer community, enhancing a collective repository of reusable solutions.

Wrapping Up

Custom hooks in React signify the framework's adaptability and expansion capabilities. They offer structured solutions for managing complex scenarios, from state handling and data fetching to animation control and event management. As the React framework evolves, proficiency in custom hooks is increasingly becoming an integral skill for developers, enabling the crafting of more refined, efficient applications.

Chapter Nine

Routing in React

Introduction to React Router

React Router stands as a pivotal library in the React framework, renowned for introducing dynamic routing functionality to web applications. It's widely recognized as the go-to solution for routing in React, empowering single-page applications (SPAs) with client-side routing that mimics the behavior of traditional multi-page websites while preserving the SPA's seamless user interface.

1. The Role of React Router

React Router comprises a set of navigational components that sync the application's user interface with the URL. It enables defining various routes in the application, linking each route to specific components, thus facilitating intricate layouts and navigational paths, all while ensuring fluid user navigation.

2. Principal Components of React Router

- BrowserRouter: This component envelops the entire application, supporting dynamic routing via the HTML5 history API.

- Route: It is responsible for rendering UI components based on the URL path, defining which component appears for each route.

- Link: Replacing the traditional `<a>` tag, the Link component allows for in-app navigation without full page refreshes.

- Switch: Utilized to render only the first matching route for the current location, as opposed to rendering all matches.

3. Variants and Versions

React Router is available in various forms, such as `**react-router-dom**` for web applications and `**react-router-native**` for mobile apps using React Native. The web-focused `**react-router-dom**` includes all core features of React Router, along with additional functionalities tailored for web apps.

4. Implementation and Integration

Integrating React Router into a React project is straightforward. Installation is achieved through npm or yarn, followed by importing its components into the React application. Typically, the setup involves wrapping the app with a `**BrowserRouter**` and placing `**Route**` components within it.

5. Advantages in Single-Page Applications

React Router revolutionizes navigation in SPAs by enabling dynamic, client-side routing. This method renders different components based on URL changes without actual page reloads, significantly boosting performance and enhancing user experience.

6. Advanced Routing Concepts

React Router supports complex routing structures like nested routing for multi-layered application layouts and protected routes that impose specific access conditions, such as user authentication.

7. Dynamic Paths and Queries

The library excels in handling dynamic route parameters and query strings, allowing components to receive and utilize dynamic information from the URL, thereby adding versatility to the application routing.

8. Navigational Control

Beyond using the `Link` component for navigation, React Router provides programmatic navigation methods, such as the `useHistory` hook or the `withRouter` higher-order component, offering more nuanced control over navigation actions.

9. Compatibility with Other Libraries

React Router seamlessly integrates with other libraries and can be combined with state management solutions like Redux or the Context API, ensuring a coherent state management ecosystem in conjunction with routing.

10. Managing Redirects and 404 Pages

The library includes functionalities for handling 'not found' scenarios and implementing redirects under specific conditions, enhancing the robustness of routing in the application.

Wrapping Up

In essence, React Router is an integral tool for developing contemporary SPAs in the React framework. Its dynamic routing capabilities, support for complex routing structures, and flexible navigation control make it indispensable for building modern web applications with rich, intuitive user interfaces. For React developers, mastering React Router is crucial, as it continues to be an essential component of the React development toolkit, adapting and evolving to meet the ever-changing demands of web application development.

Setting up and configuring routes

In the realm of web development, particularly for single-page applications (SPAs), setting up and configuring routes is a key task. Effective routing ensures users are directed to appropriate content based on URLs, enhancing user interface experience and application functionality.

1. The Role of Routing in Web Applications

Routing in web apps involves displaying different pages or components in response to URL changes. While server-side routing is typical in multi-page applications, SPAs handle routing on the client side, often using JavaScript libraries or frameworks.

2. Implementing Routing in React Using React Router

React Router is a preferred tool for routing in React applications. Its setup involves:

- Installation:

  - React Router is added to a project via npm or yarn, with `react-router-dom` being the standard package for web apps.

  - Installation command: `npm install react-router-dom` or `yarn add react-router-dom`

- Initial Configuration:

  - The setup typically involves encasing the app in a `BrowserRouter` component. Inside this, `Route` components define the mapping between URL paths and React components.

3. Route Definition

Routes are set using the `Route` component, associating URL paths with React components. A simple route setup includes:

```
<BrowserRouter>
  <Switch>
    <Route exact path="/" component={Home} />
    <Route path="/about" component={About} />
    <Route path="/contact" component={Contact} />
  </Switch>
</BrowserRouter>
```

- Usage of `**Switch**`:

  - `**Switch**` renders the first child `**Route**` matching the location. It's useful for grouping routes and ensuring only one is rendered at a time.

- `**exact**` Prop in Routes:

  - The `**exact**` prop is crucial for precise path matching, avoiding multiple component renderings for similar paths.

4. Advanced Routing Techniques

React Router supports nested routing for complex layouts and dynamic routing using route parameters for variable path segments.

5. Managing Redirects and 404 Pages

The `**Redirect**` component in React Router handles conditional route redirections. For 404 or 'not found' cases, a catch-all `**Route**` can be used.

6. Navigation Components

`**Link**` and `**NavLink**` components in React Router facilitate in-app navigation without page reloads.

- `**Link**`: Basic navigation.

- `**NavLink**`: Similar to `**Link**` but adds styling attributes when matching the current URL.

7. Programmatic Navigation Methods

React Router allows navigation to be triggered programmatically, using the `useHistory` hook in functional components or `withRouter` in class components.

8. Lazy Loading for Performance Optimization

React Router accommodates lazy loading of components, which, combined with React's `React.lazy()` and `Suspense`, allows for efficient code splitting and component loading.

9. Securing Application Routes

Creating protected routes is key for controlling access in parts of the application, implementable through wrapper components or authentication context management.

Wrapping Up

Configuring routes is an integral part of SPA development, crucial for user navigation and content rendering based on URL structures. Tools like React Router enable developers to build sophisticated routing systems, improving user experience and app performance. As applications grow in size and complexity, a deep understanding of routing setup and configuration becomes more essential, requiring developers to be well-versed in routing concepts and best practices.

Navigating between pages

Page navigation is a critical component in web development, crucial for ensuring a smooth and intuitive user journey within an application. It involves guiding users efficiently from one section or view to another, which is key to enhancing user experience and maintaining the functionality of the web application.

1. Significance of Fluid Navigation

In today's web development, especially in single-page applications (SPAs), the significance of fluid navigation cannot be overstated. It's about creating a user journey that is seamless, contextually consistent, and swift in content loading. Well-designed navigation reduces user disorientation, lowers bounce rates, and enhances overall user interaction with the application.

2. Client-Side Routing in SPAs

SPAs typically employ client-side routing, where JavaScript in the browser handles the navigation logic. This contrasts with traditional multi-page applications that rely on server-side page reloads.

- Benefits of Client-Side Routing:

    - Quicker transitions between sections as resources are initially loaded.

    - Less server demand, as many navigational actions are handled within the browser.

- Maintained state and UI consistency across the user's session.

3. Navigation Tools in React Applications

Frameworks like React often utilize libraries such as React Router for navigation management. These provide components for creating linkable elements and enable navigation control programmatically through hooks.

- Link Elements:

  - `Link` and `NavLink` components replace traditional anchor (`<a>`) tags for internal routing, preventing full page reloads in SPAs.

- Programmatic Navigation Control:

  - Hooks, notably `useHistory`, are employed for navigation in scenarios like post-form submission or after authentication processes.

4. Principles of Effective Navigation Design

Good navigation design is as much about the user experience as it is about technical execution.

- Consistent and Intuitive Design: Navigation elements should be easy to find and consistently placed.

- Clear Orientation Cues: Users should readily understand their current location in the app and how to navigate to other sections.

- Accessibility Compliance: Navigation should support diverse user interactions, including keyboard and screen reader accessibility.

5. Mobile-Responsive Navigation

Adapting navigation for mobile devices is essential due to the increasing prevalence of mobile usage.

- Compact Menus on Small Screens: Hamburger menus or dropdowns are common solutions for space constraints on mobile devices.

- Touch-Friendly Design: Ensuring navigational elements are easily interactable on touchscreens.

6. Deep Linking and Bookmarking in SPAs

Managing deep linking, where users bookmark or share URLs to specific app locations, requires thoughtful design in SPAs to ensure the server responds correctly to these direct accesses.

7. Managing Loading States and Page Transitions

Enhancing the user experience includes gracefully managing content loading states and transitions.

- Indicators for Loading: Providing visual cues when content is being loaded.

- Smooth Page Transitions: Employing animations or transitions for a better perceived performance.

8. SEO Aspects in Navigation

For web applications that need public visibility, ensuring SEO-friendly navigation is key. This includes crawlable navigation elements and user-friendly URLs.

9. Navigational Practices to Follow

- Simplicity is Key: Avoid complex navigation structures.

- Provide Instant Feedback: Users should receive immediate indications of their navigational actions.

- Uniform Navigation Experience: Consistency in navigation is vital across the application.

Summing Up

Navigating between pages transcends mere linking of application sections; it involves crafting an engaging and coherent user experience. Employing client-side routing tools like React Router, coupled with a focus on user experience, mobile adaptability, accessibility, and SEO considerations, are integral to designing successful navigation. As web technologies evolve, so do navigation strategies, highlighting their continued importance in web development.

Chapter Ten

State Management with Context API

Understanding Context API for global state management

Grasping the Context API in React is vital for developers aiming to manage global state within their applications with greater efficiency. Since its introduction in React 16.3, the Context API has offered a method to share states like user authentication, themes, or other global states across the entire app or parts of it. This approach negates the need for prop drilling, where props are passed through every level of the component tree, streamlining state management in complex applications.

1. Necessity of Global State Management

Managing state data accessible across multiple components can be challenging in intricate React applications. Traditional methods like prop drilling, passing props down the component tree, become cumbersome with deep component nesting. The Context API provides a more efficient global state management alternative.

2. Fundamentals of the Context API

The Context API in React allows for the creation of global variables that can be passed around the React component tree. It involves two key elements:

- React.createContext():

  - This function creates a Context object. Components subscribing to this Context object will read the current context value from the nearest matching `**Provider**` in the tree.

  - The createContext method yields an object with a `**Provider**` and a `**Consumer**`.

- Provider Component:

  - The Provider component wraps the component tree to supply the context value to all components within that tree. Any component can then access the context using the Consumer component or the useContext hook.

- Consumer Component:

  - The Consumer component and useContext hook are utilized to access the context value. The useContext hook is more commonly used for its simplicity, particularly in functional components.

3. Implementing the Context API

Implementing the Context API typically involves:

- Creating a Context:

  - Establish a Context using `**React.createContext()**`.

  -

- Example:

```
const MyContext = React.createContext(defaultValue);
```

- Providing Context Value:

  - The Provider component is used to envelop the app section where the context needs to be accessible.

  - Example:

```
<MyContext.Provider value={/* some value */}>
  {/* component tree */}
</MyContext.Provider>
```

- Using the Context:

  - Access the context value in components using the Consumer component or the useContext hook.

  - Example with useContext:

```
const value = useContext(MyContext);
```

4. Applications of Context API

The Context API is especially useful in situations where data needs to be accessible by many components at different levels. Typical applications include user authentication status, UI themes or preferences, and language settings for internationalization.

5. Advantages of Context API

- Streamlined State Management: It reduces the complexity of prop passing at every component level.

- Enhanced Component Reusability: By avoiding prop drilling, it increases the reusability of components.

- Efficient Performance: It can be more efficient than prop drilling across many component levels.

6. Recommended Practices and Considerations

The Context API is powerful but should be used judiciously:

- Limited Use: It should not replace all component communication but rather be used for genuinely global states.

- Performance Awareness: Be aware that updating Context values triggers re-renders of all consuming components.

7. Context API vs. Other State Management Tools

For larger applications, more comprehensive state management solutions like Redux or MobX, which offer middleware support and more predictable state transitions, might still be preferable over the Context API.

Concluding Thoughts

In summary, the Context API provides an effective solution for managing global state in React applications. It offers a streamlined way to pass data through the component tree, easing state management in large-scale applications. Proper implementation of the Context API enables developers to construct scalable, maintainable, and efficient React applications, particularly when dealing with broad state dependencies such as user preferences, themes, or authentication data. The Context API should be employed judiciously, complementing other state management solutions as necessary, depending on the application's specific requirements and complexity.

Creating and using context in React applications

In React applications, the concept of context is a sophisticated solution designed to eliminate the complexities of passing data through various component layers. This approach is particularly beneficial in extensive applications where passing props directly (prop drilling) can become cumbersome and inefficient.

1. Grasping Context in React

React's context feature allows for the distribution of values such as user settings, themes, or languages across different components, bypassing the need to pass props at each level. It's a mechanism intended for effective data dissemination throughout an application, particularly useful in scenarios demanding global state management.

2. Establishing a Context

Creating a context involves the `**React.createContext**` function. This generates a Context object with two key components: `**Provider**` and `**Consumer**`.

- Example of Context Creation:

```
const UserContext = React.createContext('defaultUser');
```

Here, a user context is established with a default value.

3. Utilizing the `**Provider**` Component

The `**Provider**` component wraps parts of the app where the context is to be accessible, using the `**value**` prop to relay data to children components.

- Implementing Provider:

```
<UserContext.Provider value={/* some value */}>
  {/* children components */}
</UserContext.Provider>
```

In this scenario, the `**UserContext.Provider**` encloses components that require access to the user context.

4. Accessing Context with `**Consumer**`

The `**Consumer**` component, part of the created context object, facilitates access to the context value in components below the provider in the tree.

- Example with Consumer:

```
<UserContext.Consumer>
  {value => /* rendering based on context value */}
</UserContext.Consumer>
```

5. The `useContext` Hook for Functional Components

The `useContext` hook is a simpler alternative for accessing context in functional components, providing the current context value.

- `useContext` Usage Example:

```
const user = useContext(UserContext);
```

6. Dynamic Context Values

Context values can be updated dynamically, and consumer components using this context will re-render with the new value upon changes in the `Provider`.

7. Context Usage Guidelines

- Limited Application: Context should not be overused; it's best employed for specific scenarios needing global state sharing.

- Encapsulating Context Logic: Wrapping context logic in custom hooks or higher-order components can streamline consuming components.

- Setting Default Values: Default values in `createContext` are beneficial for isolated component testing.

131

8. Comparing Context with State Management Libraries

The Context API, while robust for certain use cases, is not a complete alternative to state management libraries like Redux, which offer more comprehensive solutions for complex state management.

9. Context API Use Cases

Common applications of context include:

- User Authentication State Management: Efficiently handling and accessing user authentication information.

- Theme Implementation: Facilitating dynamic theme changes across an application.

- Localization Efforts: Managing and applying language preferences and localization data.

Summation

In summary, the context feature in React significantly simplifies data management across an application, especially in large-scale projects where direct data passing is not practical. Mastery of context creation and usage is essential for React developers, especially for those developing expansive applications requiring streamlined data handling. However, context should be used thoughtfully, often in tandem with other state management practices or libraries, to ensure a well-structured and manageable codebase.

Best practices for state management

State management is a pivotal element in the development of web applications, especially within frameworks like React. Properly managing state is crucial for ensuring that an application runs efficiently, scales well, and is easy to maintain. Adhering to best practices in state management can greatly enhance an application's performance and overall user experience.

1. Comprehending State in Web Development

State in a web application encompasses the data determining the application's behavior and appearance at any moment. This includes user inputs, application settings, UI states, and similar elements. Skillful state management is fundamental for ensuring an application's responsiveness and functionality.

2. Localizing State Management

- State Proximity: It's best to keep the state as close to where it's used as possible. Not all state data must be global; often, it's better managed locally, like form input states within a form component.

- Advantages of Proximity: Local state management can lead to fewer unnecessary re-renders and less complex dependencies, enhancing component reusability and application performance.

3. Implementing State Management Libraries

- Appropriate Library Utilization: For complex applications where state is shared and modified across many components, it might be beneficial to use libraries like Redux, MobX, or Context API.

- Centralized State Approach: These libraries often provide a centralized store, simplifying state management, debugging, and maintenance.

4. Immutable State Modification

- State Immutability: Always treat state as immutable; state should never be directly modified but rather updated through new object or array instances.

- Benefits of Immutability: This approach eases complex state updates and debugging, and is particularly effective when using libraries like Redux.

5. Keeping State Minimal

- Reducing State Footprint: Only store necessary data in the state, deriving any additional information as needed.

- Complexity Reduction: Minimizing state volume can decrease the likelihood of bugs and simplify overall state management.

6. Syncing with External Data

- Efficient Data Management: Be mindful of state synchronization with external sources. Efficient fetching and caching strategies are crucial to avoid excessive network requests and state updates.

7. State and Component Design

- Emphasis on Stateless Components: Aim to create stateless (functional) components where feasible, as they are generally easier to test, debug, and maintain.

- Categorizing Components: In larger applications, differentiate between 'smart' (stateful) and 'dumb' (stateless) components for better state management.

8. Managing Asynchronous Operations

- Handling Async State: Manage asynchronous operations such as API calls using patterns and libraries (e.g., async/await, Redux Thunk, or Saga) to maintain predictable state changes.

9. Regular Testing of State Logic

- State Testing: Continuously perform unit tests on state management logic to ensure reliable state behavior.

- Utilizing Testing Tools: Employ testing libraries and tools to replicate state changes and actions in test scenarios.

10. Optimizing Performance

- Monitoring Performance: Regularly check the performance implications of state changes. Tools like React DevTools can be instrumental in identifying and optimizing unnecessary renders.

- Employing Memoization: Use memoization to prevent re-computation of derived states.

11. Documenting State Flow

- State Documentation: Keep clear documentation of the state flow within your application, especially in complex projects, to aid in understanding and maintaining the state architecture.

12. Learning from Established Patterns

- Leveraging Known Patterns: Familiarize yourself with established state management patterns seen in frameworks and libraries like Redux, MobX, or React's Context API, and adapt these patterns effectively in your projects.

Summing Up

Effective state management is essential for crafting robust web applications. By localizing state, judiciously using state management libraries, maintaining immutable state updates, minimizing state, and handling asynchronous operations carefully, developers can create performant, maintainable, and scalable applications. Regular testing, performance optimization, and thorough documentation further strengthen state management practices. Keeping abreast of evolving state management strategies and best practices is vital for any web developer's toolkit.

Chapter Eleven

Fetching Data from APIs

Making HTTP requests in React

In React development, HTTP requests are integral for interacting with external APIs and services, crucial for retrieving data, submitting forms, and other server interactions. Properly managing these requests is key to ensuring a responsive application that provides timely and accurate information.

1. Significance of HTTP Requests in React

HTTP requests enable React applications to fetch and send data to external sources, crucial for displaying dynamic content, handling user inputs, and performing network-related operations. Efficiently managing these requests ensures the application remains responsive and up-to-date.

2. Popular Methods for HTTP Requests

- XMLHttpRequest: A traditional method in JavaScript for making HTTP requests. Although it's less commonly used now, it paved the way for newer, more efficient methods.

- Fetch API: A modern standard for making network requests in the browser. It's promise-based, offering a simpler and more flexible approach than XMLHttpRequest.

- Axios: A widely-used HTTP client for the browser and Node.js. Axios simplifies request and response handling and offers automatic transformation of JSON data.

3. Implementing Fetch API in React

- Executing a GET Request:

```
fetch('https://api.example.com/data')
  .then(response => response.json())
  .then(data => console.log(data))
  .catch(error => console.error('Error:', error));
```

- This snippet demonstrates a basic GET request using `fetch`, processing the response as JSON.

- Managing POST Requests:

```
fetch('https://api.example.com/submit', {
  method: 'POST',
  headers: {
    'Content-Type': 'application/json',
  },
  body: JSON.stringify({ key: 'value' })
})
.then(response => response.json())
.then(data => console.log('Success:', data))
.catch(error => console.error('Error:', error));
```

- Here's how to handle a POST request with a JSON payload.

4. Utilizing Axios for Requests

Axios is renowned for its additional features such as automatic JSON transformation and interceptors for requests and responses.

- GET Request with Axios:

```
axios.get('https://api.example.com/data')
  .then(response => console.log('Data:', response.data))
  .catch(error => console.error('Error:', error));
```

- POST Request Using Axios:

```
axios.post('https://api.example.com/submit', { key: 'value' })
  .then(response => console.log('Success:', response.data))
  .catch(error => console.error('Error:', error));
```

5. State Management for HTTP Requests in React

Managing the various states of an HTTP request, like loading, success, or error, is essential.

- Example with React Hooks:

```
const [data, setData] = useState(null);
const [isLoading, setIsLoading] = useState(false);
const [error, setError] = useState(null);

useEffect(() => {
  setIsLoading(true);
  fetch('https://api.example.com/data')
    .then(response => response.json())
    .then(data => setData(data))
    .catch(error => setError(error))
    .finally(() => setIsLoading(false));
}, []);
```

6. Robust Error Handling

Effective error handling ensures a resilient user experience, displaying appropriate messages or fallbacks when requests fail.

7. Custom Hooks for HTTP Requests

Creating custom hooks can encapsulate HTTP request logic, enhancing code reusability and simplicity.

- Custom Hook for Fetching Data:

```
function useDataFetch(url) {
  const [data, setData] = useState(null);
  const [isLoading, setIsLoading] = useState(true);
  const [error, setError] = useState(null);

  useEffect(() => {
    fetch(url)
      .then(response => response.json())
      .then(data => setData(data))
      .catch(error => setError(error))
      .finally(() => setIsLoading(false));
  }, [url]);

  return { data, isLoading, error };
}
```

Final Thoughts

Managing HTTP requests is a critical part of building dynamic, interactive React applications. Whether utilizing Fetch API, Axios, or other HTTP clients, understanding how to make requests, handle responses, and manage states is crucial. Developing efficient practices for HTTP requests, including the use of custom hooks, allows developers to create React applications that seamlessly integrate with external APIs and services, enhancing functionality and user experience. As web technologies evolve, keeping up-to-date with current methods and best practices in HTTP request handling remains vital for React developers.

141

Fetching data from APIs using Axios

In modern web development, particularly within React environments, making HTTP requests to fetch data from APIs is a fundamental task. Axios, a prominent promise-based HTTP client, is favored for this role due to its user-friendly interface, versatility, and comprehensive set of features. It's particularly adept at handling various network requests and responses, a crucial aspect of interactive and data-driven web applications.

1. Introduction to Axios for HTTP Requests

Axios is an esteemed HTTP client library that eases the process of sending asynchronous HTTP requests to interact with REST endpoints. Its standout feature is the automatic transformation of JSON request and response data, facilitating a smoother interaction with JSON APIs. Axios is also recognized for its ability to handle a diverse range of HTTP request and response configurations.

2. Core Features of Axios

- Promise-Based Approach: Axios operates on JavaScript promises, providing a structured approach to handling asynchronous operations.

- Interceptors for Request and Response Handling: Axios allows for the definition of interceptors, useful for tasks like logging or authentication.

- Auto-Conversion to JSON: It automatically converts request and response data to JSON, streamlining interactions with JSON data.

- Request Cancellation: Axios supports the cancellation of requests, which is particularly useful in scenarios like search autocompletes.

- Configurable Request and Response Options: It offers a plethora of configuration options for requests and responses, including custom headers, query parameters, and timeout settings.

3. Incorporating Axios into a Project

Axios can be integrated into a project using npm or yarn:

```
npm install axios
```

or

```
yarn add axios
```

4. Performing GET Requests with Axios

GET requests are commonly used to retrieve data. Axios simplifies this process with its straightforward syntax.

- Example of a GET Request:

```
axios.get('https://api.example.com/data')
  .then(response => console.log(response.data))
  .catch(error => console.error('Error:', error));
```

5. Executing POST Requests via Axios

POST requests, typically used to send data to a server, are also efficiently managed by Axios.

- **Example of a POST Request:**

```
axios.post('https://api.example.com/data', { key: 'value' })
  .then(response => console.log('Success:', response.data))
  .catch(error => console.error('Error:', error));
```

6. Customizing Request Configurations with Axios

Axios allows for detailed customization of request configurations, suitable for various application needs.

- **Configuring Headers:**

```
axios.get('https://api.example.com/protected-data', {
  headers: { 'Authorization': `Bearer ${token}` }
});
```

- **Setting Timeouts and Parameters:**

```
axios.get('https://api.example.com/data', {
  params: { key: 'value' },
  timeout: 5000
});
```

7. Implementing Axios Interceptors

Axios interceptors are invaluable for consistently managing request and response operations across the application.

- Establishing an Interceptor:

```
axios.interceptors.response.use(response => response, error => Promise.reject(error));
```

8. Handling Errors in Axios Requests

Effective error management is essential for maintaining a user-friendly application. Axios aids in capturing and handling errors efficiently.

- Error Handling Strategy:

```
axios.get('https://api.example.com/data')
  .catch(error => {
    // Process error based on its type
    console.error('Error:', error);
  });
```

9. Utilizing Axios Instances for Frequent API Interactions

For applications regularly interacting with a specific API, creating an Axios instance configured for that API can simplify the process.

- Creating an Axios Instance:

```
const apiClient = axios.create({
  baseURL: 'https://api.example.com',
  timeout: 1000,
  headers: {'X-Custom-Header': 'value'}
});

apiClient.get('/data');
```

Summing Up Axios for Data Fetching

Axios stands as a robust and flexible tool for making HTTP requests in web applications. Its extensive features, including promise-based operation, interceptors, JSON auto-conversion, and customizable options, make it a preferred choice among developers. Effectively leveraging Axios for network requests, alongside proper error handling and the use of features like interceptors and instances, allows developers to create responsive, data-rich web applications. As the web development landscape evolves, Axios continues to be a reliable, widely-used tool for API interactions.

Handling asynchronous operations

Managing asynchronous operations is a key component in the realm of web development. Asynchronous tasks allow programs to perform time-intensive operations, such as fetching data or processing files, without halting other functionalities. This approach is pivotal for creating web applications that are responsive and user-centric.

1. The Essence of Asynchronous Operations in Web Applications

Asynchronous operations in web applications refer to tasks executed independently from the primary execution thread, enabling the application to stay responsive. These operations are integral for tasks like API communications, file processing, or any other processes that necessitate waiting for a response or event.

2. Asynchronicity in JavaScript

JavaScript's core design is intrinsically asynchronous, employing an event-driven, non-blocking model. This makes it well-equipped to handle operations that might vary in completion time.

3. Early Asynchronous Patterns: Callback Functions

Originally, JavaScript used callback functions for asynchronous tasks. These are functions provided as arguments to another function and executed after a task finishes.

- Drawback of Callbacks: The use of callbacks can lead to nested, complex code structures, often termed "callback hell," which complicates readability and maintainability.

4. Promises: An Evolution in Asynchronous JavaScript

Promises represent a significant advancement in managing asynchronous operations. They are objects that signify the eventual completion or failure of an operation.

- States of Promises: Promises exist in one of three states: pending, fulfilled, or rejected.

- Sequential Operations with Promises: They allow for the execution of asynchronous operations in sequence, avoiding the nested structure of callbacks.

5. Simplifying Asynchrony with `async/await`

The `async/await` syntax, introduced to simplify working with promises, allows asynchronous code to be written in a more synchronous manner.

- Async Functions: Functions declared with `async` return a promise, and the `await` keyword pauses function execution until the awaited promise settles.

6. Error Handling in Asynchronous JavaScript

Proper error handling is crucial in asynchronous operations. With promises and `async/await`, errors are typically managed using `catch` blocks or `try...catch` constructs.

7. Applying Asynchronous Operations in Applications

- API Data Retrieval: Fetching data from external APIs is a common use case for asynchronous operations, employing methods like `fetch` or libraries such as Axios.

- File Operations in Node.js: In Node.js, asynchronous operations are often used for reading and writing files, ensuring non-blocking input/output.

8. Parallel Execution in Asynchronous JavaScript

JavaScript allows handling multiple asynchronous tasks concurrently or in parallel, such as with `Promise.all`.

9. Managing UI State with Asynchronous Tasks

Frameworks like React manage UI state changes in response to asynchronous task outcomes using state hooks and effects.

10. Best Practices for Asynchronous Operations

- Avoiding Callback Nesting: Prefer using promises or `async/await` over complex callback nesting.

- Comprehensive Error Management: Ensure thorough error handling for all asynchronous operations.

- Network Request Optimization: Monitor the number and frequency of network requests to prevent performance issues.

- Leveraging Latest JavaScript Features: Employ contemporary JavaScript functionalities, like `async/await`, for cleaner and more intuitive asynchronous code.

Summary

Asynchronous operations form the backbone of effective web application development. Utilizing JavaScript's capabilities, such as callbacks, promises, and `async/await`, developers can efficiently manage lengthy tasks. This leads to the creation of applications that are both high-performing and aligned with user expectations. As web technologies advance, proficiency in asynchronous operations remains vital for web developers, enabling them to craft interactive, data-driven, and responsive applications.

Chapter Twelve

Styling React Components

Basics of styling in React

Styling in React is a pivotal element of web development, encompassing a range of techniques to apply aesthetic designs to React components. React's versatility allows for multiple styling approaches, each catering to different needs and preferences. Mastering these styling methods is essential for creating visually compelling and responsive applications.

1. Inline Styling Approach

Inline styling in React involves directly assigning styles to elements using the `style` attribute, where styles are defined as JavaScript objects.

- Inline Styling Example:

```
const styleExample = { color: 'blue', backgroundColor: 'lightgray' };
<div style={styleExample}>Example Styled Component</div>
```

- Pros and Cons:

    - Inline styling is convenient for simple or dynamic styling but may lead to redundancy and is less effective for complex styling scenarios.

2. Traditional CSS Stylesheets

Using standard CSS stylesheets is a common practice in React. This method involves creating and importing a separate CSS file into React components.

- CSS Stylesheets Usage:

    - Craft a `.css` file and import it into your React component.

    - Example: `import './MyComponent.css'`;

- Benefits:

    - Utilizes the full capabilities of CSS and is familiar to those experienced with traditional web development.

3. CSS Modules for Scoped Styling

CSS Modules provide a way to write CSS classes scoped locally to the component rather than globally.

- Applying CSS Modules:

    - Create a `.module.css` file and import it as an object into React components.

    - Example:` **import styles from './MyComponent.module.css'`**;

- Advantages:

    - Prevents global scope pollution and class name clashes, offering reusability and modularity.

4. Styled-components Library

Styled-components is a library enabling the creation of component-level styles using tagged template literals, blending JavaScript and CSS.

- Styled-components Usage:

```
const StyledExample = styled.div`
  color: blue;
  background-color: lightgray;
`;
<StyledExample>Styled Component</StyledExample>
```

- Key Features:

  - Facilitates dynamic styling and theming, integrating styles within JavaScript.

5. Leveraging Sass/SCSS

Sass is a CSS preprocessor that extends CSS with features like variables, mixins, and nested rules, offering more advanced styling capabilities.

- Incorporating Sass in React:

  - Use `.scss` or `.sass` files for more complex styling structures.

- Sass Benefits:

  - Enhances CSS with powerful features, allowing for more maintainable style sheets.

6. CSS-in-JS Solutions

Beyond styled-components, there are other CSS-in-JS libraries like Emotion or JSS, offering similar capabilities to define styles within JavaScript files.

- Characteristics of CSS-in-JS:

    - These libraries typically allow CSS styling directly within JavaScript, supporting dynamic styling and isolated component styles.

7. Styling Best Practices in React

- Consistency in Styling: It's important to maintain consistent styling throughout the application, regardless of the chosen method.

- Performance Considerations: Be aware of the impact on performance, especially with dynamic or intricate styles.

- Maintaining Separation of Concerns: Even with CSS-in-JS, keeping a clear distinction between styling and logic is beneficial.

- Adaptive and Responsive Design: Styles should accommodate different devices and screen sizes.

Final Thoughts on Styling in React

In React development, styling is crucial for crafting effective user interfaces. From traditional CSS and Sass to CSS Modules, inline styles, and CSS-in-JS libraries, each method serves specific purposes. Understanding these various approaches and when to use them is vital for any React developer, enabling the creation of both functional and visually appealing applications. Keeping up with evolving trends and practices in React styling remains important for developing cutting-edge web applications.

Using CSS, SASS, and styled-components

In the realm of web development with frameworks like React, styling is a key factor that defines an application's aesthetic and user experience. Among various styling methodologies, CSS, Sass, and styled-components are notably prominent, each offering distinct benefits and functionalities suited to different development needs.

1. CSS: The Fundamental Styling Technique

Cascading Style Sheets (CSS) is the bedrock technology for styling web interfaces. It enables developers to define the appearance of HTML elements, including layout, color schemes, and typography.

- React Integration with CSS:

    - CSS is often written in separate **.css** files and imported into React components.

    - Example usage: `**import './App.css'**`;

- Advantages of Using CSS:

    - Universally Recognized: CSS is a standard across all web platforms.

154

- Straightforward Implementation: It offers an easy way to apply styles using selectors and property declarations.

- Optimal Performance: Native browser support for CSS ensures efficient performance.

- Downsides:

  - Global Scope Issues: CSS can lead to potential conflicts and maintenance difficulties due to its global nature.

2. Sass: Enhanced CSS with Preprocessing

Sass, a CSS preprocessor, augments standard CSS capabilities with additional features like variables, mixins, and nested syntax.

- Incorporating Sass in React Projects:

  - Sass files, with `.scss` or `.sass` extensions, are compiled into CSS.

  - Additional setup, like node-sass, may be required in React environments.

  - Example:` **import './App.scss'`**;

- Benefits of Sass:

  - Rich Features: Offers variables, mixins, and nesting to streamline CSS code.

  - Advanced Capabilities: Provides functions and directives for dynamic styling.

- Considerations:

  - Learning Requirements: Sass has its own syntax and features to learn.

  - Compilation Requirement: Needs to be compiled into CSS, adding a step to the development process.

3. Styled-components: Embracing CSS-in-JS

Styled-components is a library that merges CSS and JavaScript, enabling component-level styling directly within JavaScript files using tagged template literals.

- Utilizing Styled-components:

  - Styles are scoped to components and written within JavaScript files.

  - Example:

```
import styled from 'styled-components';

const ButtonStyled = styled.button`
  background: blue;
  color: white;
`;
```

- Pros of Styled-components:

  - Component-Specific Styling: Facilitates tight coupling of styles and components.

- Dynamic Styling Flexibility: Allows the use of props and themes in styling.

- Conflict-Free Class Names: Auto-generates unique class names to avoid styling conflicts.

- Potential Limitations:

  - Familiarity Requirement: Involves understanding both CSS and JavaScript.

  - Performance Aspects: May have performance implications in extensive applications due to dynamically generated styles.

4. Selecting an Appropriate Styling Method

Choosing between CSS, Sass, or styled-components depends on several factors:

- Project Scale and Dynamics: Larger or dynamic style-centric projects may benefit more from Sass or styled-components.

- Team's Skill Set: The choice may be influenced by the team's proficiency with CSS, Sass, or JavaScript-focused styling.

- Performance Priorities: Standard CSS might be favored for performance-critical applications.

- Maintenance and Growth: The impact of each styling method on long-term project maintenance and scalability should be considered.

5. Styling Best Practices

Irrespective of the chosen approach, adhering to certain best practices is essential:

- Style Consistency: Ensure uniform styling practices across the application.

- Style Modularity: Aim for modular and component-specific styles in large projects.

- Optimizing for Performance: Be conscious of the performance impacts of various styling techniques, especially for dynamic and elaborate styles.

- Responsive and Adaptive Design: Styles should accommodate various devices and screen sizes.

Styling in Modern Web Development

In conclusion, CSS, Sass, and styled-components each present unique advantages for styling in web applications. While CSS lays the foundation, Sass extends its functionality, and styled-components integrate styling within JavaScript, offering component-specific and dynamic styling capabilities. The choice among these methods hinges on project specifications, developer expertise, and application complexity. By following best practices and understanding each method's strengths and limitations, developers can adeptly style their React applications, creating interfaces that are both visually appealing and functionally robust. Keeping abreast of evolving styling trends and practices is crucial for developers in the ever-changing landscape of web development.

Responsive design principles

Responsive design is a key component in today's web development, focusing on creating websites and applications that adapt fluidly across a variety of devices, from smartphones to desktops. This design approach is vital in ensuring a consistent and engaging user experience, regardless of device specifics like screen resolutions or user interfaces.

1. Fluid Grids as a Core Element of Responsive Design

Fluid grids use relative units (like percentages) instead of fixed units (such as pixels) to define elements in web layouts. This approach allows layouts to adapt dynamically to different screen sizes.

- Application of Fluid Grids:

    - Techniques like CSS grid and flexbox are instrumental in creating fluid grids.

    - Fluid grids typically involve column-based designs that adjust based on the viewport size.

2. Responsiveness of Images and Media

A responsive design must ensure that all media, including images and videos, adjust appropriately within their containers.

- Making Media Responsive:

    - CSS properties like `**max-width: 100%**` help media scale proportionally.

- For complex scenarios, CSS properties like object-fit can be utilized.

3. The Role of Media Queries

Media queries allow for the application of different CSS styles based on certain conditions, such as screen width or height.

- Implementing Media Queries:

    - Media queries can alter layouts, typography, or visibility of elements based on the device's screen size.

    - Example:

```
@media (min-width: 600px) {
    .navigation { width: 25%; }
}
```

4. Adapting Typography

Typography in responsive design should be flexible to ensure readability across devices.

- Responsive Typography Techniques:

    - Use relative units like ems or rems instead of fixed pixels.

    - Media queries can be employed to adjust font sizes for different resolutions.

5. Embracing a Mobile-First Strategy

Designing for mobile devices first and then scaling up for larger screens is the essence of the mobile-first approach.

- Benefits of Mobile-First Design:
    - Prioritizes mobile user experience, focusing on essential content and functionality.

6. Designing for Touch Interfaces

Responsive design must cater to touchscreen interfaces, ensuring interactive elements are easily accessible.

- Considerations for Touchscreens:
    - Interactive elements should be adequately sized and spaced for touch accuracy.
    - The design should account for various touch gestures.

7. Responsive Design Testing

Testing across various devices and browsers is essential to ensure a uniform user experience.

- Practices for Testing Responsive Designs:
    - Utilize browser-based device emulation tools.
    - Conduct real-world testing on multiple devices.

8. Focusing on Performance

Optimizing performance is especially critical in responsive design to accommodate varying network conditions.

- Performance Optimization Strategies:

    - Optimize images and media for quick loading.

    - Limit the use of large scripts and frameworks.

9. Integrating Accessibility

Responsive design should be inclusive, ensuring accessibility for users with disabilities.

- Accessible Design Practices:

    - Responsive layouts should be navigable via keyboard.

    - Use semantic HTML and ARIA attributes to enhance accessibility.

Summary

Responsive design is fundamental in modern web development, encompassing various principles to create adaptive, user-friendly experiences across all devices. It combines fluid grids, responsive media, media queries, adaptable typography, and a mobile-first approach. Other important factors include touch-friendly interfaces, performance considerations, and accessibility. Staying updated with responsive design trends is crucial for developers and designers in creating versatile, user-centric web applications and sites. As technology evolves, so does the importance of responsive design in delivering comprehensive digital experiences.

Chapter Thirteen

Deploying React Applications

Preparing the application for production

Transitioning an application from development to production is a vital phase in software development, involving meticulous preparation to ensure the application is robust, secure, and ready for real-world deployment. This stage includes a series of important steps and considerations to optimize the application's performance and functionality.

1. Code Refinement and Optimization

Preparing for production involves a thorough review and enhancement of the application code:

- Code Refinement: Streamlining code architecture and enhancing readability while maintaining the existing functionality.

- Elimination of Development Residues: Removing any code or files that were solely used for development and are not required in the production environment.

- Performance Enhancement: Boosting the efficiency of the code to reduce load times and enhance the application's speed.

2. Comprehensive Testing Regimen

Rigorous testing is essential to ensure the application is free from defects and functions correctly:

- Component Testing: Verifying the correctness of individual parts or functions.

- Holistic Testing: Ensuring that different components of the application work together effectively.

- User Scenario Testing: Mimicking real-user actions to validate the overall application workflow.

- Load Testing: Confirming that the application can sustain the anticipated user load and traffic.

3. Strengthening Security Measures

Security is a top priority, especially when handling sensitive data:

- SSL/TLS Deployment: Implementing encrypted communication protocols for secure data transmission.

- Endpoint Security: Fortifying APIs and data access points against unauthorized usage and cyber threats.

- Data Safeguarding: Implementing robust encryption and secure storage practices for user data.

4. Asset Optimization

Frontend asset optimization is crucial for ensuring quick load times:

- Code Minification: Compressing HTML, CSS, and JavaScript files to eliminate unnecessary characters without impacting functionality.

- Asset Bundling: Merging multiple files into fewer packages to minimize server requests.

5. Setting Up the Production Environment

Proper configuration of the production environment is critical:

- Configuring Environment Variables: Setting up specific variables for things like database connections and API paths.

- Server Preparation: Ensuring that the server is optimally configured for performance and resource utilization.

6. Deployment Planning

An effective deployment strategy is crucial for a smooth transition:

- Automated Deployment Processes: Implementing CI/CD pipelines for efficient and reliable software releases.

- Dual-Environment Strategies: Utilizing techniques like blue-green deployment to minimize downtime and risk.

7. Scalability Strategies

The application should be prepared to scale based on user demand:

- Traffic Management: Implementing load balancing to evenly distribute user requests across servers.

- Elastic Architecture: Designing the system to efficiently manage increases in load, possibly through cloud-based solutions.

8. Data Backup and Recovery Systems

Establishing reliable backup and disaster recovery plans is essential for data integrity:

- Automated Data Backups: Setting up systems for regular data backups.

- Crisis Management Plans: Developing strategies to quickly recover data and resume operations in case of system failures.

9. Monitoring Systems and User Analytics

Implementing tools to monitor performance and user interaction is essential:

- Application Performance Monitoring: Using tools to keep an eye on server health and application performance.

- Analyzing User Behavior: Collecting data on how users interact with the application to inform future updates.

10. User Feedback Mechanisms and Support

Setting up systems for gathering user feedback and providing support post-launch is important:

- User Communication Channels: Enabling users to report issues or provide feedback.

- Support Infrastructure: Having a dedicated team to handle user inquiries and technical issues.

11. Compliance and Privacy Considerations

Ensuring the application adheres to legal standards and privacy regulations is crucial:

- Adherence to Privacy Laws: Complying with regulations like GDPR and CCPA.

- Transparent User Agreements: Clearly outlining terms of service and privacy policies.

12. Launch Preparations

Final steps before launching include:

- Promotional Strategies: Planning the announcement and marketing approaches for the launch.

- Initial Limited Release: Considering a soft launch to a restricted audience as a preliminary step.

13. Post-Launch Management

After the application goes live, focus shifts to:

- Ongoing Monitoring: Continuously observing system performance and user feedback.

- Iterative Development: Making regular updates and improvements based on user input and performance data.

Final Thoughts

Preparing an application for production encompasses a range of activities from code optimization and security fortification to deployment strategies and scalability considerations. This stage is fundamental in ensuring that the application is primed for real-world usage, balancing performance, reliability, and user experience. Continual adaptation and meticulous planning in this phase are critical for the success of the application launch. As the field of software development evolves, the process of preparing for production remains an integral and dynamic aspect of delivering high-quality, resilient, and user-centric applications.

Deployment strategies and platforms

Deployment strategies and platforms play a pivotal role in the lifecycle of software development, guiding how applications are distributed to users. The choices made in deployment have significant impacts on the application's reliability, scalability, and ease of maintenance. With the diverse array of technologies available today, a deep understanding of the various deployment methodologies and platforms is crucial for ensuring successful, efficient, and scalable software deployments.

1. Approaches to Deployment

Various methodologies exist for deploying software, each with its own implications for downtime, risk management, and resource allocation.

- Blue-Green Deployment: This method utilizes two identical production environments, alternating between them to reduce downtime and facilitate smooth transitions.

- Canary Deployment: This gradual approach releases updates to a small user base initially, allowing teams to assess performance before a full rollout.

- Rolling Deployment: This technique updates instances sequentially, minimizing downtime but potentially causing version inconsistency during the process.

- A/B Testing Deployment: This strategy is used to test new features, deploying different versions to separate user segments to evaluate each version's performance.

2. Choices in Deployment Platforms

Deployment platforms are the environments where applications reside and operate. The platform chosen influences the management, scaling, and upkeep of applications.

- Cloud-Based Solutions: Providers like AWS, Azure, and Google Cloud offer versatile, scalable hosting options, providing a suite of services for diverse computing needs.

- Container Orchestration Tools: Kubernetes and Docker Swarm manage the deployment and scaling of containerized apps, ensuring consistency across environments.

- Platform as a Service (PaaS) Offerings: Platforms such as Heroku and OpenShift allow for direct application deployment, removing the need to manage underlying infrastructure.

- Serverless Frameworks: Solutions like AWS Lambda enable running code without server management, suitable for sporadic, demand-based tasks.

3. Implementing CI/CD Pipelines

CI/CD automates the stages of application development to frequently and reliably deliver applications to customers.

- Continuous Integration: This practice involves regular code integrations to a shared repository, where automated builds and tests are run.

- Continuous Deployment: Automates the release process, allowing for seamless and frequent deployments to production.

4. Emphasizing Security and Regulatory Compliance

Security and adherence to regulations are critical considerations in the deployment process.

- Best Practices for Secure Deployments: These include using SSL/TLS protocols, performing security assessments, and adhering to standards like GDPR.

- Incorporating DevSecOps: This integrates security measures within the DevOps process to ensure holistic application security.

5. Post-Deployment Monitoring and Upkeep

Continuous monitoring and maintenance are key to sustaining application performance post-deployment.

- Utilizing Monitoring Solutions: Tools like Prometheus and Grafana offer insights into application performance, aiding in quick issue resolution.

- Routine Maintenance: Regular updates and patching are necessary to maintain security and functionality.

Summarizing Deployment Strategies and Platforms

In the software delivery process, the strategies and platforms chosen for deployment are fundamental. Deciding on a deployment strategy, such as blue-green, canary, or rolling, depends on the specific needs of the application and the team's ability to handle various risks. The selection of a deployment platform, whether it be cloud-based, container-based, PaaS, or serverless, is influenced by the application's specific requirements and scalability objectives. Practices like CI/CD, security integration, and diligent post-deployment monitoring form integral parts of a comprehensive deployment approach. Keeping abreast of evolving deployment trends and practices is vital in the dynamic field of software development, ensuring the delivery of robust, secure, and user-friendly applications.

Maintaining and updating live applications

The ongoing maintenance and updating of live applications are pivotal activities in the software development lifecycle, ensuring that applications remain functional, secure, and aligned with user needs. This continuous process is critical for addressing operational issues, incorporating user insights, and keeping pace with technological advancements.

1. Necessity of Consistent Maintenance

Consistent maintenance is essential for the smooth operation of any live application. It includes:

- Performance Monitoring: Regularly checking the application's performance indicators to identify and resolve any issues.

- Dependency Management: Keeping libraries and frameworks up to date to maintain security and efficiency.

- Database Management: Periodically optimizing the database for improved response times and efficiency.

2. Security Enhancements and Patching

In a constantly evolving digital landscape, maintaining robust security is imperative:

- Security Assessments: Performing thorough security checks to find and mitigate vulnerabilities.

- Timely Security Updates: Quickly applying security patches to address vulnerabilities.

- SSL Certificate Management: Ensuring SSL certificates are current for secure communication.

3. Leveraging User Feedback for Improvement

User feedback is invaluable for enhancing application functionality and user satisfaction:

- Feedback Collection: Utilizing various tools and methods to gather user insights.

- Feature Development Based on Feedback: Iteratively developing and releasing new features in line with user preferences and market demands.

- Effectiveness Testing of New Features: Employing A/B testing to evaluate the impact of new features or modifications.

4. Optimizing for Scalability and Performance

Adjusting the application to handle increased usage and data is critical:

- Infrastructure Scaling: Expanding server capabilities or using scalable cloud solutions.

- Code and Resource Optimization: Refining code and resources for optimal performance under higher loads.

5. Implementing CI/CD for Smooth Updates

CI/CD practices are vital for streamlined maintenance and updates:

- Regular Integration: Frequently integrating code changes and conducting automated testing to catch issues early.

- Automated Deployment: Ensuring swift and consistent updates to the production environment.

6. Update Strategies to Minimize Downtime

Reducing downtime during updates is key to a positive user experience:

- Planned Update Times: Conducting updates during periods of low user activity.

- Incremental Rollouts: Gradually releasing updates to a limited user base initially to ensure stability.

- Alternate Environment Deployments: Utilizing methods like blue-green deployment to minimize interruption during updates.

7. Ensuring Data Integrity

Regular backups and a robust disaster recovery strategy are essential:

- Automated Data Backups: Setting up systems for consistent data backups.

- Efficient Disaster Recovery: Developing quick recovery mechanisms in the event of system breakdowns.

8. Maintaining Regulatory Compliance

Compliance with legal and regulatory standards is essential, especially for data-sensitive applications:

- Adherence to Data Regulations: Compliance with laws like GDPR and CCPA.

- Software License Management: Ensuring all software and services used comply with licensing agreements.

9. Focus on Accessibility and Inclusivity

Ensuring the application is accessible to all users, including those with disabilities, is crucial:

- Regular Accessibility Reviews: Conducting audits to maintain adherence to standards like WCAG.

- Inclusive User Interface Design: Continuously enhancing the UI to be more inclusive and user-friendly.

10. Keeping Documentation and Knowledge Current

Updated documentation and effective knowledge sharing within the team are vital for efficient maintenance:

- Documentation Updates: Keeping all documentation reflective of the latest application changes.

- Knowledge Sharing Practices: Facilitating the transfer of knowledge and insights across the team.

Wrapping Up

The maintenance and updating of live applications are dynamic processes that require careful management across various dimensions, including regular upkeep, security, user responsiveness, scalability, and legal compliance. Effective strategies for continuous updates, data protection, and ensuring accessibility form the cornerstone of these activities. Keeping applications updated and well-maintained is key to meeting current user requirements and adapting to future challenges and opportunities in the ever-evolving digital landscape. This holistic approach to application management ensures that software not only meets but exceeds user expectations while remaining ready for future advancements.

Conclusion

Recap of key concepts learned

In the dynamic field of software development, constant learning and revisiting key concepts are imperative for professional growth and adaptation to new technological trends. This overview serves to reinforce essential knowledge, highlight areas for further learning, and guide future educational endeavors in various areas of software development.

1. Proficiency in Programming Languages and Frameworks

A thorough understanding of diverse programming languages and their corresponding frameworks is crucial:

- JavaScript and Its Ecosystem (React, Node.js): Integral for both front-end and back-end web development.

- Python's Versatility: Employed in a range of applications from web development to data analysis.

- Java's Role in Large-scale Systems: Known for its robustness and scalability in enterprise-level applications.

2. Mastery of Database Technologies

Competence in database technologies, including both SQL and NoSQL systems, is essential:

- SQL Databases (e.g., MySQL, PostgreSQL): Important for handling structured data and relationships.

- NoSQL Databases (e.g., MongoDB, Cassandra): Suitable for unstructured data and scenarios requiring scalability.

3. Front-End Development Skills

Front-end development is focused on crafting the user interface and experience:

- HTML/CSS Foundations: Fundamental for structuring and styling web pages.

- Principles of Responsive Design: Ensures cross-device compatibility and usability.

- Frameworks and Libraries in JavaScript: Enhance user interfaces and interaction (examples include React, Angular, Vue.js).

4. Back-End Development Proficiencies

Back-end development involves managing server-side logic, database interactions, and application integration:

- Server-Side Scripting: Writing server-executable scripts in languages like Node.js, Python, or Ruby.

- API Development and Management: Essential for facilitating effective data exchange between software components.

- Adopting Microservices Architecture: Enhances application modularity and scalability.

5. DevOps and CI/CD Practices

DevOps integrates development and operations, emphasizing continuous collaboration and automation:

- **Streamlined CI/CD Processes:** Automated pipelines that facilitate rapid and reliable software delivery.

- **Containerization Technologies:** Such as Docker and Kubernetes, which standardize and simplify deployment across environments.

6. Utilizing Version Control Systems

Implementing version control systems like Git is vital for tracking code changes and facilitating team collaboration.

7. Comprehensive Software Testing Approaches

Testing is key to ensuring the quality and functionality of applications:

- **Unit Testing:** Verifying the functionality of individual components.

- **Integration Testing:** Testing the interoperability of combined application parts.

- **End-to-End Testing:** Validating the complete workflow of the application.

8. Leveraging Cloud Computing Platforms

Cloud computing has transformed service delivery, offering scalable and efficient solutions:

- Infrastructure as a Service (IaaS): Provides foundational computing and storage resources.

- Platform as a Service (PaaS): Offers a development platform for application creation and hosting.

- Software as a Service (SaaS): Delivers application functionality over the internet.

9. Cybersecurity Fundamentals

Knowledge of cybersecurity practices is crucial for protecting applications and sensitive data:

- Encryption Techniques: Essential for securing data in transmission and at rest.

- Network Security Protocols: Critical for safeguarding data within networked environments.

- Understanding Cyber Threats: Recognizing common threats like malware and phishing attacks.

10. Agile and Scrum Methodologies

Agile methodologies, particularly Scrum, focus on adaptability, iterative development, and customer-centric project management.

11. UX/UI Design Principles

Emphasizing user experience (UX) and user interface (UI) design is vital for creating engaging digital interfaces:

- User-Centric Design Approaches: Designing with a focus on the end-user's requirements.

- Enhancing Interaction Design: Focusing on the interactive elements of the user interface.

12. Inclusive Design for Accessibility

Creating accessible and inclusive designs ensures applications are usable by a broad audience, including individuals with disabilities.

13. Basics of AI and Machine Learning

A foundational understanding of artificial intelligence and machine learning is increasingly important in modern application development.

Wrapping Up the Recap

In conclusion, the field of software development encompasses a broad spectrum of skills, from programming languages to cloud computing. Each concept plays a significant role in the overall landscape of software development. Continually revisiting these concepts is critical for staying current in the rapidly evolving tech world. Continuous learning, adaptation, and a willingness to embrace new technologies are the hallmarks of a successful career in software development, no matter one's experience level. As the tech landscape continues to evolve, this evergreen approach to learning and development remains crucial for professionals in the field.

Next steps in the journey of mastering React JS

Advancing in React JS, a prominent library for building dynamic user interfaces, entails a journey of ongoing education and skill refinement. As the technological landscape shifts, React developers must adapt to new tools, practices, and methodologies. For those aiming to deepen their expertise in React JS, there are several critical areas to focus on.

1. Exploring Complex Component Patterns

Delving into complex component patterns is essential for React mastery:

- Higher-Order Components (HOCs): A technique for reusing component logic efficiently.

- Render Props Method: A pattern that allows sharing of code through a function prop.

- Advanced Use of Hooks: Leveraging hooks to manage state and side effects in functional components.

- Context API Utilization: Effectively managing and distributing state with the Context API.

2. Advanced State Management Techniques

Beyond basic React state tools, exploring comprehensive state management solutions is key:

- Redux Mastery: Deepening knowledge of Redux for global state management.

- MobX Exploration: Understanding MobX as an alternative to Redux.

- Experimenting with Recoil: Investigating modern libraries like Recoil designed for React.

3. Enhancing Application Performance

Optimizing the performance of React applications is crucial:

- Implementing Code Splitting: Reducing initial load size to enhance performance.

- Effective Memoization: Using memoization to avoid unnecessary rendering.

- Lazy Loading Strategies: Implementing lazy loading for resources and components.

4. Proficient Testing and Debugging

Strong testing and debugging practices are vital:

- Unit Testing with Jest: Mastering Jest for component testing.

- End-to-End Testing Proficiency: Gaining skills in frameworks like Cypress for comprehensive testing.

- Advanced Debugging: Utilizing React Developer Tools for efficient debugging.

5. Integrating with Back-End Services

Skill in integrating React with back-end services enhances full-stack development capabilities:

- REST API Integration: Connecting React with RESTful services.

- GraphQL Usage: Employing GraphQL for optimized data fetching.

- Server-Side Rendering Techniques: Using server-side rendering for performance and SEO benefits.

6. Diving into React Native for Mobile Development

Expanding into mobile development with React Native:

- Developing Cross-Platform Apps: Building native apps for Android and iOS using React Native.

- Exploring the React Native Ecosystem: Learning about navigation, state management, and UI components in React Native.

7. Leveraging Sophisticated Tools and Libraries

Utilizing advanced tools and libraries can significantly enhance React development:

- Webpack Understanding: Deepening knowledge of Webpack for module bundling.

- Adopting TypeScript: Incorporating TypeScript in React projects.

- Animation Library Integration: Using libraries like Framer Motion for interactive UI animations.

8. Adherence to Best Practices

Employing best practices and design patterns is fundamental:

- Functional Programming Principles: Applying functional programming concepts in React.

- Architectural Best Practices: Building scalable and maintainable component architectures.

- Focus on Accessibility: Ensuring applications comply with accessibility standards.

9. Active Community Participation and Lifelong Learning

Staying engaged with the React community and continually updating skills:

- Contributing to Open Source: Active participation in open-source React projects.

- Community Involvement: Engaging in forums, attending conferences, and participating in meetups.

- Keeping Up-to-Date: Staying informed about the latest React updates and features.

10. Real-World Application Development

Applying learning in practical scenarios:

- Developing Personal Projects: Building personal projects to apply new knowledge and tools.

- Creating a Professional Portfolio: Developing a portfolio to showcase React skills and projects.

Wrapping Up the Learning Path

Progressing in React JS requires a commitment to ongoing learning, exploring advanced concepts, embracing new tools, and staying current with the latest developments in the React ecosystem. It involves practical application, community engagement, and a continuous effort to refine and update skills. As React continues to evolve, developers must adapt and enhance their abilities to build effective, scalable, and maintainable applications. Engaging with the broader community and contributing to open-source are also excellent ways to deepen understanding and expertise in React JS, placing oneself at the cutting edge of web development.

Resources for further learning and exploration

For individuals keen on expanding their expertise, especially in technology and software development, there exists a myriad of resources for further education and exploration. Identifying the right mix of resources is key to staying abreast of the latest advancements and honing one's skills in this constantly evolving field. This guide outlines various resources, ranging from digital courses and printed literature to interactive community platforms and professional events, suitable for different learning preferences and goals.

1. Digital Learning Platforms and Interactive Tutorials

The internet offers a wealth of online courses and interactive tutorials, covering a broad spectrum of topics:

- Educational Websites like Coursera, Udemy, and Pluralsight: These platforms offer a diverse range of courses in programming, web development, data science, AI, and more, taught by experts in the field.

- Interactive Coding Platforms: Websites like Codecademy and freeCodeCamp provide hands-on coding exercises and project-based learning.

2. Books and Digital Publications

Traditional and digital books are fundamental resources for comprehensive subject understanding:

- Classic Texts: Titles such as "The Pragmatic Programmer" or "Clean Code" provide enduring insights into software development.

- Focused Learning Material: Books targeting specific technologies or languages, like "Eloquent JavaScript" or "Python Crash Course," are recommended for focused learning.

3. Official Documentation and Guides

Official documentation and guides serve as primary resources for mastering new tools or languages:

- Official Language Guides: Documentation for languages like Python or JavaScript is crucial for deep understanding.

- Framework and Library Documentation: Manuals for tools like React or libraries like Pandas are essential for specialized skill development.

4. Video-Based Learning and Screencasts

For those who prefer visual and auditory learning, video tutorials and screencasts are invaluable:

- Educational YouTube Channels: Channels such as Traversy Media and Academind offer extensive, freely accessible tutorials.

- Specialized Video Platforms: Websites like Laracasts or Egghead.io provide focused video content on specific technologies.

5. Podcasts and Online Seminars

Podcasts and webinars provide flexible learning options, featuring expert discussions and industry insights:

- Technology Podcasts: Shows like "Syntax" offer discussions on a wide range of software development topics.

- Educational Webinars: Regular webinars hosted by tech companies or organizations provide insights into current trends and practices.

6. Blogs and Tech News Websites

Tech blogs and online articles are great for quick, up-to-date insights and news:

- Individual Tech Blogs: Following industry leaders' blogs for personal insights and experiences.

- Technology News Platforms: Websites such as TechCrunch or Smashing Magazine offer the latest news and trends in the tech world.

7. Online Forums and Q&A Platforms

Online forums and Q&A sites offer practical problem-solving and community-based learning:

- Stack Overflow: A go-to platform for developers seeking solutions to specific technical issues.

- Tech Communities on Reddit and Discord: Platforms for discussions, advice, and community support.

8. Contributions to Open Source Projects

Active participation in open-source projects on platforms like GitHub or GitLab can sharpen practical skills and expose developers to collaborative project environments.

9. Intensive Workshops and Bootcamps

Workshops and coding bootcamps offer focused, immersive experiences in various tech disciplines:

- Coding Bootcamps: Institutions like General Assembly provide intensive, structured learning paths in software development and related fields.

10. Professional Conferences and Local Gatherings

Attending tech conferences and local meetups facilitates networking and learning from industry peers and leaders:

- Major Tech Conferences: Events like Google I/O offer insights into the latest industry developments.

- Local Meetups: Community meetups provide opportunities for networking and knowledge exchange.

11. Engaging with Online Tech Communities

Participation in digital communities on platforms like LinkedIn or Twitter, and following key industry figures, can provide valuable learning and networking opportunities.

Wrapping Up

In summary, the resources available for advancing knowledge and skills in technology and software development are diverse and plentiful. From online educational platforms to real-world project involvement, each resource offers unique advantages. Traditional books provide in-depth theoretical knowledge, while podcasts and webinars offer learning flexibility. Staying updated with the latest industry news, engaging with online communities, and attending workshops or conferences are crucial for keeping pace with evolving trends and practices. Whatever the preferred method of learning or area of interest, these resources present ample opportunities for continuous growth and skill enhancement in the ever-changing field of technology.

Introduction

Overview of integrating React JS with modern web technologies

Incorporating React JS into the fabric of contemporary web development is an essential strategy for modern web developers. React JS, originating from Facebook's tech labs, is a dynamic JavaScript library primarily utilized for crafting interactive user interfaces, especially adept for single-page applications. Its component-driven structure, combined with efficient rendering mechanisms, has cemented its popularity in the development community. This overview focuses on how React JS seamlessly integrates with a variety of current web technologies, highlighting the synergistic relationships and methodologies that are prevalent in today's web development arena.

1. Advanced State Management with React

Managing application state in React can often extend beyond its intrinsic capabilities, calling for more robust solutions:

- Redux Integration: A widely-used state management system that introduces a centralized store for managing state in a predictable manner.

- MobX as an Alternative: MobX offers a simpler, more scalable approach to state management through transparent functional reactive programming.

2. Navigational Structures in React Apps

For single-page applications using React, implementing routing solutions is fundamental:

- React Router and Alternatives: React Router remains the de facto standard for handling in-app routing, with alternatives like Reach Router or Next.js offering similar functionalities.

3. Backend Connectivity

React's primary role in front-end development doesn't hinder its ability to integrate with back-end systems:

- RESTful API Integration: React can efficiently interact with various backend services through RESTful APIs.

- GraphQL Usage: An alternative to REST, GraphQL provides a more efficient data fetching method, often used with tools like Apollo Client in React applications.

4. Server-Side Rendering with React

Server-side rendering (SSR) in React enhances both performance and SEO:

- Frameworks like Next.js: These support SSR and static site generation for React applications.

- Gatsby for Static Sites: Gatsby integrates React with GraphQL to produce static web pages.

5. Embracing TypeScript in React

Incorporating TypeScript into React projects adds an extra layer of type safety and code reliability:

- TypeScript Integration: Offers enhanced code quality and predictability through strong typing.

6. CSS-in-JS for Styling

React's approach to styling has evolved to embrace CSS-in-JS methodologies:

- Styled-components Usage: This popular library allows for the inclusion of CSS directly within JavaScript files.

- Emotion Library: Another growing library in the CSS-in-JS paradigm within the React ecosystem.

7. Interfacing with Web APIs and Microservices

React applications commonly interact with a variety of web APIs and follow microservices architecture for enhanced flexibility:

- Microservices Compatibility: React apps are adept at integrating with microservices architectures.

- Web API Integration: They can effectively work with advanced web APIs for added functionalities.

8. Developing Progressive Web Apps (PWAs)

React is an excellent choice for building Progressive Web Apps, providing a native app-like experience:

- Service Workers in React: They are used for adding offline functionalities to applications.

- Responsive Design with React: The library's component-based architecture aids in developing responsive applications.

9. Utilizing Cloud Services

Cloud services play a significant role in hosting and providing additional functionalities for React applications:

- Platforms like AWS Amplify and Firebase: These services are popular for deploying and managing React applications, offering hosting, authentication, and database services.

10. Accessibility and Globalization

Ensuring applications are accessible and globally adaptable is a priority in modern web development:

- Accessibility Standards: Adhering to accessibility guidelines to make React applications usable by a wider audience.

- Internationalization Techniques: Tools like react-intl help in adapting applications for multiple languages and regions.

Wrapping Up the Integration Overview

The integration of React JS with contemporary web technologies encompasses understanding and implementing a variety of tools, frameworks, and methodologies. From sophisticated state management and server-side rendering to embracing TypeScript and building PWAs, the React ecosystem is rich and diverse, aligning well with the latest trends in web technology. Staying current with these integrations and practices is crucial for developers aiming to create advanced, efficient, and user-centric web applications. React JS continues to be a pivotal element in web development, enabling developers to craft applications that are both powerful and adaptable to the ever-changing digital landscape.

How this book differs from the beginner's guide

Moving from a foundational guide to a more advanced text marks a significant evolution in the learning journey, especially in fields like technology and software development. This shift becomes particularly pronounced in resources dedicated to React JS, a widely-used JavaScript library for building interactive user interfaces. The difference between a book designed for beginners and one aimed at more experienced learners in React JS can be highlighted across various facets of content and approach.

1. Depth and Range of Concepts

- Beginner's Guide: These texts typically focus on introducing the essentials of React JS, like JSX syntax, basic component creation, elementary state management, and simple event handling techniques.

- Advanced Text: Advanced books delve into more intricate subjects such as sophisticated state management using Redux, advanced hook patterns, context API, and nuanced performance tuning methods.

2. Comprehensive Nature of Content

- Beginner's Guide: Limited mostly to the essential aspects of React, beginner books offer a foundational understanding, ensuring new learners are not overwhelmed.

- Advanced Text: More comprehensive, these texts branch out to include integrations with other technologies, detailed case studies, and addressing complex development scenarios, encompassing areas like server-side rendering with tools like Next.js or mobile app development with React Native.

3. Project Complexity and Application

- Beginner's Guide: Typically featuring simple, illustrative exercises, these books focus on basic React applications to consolidate fundamental concepts.

- Advanced Text: Contrarily, advanced guides present more complex, real-world project examples that mirror professional development standards, offering a deeper dive into professional coding practices and architectural considerations.

4. Exploration of Best Practices

- Beginner's Guide: Introductory guides skim the surface of best practices in a more generalized manner, primarily concentrating on familiarizing learners with the React environment.

- Advanced Text: Advanced texts, however, offer a thorough exploration of best practices, delving into aspects of code organization, optimization, comprehensive testing strategies, and security best practices, emphasizing clean, maintainable, and scalable code development.

5. Integration with Professional Tools and Techniques

- Beginner's Guide: These texts introduce the fundamental tools and techniques adequate for developing simple React applications.

- Advanced Text: Advanced manuals discuss in detail professional-grade tools and methodologies, covering aspects like complex state management tools, TypeScript integration, advanced CSS techniques, and production deployment strategies.

6. Advanced Problem-Solving and Debugging Approaches

- Beginner's Guide: These typically cover foundational troubleshooting and debugging skills, focusing on common errors encountered by beginners.

- Advanced Text: In contrast, advanced guides delve into sophisticated problem-solving and debugging techniques, including detailed error handling, performance profiling, and effective use of development tools.

7. Engaging with the React Community and Ecosystem

- Beginner's Guide: Introductory books may offer a brief overview of the React ecosystem and community resources.

- Advanced Text: More comprehensive texts provide deeper insights into the React community, covering open-source contributions, an in-depth understanding of the library ecosystem, and keeping up with React's latest developments.

8. Orientation Towards Professional Development Practices

- Beginner's Guide: These are often oriented towards individual learning and personal projects.

- Advanced Text: Conversely, advanced books are tailored to prepare readers for professional development settings, addressing team collaboration, advanced version control, CI/CD practices, and Agile/Scrum methodologies.

Summary

In essence, transitioning from a beginner's guide to an advanced book in React JS signifies a move from foundational principles and basic applications to exploring complex topics, engaging in sophisticated projects, and adhering to professional standards. While the beginner's guide establishes the groundwork, an advanced text builds upon this foundation, equipping learners with skills and knowledge necessary for high-level software development with React JS. This progression in content sophistication and instructional approach mirrors a learner's evolution from a novice to a skilled developer, poised to address complex challenges and thrive in professional software development environments.

Setting the stage for intermediate to advanced development

Progressing from an intermediate to an advanced stage in software development entails a significant upgrade in skills, a deeper comprehension of complex concepts, and an engagement with more sophisticated development methodologies. This progression is vital for developers striving to excel in the ever-changing technology sector, where advanced skills are increasingly becoming a standard requirement. Preparing for this advancement involves a comprehensive approach that includes a solid grasp of complex programming principles, expertise in diverse development tools and frameworks, involvement in intricate project work, and a continuous commitment to learning and skill enhancement.

1. Advanced Programming Knowledge

Moving into advanced stages, developers are expected to have an in-depth understanding of more intricate programming concepts:

- Proficient in Algorithms and Data Structures: An advanced developer should possess a deep knowledge of complex algorithms and data structures, applying them effectively to solve practical problems.

- Acquaintance with Design Patterns: Familiarity with various design patterns and architectural principles is essential for creating scalable and maintainable software.

2. Tools and Framework Expertise

Advanced development often demands expertise in a broad spectrum of development tools and frameworks:

- Framework Specialization: Depending on their focus, developers should have in-depth knowledge of specific frameworks, such as React for front-end or Node.js for backend development.

- Advanced Database Skills: Proficient handling of both SQL and NoSQL databases, including optimization and complex query management, is crucial.

3. Tackling Complex Development Projects

An indicator of advanced development is the ability to manage and contribute to larger, more complex projects:

- Handling Large Codebases: Experience in working with extensive and intricate codebases is vital.

- Leadership and Project Management: Advanced developers should be capable of leading projects, making key architectural decisions, and managing development teams.

4. Adoption of Modern Development Methodologies

Staying abreast of and implementing modern development practices is a hallmark of an advanced developer:

- DevOps and Agile Practices: A thorough understanding of DevOps, CI/CD, and agile methodologies is crucial.

- Emphasis on Test-Driven Development (TDD): A strong focus on TDD practices to ensure the reliability and maintainability of code.

5. Cloud Computing and Distributed Systems

In the realm of cloud computing and distributed systems, advanced knowledge is key:

- Cloud Services Proficiency: Skilled use of cloud platforms for application deployment and management is essential.

- Distributed Systems: Understanding distributed computing principles and practices is important for advanced development tasks.

6. Security and Performance Focus

In advanced software development, a strong emphasis on security and performance is non-negotiable:

- Implementing Security Measures: Advanced developers should employ robust security protocols and understand common vulnerabilities.

- Performance Optimization Skills: Expertise in enhancing application performance, scalability, and handling high traffic is required.

7. Lifelong Learning and Evolution

Continuous education and adaptation to new technologies are fundamental in advanced development:

- Staying Current with Trends: Keeping up-to-date with emerging technologies and industry practices is crucial.

- Diverse Learning Sources: Utilizing various resources such as technical blogs, conferences, and online forums for learning.

8. Engagement with Open Source and Developer Communities

Active involvement in open-source projects and developer communities offers substantial benefits:

- Contributing to Open Source: Engaging with open-source projects to refine skills and interact with the community.

- Active Community Participation: Being involved in developer communities for networking and knowledge exchange.

9. Enhancing Soft Skills

Soft skills are critical for advanced developers:

- Advanced Problem-Solving Abilities: Tackling complex development challenges effectively.

- Strong Communication and Collaboration: Effective interaction with team members, stakeholders, and across departments is essential.

10. Specialization and In-depth Research

Choosing a specialization and engaging in research can further elevate a developer's expertise:

- Focusing on a Specific Domain: Specializing in areas like AI, mobile development, or cybersecurity.

- Research Engagement: Staying informed about the latest research in the chosen area can provide insights into innovative technologies and methods.

Summary

Elevating from intermediate to advanced software development is a journey that encompasses a variety of skills and practices. It involves mastering intricate technical concepts, developing proficiency in various development tools, participating in complex projects, and maintaining a lifelong commitment to learning and community engagement. Additionally, fostering strong soft skills and possibly focusing on a particular specialization can significantly boost a developer's capabilities. As the tech industry continues to evolve, this path from intermediate to advanced development requires dedication, adaptability, and a proactive stance in embracing new challenges and opportunities in the field.

Chapter One

Advanced Component Design

Exploring advanced patterns for React components

Advancing in React JS development involves embracing more nuanced and sophisticated component patterns. These advanced patterns address a variety of development challenges, enabling developers to create applications that are not only efficient but also maintainable and scalable. This deep dive into advanced React component patterns reveals techniques that are considered best practices within the React community.

1. Utilizing Higher-Order Components (HOCs)

Higher-Order Components are advanced functions that accept a component and return a new enhanced component, offering a method to reuse component logic.

- Applications: Commonly used for concerns like data fetching and conditional rendering.

- Example: A HOC that enhances a component with data-fetching capabilities.

- Advantages: Promotes reusability and composition in code.

205

2. Implementing Render Props

Render Props is a pattern where a function prop determines what a component renders, allowing for logic sharing between components.

- Applications: Beneficial for stateful logic sharing or component interaction.

- Example: A `MouseTracker` component that provides mouse location data to its render prop.

- Advantages: Offers flexibility in logic sharing and can simplify component structures.

3. Crafting Compound Components

Compound components follow a pattern where multiple components share an implicit state, functioning together seamlessly.

- Applications: Best suited for grouped UI elements like form controls.

- Example: A `Tabs` setup where individual `Tab` components interact seamlessly.

- Advantages: Clarifies component relationships and enhances structural cohesiveness.

4. Leveraging Hooks

Hooks in React enable function components to use state and other React features without needing to write a class.

- Applications: Widely used for state handling, lifecycle management, and context sharing.

- Example: Employing `**useState**` and `**useEffect**` for managing state and side effects.

- Advantages: Streamlines component logic and encourages functional component patterns.

5. Applying Context API

The Context API in React provides a method to pass data globally across the component tree.

- Applications: Suitable for managing themes, user authentication states, or any global context.

- Example: Utilizing `**UserContext.Provider**` to manage and distribute user authentication data.

- Advantages: Simplifies global state management and avoids prop drilling.

6. Developing Custom Hooks

Custom Hooks are functions that encapsulate stateful logic for reuse in multiple components.

- Applications: Designed to abstract complex functionalities like data fetching or form handling.

- Example: A `**useForm**` hook that manages form state and validation.

- Advantages: Modularizes complex stateful logic for reuse across components.

7. Differentiating Controlled and Uncontrolled Components

Controlled components in React are managed by React's state, while uncontrolled components manage their own state using refs.

- Applications: Controlled components are used for more predictable state handling; uncontrolled components are typically for integrating with non-React code.

- Example: An input field is controlled if React manages its value.

- Advantages: Controlled components align with React's declarative approach and offer more predictability.

8. Adopting Lazy Loading with Suspense

Lazy loading and Suspense are modern techniques for optimizing React application performance.

- Applications: Ideal for reducing the initial load time in large applications.

- Example: Dynamically importing components with `**React.lazy**` and managing loading states with `**Suspense**`.

- Advantages: Reduces initial payload size, enhancing application performance.

9. Implementing Error Boundaries

Error boundaries are components that catch and handle errors in their child component tree.

- Applications: Used to gracefully handle UI errors without crashing the entire app.

- Example: An error boundary component that catches unexpected JavaScript errors in its child components.

- Advantages: Adds robustness to applications by managing runtime errors effectively.

Summary

Mastering these advanced patterns in React components is essential for developers aiming to reach higher proficiency in React JS. From enhancing component logic with HOCs and Render Props to optimizing application performance with lazy loading and Suspense, these patterns provide solutions to common challenges in React development. Understanding and implementing these patterns not only enriches the developer's skill set but also contributes to building a more efficient, scalable, and maintainable codebase. As React continues to evolve, proficiency in these patterns remains crucial for developing sophisticated, high-quality React applications that align with contemporary web development standards.

Higher-order components and render props

In React development, grasping the intricacies of higher-order components (HOCs) and render props is pivotal for developers aiming to enhance the versatility and reusability of their components. These advanced concepts enable developers to write more dynamic, clean, and scalable React code, each offering unique approaches to logic sharing in a React application.

1. Higher-Order Components (HOCs)

Higher-Order Components are advanced functions that take a component and return a new, enhanced version of it. This pattern stems from React's compositional nature and is similar to higher-order functions in JavaScript.

- Usage and Purpose: HOCs are predominantly used for injecting additional functionality into components, such as shared data fetching logic, state handling, or conditional rendering capabilities.

- Implementation Details: A typical HOC function wraps a component and returns a new component enhanced with added properties or state. An example could be a HOC that enriches a component with data fetched from an API.

- Advantages: The primary strength of HOCs lies in their ability to encourage code reuse and modularity. They align with the principle of keeping components focused on UI rendering, thus maintaining a separation of concerns.

- Challenges: HOCs, while powerful, can introduce complexities like prop name clashes and excessive nesting, sometimes affecting the maintainability and readability of components.

2. Render Props Technique

Render props is a term for a technique in React where a component uses a function prop to determine what it renders, thus enabling a more explicit way of sharing logic between components.

- Usage and Purpose: This pattern is suitable for cases where components need to share behavior or state. It is ideal for crafting flexible and reusable components that encapsulate behavior and let the consumer determine the rendering.

- Implementation Details: Components using render props accept a function that returns a React element. For instance, a `MouseTracker` component might provide mouse position data to a function prop, which is then utilized by other components for rendering.

- Advantages: Render props offer greater control over how components are rendered compared to HOCs. They make the logic sharing process more transparent within the component's JSX.

- Challenges: The main drawback of render props is the potential for deep nesting in the render method, which can hinder readability. It also requires a solid grasp of functional programming concepts in JavaScript.

3. HOCs vs. Render Props: A Comparative Overview

HOCs and render props each have their own strengths and ideal use cases:

- Composition vs. Flexibility: HOCs are more suitable when composition takes precedence over flexibility in rendering. In contrast, render props offer enhanced control over a component's output.

- Ease of Use: HOCs might be more straightforward for those familiar with higher-order functions, while render props require a deeper understanding of JSX and functions as children.

- Performance Implications: Improper use of render props can lead to performance issues, especially if it leads to the creation of new components in each render cycle.

4. Application Best Practices

When deciding between HOCs and render props, it's essential to consider the specific needs of the application. HOCs are generally better for abstracting higher-level functionalities across multiple components. Render props are more apt for creating customizable components where control over rendering is crucial. It's not uncommon to see both patterns used together to leverage the advantages of each.

Conclusion

Understanding higher-order components and render props in React is essential for developers who wish to advance their React skills. Each pattern provides a unique method for reusing logic across components, contributing to the development of sophisticated and efficient React applications. Mastering these patterns not only enhances the developer's toolkit but also leads to the creation of more maintainable and scalable codebases. As React continues to evolve, these patterns maintain their relevance, underscoring their importance in modern web application development.

Reusability and composition in component design

In contemporary web development, especially within frameworks like React, the principles of reusability and composition are integral to effective component design. These concepts are essential for developing applications that are not only efficient but also easy to maintain and scale. Emphasizing reusability and composition allows developers to craft modular components that can be easily integrated and reused, streamlining the development process and enhancing the application's adaptability.

1. The Role of Reusability in Component Design

Reusability pertains to creating components that can be effectively utilized in multiple contexts within an application or across different projects.

- Modularity of Code: Reusable components are designed as self-contained units, each handling specific functionality.

- Advantages: This approach minimizes code redundancy, eases maintenance, and accelerates development. It enables the creation of a component library that can be applied across various parts of an application.

- Approaches to Enhance Reusability: Developing versatile components that can be customized through properties, utilizing patterns like higher-order components for common logic abstraction, and applying utility functions for frequently executed tasks.

2. Composition in Building Complex UIs

Composition involves creating complex user interfaces by combining smaller, reusable components, akin to using building blocks.

- Assembling with Simpler Components: This strategy enables the construction of intricate UIs from basic, well-defined components.

- Benefits: Composition results in a codebase that is more manageable and intuitive, where each component maintains a single focus and can be independently tested and debugged.

- Preference for Composition Over Inheritance: Modern JavaScript frameworks, including React, generally favor composition over inheritance as a means of code reuse.

3. Adhering to Component Design Best Practices

Following established best practices in component design ensures that reusability and composition are effectively achieved:

- Focusing on Single Responsibilities: Designing components with a singular focus enhances understandability and reusability.

- Design Driven by Properties: Configuring components to accept data and callbacks via properties enhances their flexibility.

- Minimizing Prop Drilling: Utilizing Context API or state management solutions to handle widespread state prevents the complexity of prop drilling.

4. Strategies to Maximize Reusability and Composition

Several strategies can be implemented to foster component reusability and composability:

- Incorporating Custom Hooks: Leveraging React hooks to abstract stateful logic into reusable functions.

- Utilizing Utility Libraries: Applying libraries like Lodash for common functions across components.

- Adopting Component Libraries: Building or employing existing component libraries ensures consistency and reusability.

5. Addressing Challenges in Reusability and Composition

While these principles offer numerous benefits, certain challenges must be navigated:

- Avoiding Over-Generalization: Excessively generic components can lead to convoluted codebases; balance is key.

- Performance Impacts: Misuse of certain patterns, such as higher-order components, can lead to performance drawbacks.

6. Emphasizing Testing and Documentation

Robust testing and clear documentation are crucial for successful implementation:

- Comprehensive Testing: Rigorous unit and integration testing of components, both standalone and in conjunction, is vital.

- Detailed Documentation: Well-documented components, complete with usage guidelines and examples, facilitate easier reuse and composition by other developers.

Conclusion

Incorporating reusability and composition in component design is fundamental in modern web development frameworks like React. These principles enable the development of modular, maintainable, and scalable applications. They require thoughtful design, adherence to best practices, and a balance between general abstraction and practical functionality. By effectively applying these concepts, the development process is streamlined, leading to robust and adaptable applications. As web development continues to progress, the principles of reusability and composition remain central to crafting sophisticated and efficient web applications.

Chapter Two

State Management with Redux

Introduction to Redux in React

Redux, renowned as a state management library, has become an essential aspect of advanced React application development. It introduces a streamlined approach to handling the state in React apps, centralizing it in a single, manageable entity. This detailed overview provides insights into Redux's core concepts, its integration with React, and its role in managing complex application states with greater efficiency.

1. The Essence of Redux

Redux serves as a centralized state container for JavaScript apps, commonly coupled with React. It centralizes the application state in a single store, enforcing unidirectional data flow, which simplifies state management.

- Foundational Principles: Redux's architecture is built on three key principles: the single source of truth (the store), read-only state (state changes are made through actions), and pure functions (reducers).

- The Store Concept: In Redux, the store is the central repository of the entire state of the application.

- Actions and Reducers Role: Actions in Redux are payloads of information that send data from the application to the store. Reducers are pure functions that specify how the state changes in response to actions.

2. Merging Redux with React

Integrating Redux into a React application involves understanding the synergy between the two.

- Provider and connect(): The React-Redux library offers `**Provider**` to make the Redux store available to React components and `**connect()**` to link React components with the Redux store.

- Role of Actions and Action Creators: In React-Redux apps, components dispatch actions, which are generated by action creators.

- Function of Reducers and combineReducers(): Reducers process state changes in response to dispatched actions. For complex apps, multiple reducers can be combined using `**combineReducers()**`.

3. Benefits of Redux in React Development

Redux brings several advantages to React applications, especially those of significant complexity:

- Consistent State Management: Redux's centralized store ensures state management is predictable and streamlined.

- Enhanced Maintainability and Scalability: The structured nature of Redux aids in maintaining and scaling applications.

- Developer Tools: Tools like Redux DevTools offer advanced features like time-travel debugging for enhanced development experiences.

4. Applicability of Redux

While powerful, Redux may not be necessary for all React applications:

- Complex State Scenarios: Redux proves most beneficial in apps with intricate state interactions among multiple components.

- Suitability for Large Applications: In larger applications, where local state management is inefficient, Redux offers a more effective solution.

5. Established Patterns in Redux Usage

Redux usage has led to the development of certain patterns and practices to optimize its integration with React:

- Implementing Middleware: Middleware like Redux Thunk or Redux Saga handles side effects and asynchronous actions.

- State Normalization: Normalizing the state shape helps manage data more efficiently.

- Utilizing Selectors: Selectors are employed for accessing Redux state, leading to more maintainable code.

6. Considerations and Challenges in Redux

Despite its benefits, Redux introduces specific challenges:

- Inherent Complexity: Redux can add complexity to applications, particularly smaller ones where simpler state management might be adequate.

- Boilerplate Code: Redux traditionally requires substantial boilerplate, which can be reduced using modern tools like Redux Toolkit.

7. Recent Developments

The Redux ecosystem is continually evolving with new tools and approaches:

- Introduction of Redux Toolkit: This toolkit streamlines Redux development by reducing boilerplate.

- Hooks API in Redux: The newer hooks API (`useSelector` and `useDispatch`) in Redux aligns with React's hooks feature for a more straightforward approach to interacting with the Redux store.

Conclusion

Redux remains a critical component in the toolkit of a React developer, especially useful for complex and sizable applications. Its approach to state management adds structure and predictability to React applications. Proficiency in implementing Redux, along with an understanding of associated best practices and emerging patterns, is essential for developers immersed in the React ecosystem. As React and

Redux continue to evolve, keeping updated with these advancements is key to developing effective, scalable, and robust applications.

Setting up Redux and understanding its core principles

Implementing Redux within a React framework is a critical endeavor for developers seeking to harness its potent state management features. Grasping the fundamental principles of Redux is pivotal for its effective deployment. This in-depth exploration focuses on guiding you through the Redux setup process in React and explicates the core principles underlying Redux, shedding light on its transformative impact on state management in contemporary web applications.

1. Introduction to Redux

Redux, a standalone library for managing application state, is often coupled with React, though it can be used with any JavaScript framework or library. Its main function is to centralize an application's state in a single store, ensuring predictable and manageable state transitions.

2. Fundamental Principles of Redux

Redux's architecture is underpinned by three primary principles:

- Single Source of Truth: Redux centralizes the application's state in a single store, simplifying state management and enhancing traceability and debugging capabilities.

- Immutable State: In Redux, the state is immutable and can only be altered through actions, which are objects that describe what happened. This immutability guarantees the consistency and predictability of state changes.

- Pure Functions for State Changes: Redux relies on reducers, which are pure functions, to dictate how the state changes in response to actions.

3. Integrating Redux in React Applications

Incorporating Redux into a React application involves specific steps and configurations:

- Installation Requirements: Install Redux and React-Redux to begin integration.

```
npm install redux react-redux
```

- Store Creation: Use Redux's `createStore` function to set up the store. Typically, a rootReducer combining various reducers is provided to this function.

```
import { createStore } from 'redux';
import rootReducer from './reducers';
const store = createStore(rootReducer);
```

- Store Provision: Use React-Redux's `Provider` component to make the store accessible across the application.

```
import { Provider } from 'react-redux';
ReactDOM.render(
  <Provider store={store}>
    <App />
  </Provider>,
  document.getElementById('root')
);
```

4. Comprehending Actions and Action Creators

Actions in Redux are the only way to communicate data from the application to the store. They must be dispatched using `store.dispatch()`.

- Action Construction: Actions are simple objects with a `type` property defining the action's nature.

- Defining Action Creators: These are functions that facilitate the creation of actions, encapsulating the action construction process.

5. The Role of Reducers in State Transition

Reducers are essential in Redux for handling state changes. They are pure functions that take the current state and an action, and return the new state.

- Reducer Formulation: Reducers are designed to manage specific parts of the state and must adhere to purity constraints.

- Combining Multiple Reducers: For extensive applications, `combineReducers` from Redux is used to amalgamate various reducers into one.

224

6. Middleware Implementation

Middleware in Redux serves as an intermediary between dispatching an action and reaching the reducer. It's used for tasks like handling asynchronous actions or for logging purposes.

7. Debugging Tools

Redux DevTools significantly enhance debugging capabilities, allowing developers to inspect and track state and action payloads and navigate through state changes.

Conclusion

Incorporating Redux into React applications and grasping its foundational principles is key to mastering sophisticated state management. Redux's approach of maintaining a centralized, read-only state, managed through pure reducer functions, provides a structured and efficient method of state handling. As developers weave Redux into their React projects, understanding these core principles and setup instructions is instrumental in crafting robust, scalable, and maintainable web architectures.

Building a robust state management system

Developing a solid state management system is a critical aspect of contemporary application development, especially for complex web and mobile environments. Effective state management ensures the seamless function and data consistency of an application. This detailed exposition focuses on vital aspects, strategies, and methodologies crucial for constructing a reliable state management system.

1. Fundamentals of State Management

State management is the process of controlling the data and its status within an application.

- Importance: Efficient state management is key to consistent data rendering and synchronization across the user interface.

- Challenges: The main challenges include ensuring data consistency, managing state transitions, and upholding performance and scalability.

2. Essential Principles of State Management

Building a robust state management system hinges on certain fundamental principles:

- Centralized State: Keeping the application's state in a singular location ensures uniformity and eases state manipulation.

- Immutable State: This principle involves treating the state as read-only, with state changes generating new state instances.

- Predictable State Changes: The state should change in a predictable manner, a goal often achieved through structured patterns or specific state management libraries.

3. Selecting an Appropriate State Management Tool

The choice of state management tools is crucial:

- Comparing Tools: For React, options include Context API, Redux, and MobX, while Angular and Vue.js have their own preferred methods.

- Tool Selection Criteria: The choice depends on factors like the application's complexity, the development team's familiarity, and specific project needs.

4. State Structuring Strategies

Effective state structuring is vital for managing it efficiently:

- State Normalization: This approach simplifies complex data models and reduces redundancy.

- State Modularization: Dividing the state into smaller sections aids in managing large applications.

5. Distinguishing Global and Local State

Differentiating between global and local state types is crucial:

- Global State: This includes data required across multiple components or the entire app, such as user authentication details.

- Local State: Local state pertains to specific components or parts of the app, like form inputs.

6. Asynchronous Operations Management

Handling asynchronous actions, such as API calls, is an integral part of state management:

- Asynchronous Middleware: Middleware in tools like Redux Thunk or Redux Saga helps in managing these operations.

7. Performance Optimization

A well-designed state management system should not hinder the application's performance:

- Reducing Unnecessary Component Rerenders: Efficient state management should prevent unnecessary component updates.

- Implementing State Memoization: Memoization can optimize performance in operations requiring significant computation.

8. State Management in Server-Side Rendered Applications

Managing state in server-side rendered applications adds complexity:

- Client and Server State Alignment: It's important to align the client-side state with the server-rendered content.

9. Testing and Debugging Approaches

Comprehensive testing and efficient debugging are vital for a reliable state management system:

- Rigorous Testing: Thorough testing of state functions and their integration within the app is essential.

- State Debugging Tools: Tools specific to state management libraries assist in monitoring state changes and troubleshooting.

10. Documentation and Adherence to Best Practices

Effective documentation and following best practices are key to a system's longevity:

- Thorough Documentation: Documenting state management approaches and patterns aids in maintaining uniformity.

- Upholding Best Practices: Practices like minimizing component state and proper side effect management lead to a cleaner codebase.

Conclusion

Establishing a robust state management system is a nuanced and essential part of modern application development. It demands a balanced application of appropriate tools, effective state structuring, and adherence to best practices. As applications grow in complexity, the role of proficient state management becomes increasingly crucial. Implementing a well-conceived state management strategy is fundamental to ensuring the application's reliability, maintainability, and scalability.

Chapter Three

Advanced Hooks and Context API

Deep dive into advanced hooks

The introduction of hooks in React version 16.8 brought a transformative change in handling state and lifecycle features in functional components. Previously exclusive to class components, these features can now be accessed in functional components, thanks to hooks. This in-depth exploration into advanced hooks will shed light on their capabilities, intricacies, and practical applications, which are integral for proficient React development.

1. The Basics of Hooks in React

Hooks are special functions that enable functional components to "hook into" React's state and lifecycle features. They represent a more straightforward approach to using React concepts like state, lifecycle, context, and refs.

2. State Management with useState

The `useState` hook is a fundamental tool for incorporating state into functional components.

- Functionality: `useState` facilitates the declaration and manipulation of state within functional components. It provides both the current state value and a function to update it.

- Example:

```
const [count, setCount] = useState(0);
```

3. Managing Side Effects with useEffect

The `useEffect` hook serves a purpose similar to lifecycle methods in class components, handling side effects in functional components.

- Applications: It's used for tasks like data fetching, setting up subscriptions, or manually altering the DOM.

- Example:

```
useEffect(() => {
  document.title = `You clicked ${count} times`;
});
```

4. Simplified Context Access with useContext

`useContext` simplifies the process of accessing the context within functional components.

- Usage: It takes a context object (from `React.createContext`) and returns the current context value provided by the nearest context provider.

- Example:

```
const value = useContext(MyContext);
```

5. useReducer for Complex State Logic

`useReducer` is often a better choice than `useState` for complex state logic that involves multiple sub-values or when the new state depends on the previous one.

- Advantage: It's beneficial for optimizing performance in components that trigger deep updates by allowing dispatch to be passed down instead of callbacks.

- Example:

```
const [state, dispatch] = useReducer(reducer, initialArg, init);
```

6. Performance Optimization with useCallback and useMemo

These hooks are designed for performance enhancements:

- useCallback: It provides a memoized callback function, useful for optimizing child components that rely on reference equality to avoid unnecessary renders.

- useMemo: It returns a memoized value, recalculating only when dependencies change, ideal for costly calculations.

7. Direct DOM Access with useRef

`useRef` gives access to DOM elements and persists mutable values across renders.

- Common Use: It's mainly utilized for direct DOM interactions but can also hold any mutable value.

8. Custom Hooks for Reusable Logic

Custom hooks allow for the reuse of stateful logic by extracting component logic into reusable functions.

- Creation: A custom hook is a function starting with "use" that can call other hooks.

- Use Case: For instance, a custom hook for API data fetching.

9. Implementing Advanced Hook Patterns

Advanced patterns with hooks include:

- State Colocation: Keeping state within close proximity to where it's utilized.

- Solving Prop Drilling: Utilizing context and hooks to pass data efficiently without extensive prop drilling.

- Encapsulating State Logic: Using custom hooks for isolating state logic, enhancing the separation of concerns.

10. Best Practices and Considerations in Hook Usage

When using hooks, it's essential to follow certain practices and considerations:

- Adherence to Hook Rules: Hooks should only be called at the top level, not inside loops, conditions, or nested functions.

- Thorough Testing: Custom hooks, especially those with complex logic, should be rigorously tested.

- Judicious Use: While powerful, excessive reliance on hooks, like `useEffect`, can lead to complicated components.

Conclusion

Hooks have redefined how developers approach state and lifecycle management in functional components in React. Understanding and correctly applying these advanced hooks empower developers to create more intuitive, maintainable, and efficient React applications. As React evolves, hooks exemplify its commitment to functional programming, offering developers a more expressive and concise way of crafting components.

useContext and useReducer for complex state management

In the realm of React development, effectively handling intricate application states is a task of paramount importance. The advent of hooks like `useContext` and `useReducer` has revolutionized state management, especially in situations where traditional methods like prop drilling become cumbersome. These hooks, when synergized, pave the way for a more streamlined and scalable approach to managing state in React applications.

1. Delving into useContext

`useContext` is a crucial part of React's Context API, enabling effortless state sharing across the component hierarchy without resorting to prop drilling.

- Purpose of Context API: Initially aimed at disseminating "global" data like user authentication or theme settings across React components, it alleviates the complexity of passing props at every level.

- Streamlining Data Transmission: `useContext` simplifies the process of distributing state throughout components, thus maintaining a cleaner and more readable component structure.

2. The Versatility of useReducer

`useReducer` is another vital hook in React for state management, offering a more nuanced method than `useState`, especially suitable for complex state scenarios.

- Complex State Handling: It excels in situations where the state's next iteration depends on its current state or when the state logic is multifaceted.

- Functionality of useReducer: The hook takes a reducer function and an initial state as inputs, with the reducer encompassing the logic for state updates based on actions.

3. Synergizing useContext and useReducer

In tandem, `useContext` and `useReducer` can effectively mimic a global state store, akin to Redux.

- Forming a Global Store: This combination allows the creation of a store-like structure, offering global state access and manipulation across the component tree.

- Implementation Approach: A typical implementation involves a custom hook that combines `useReducer` for state logic and `useContext` to disperse the state and dispatch function throughout the application.

4. Advantages of This Combination

Using `useContext` and `useReducer` together brings several benefits:

- Enhanced Scalability and Organization: The pattern is apt for large applications, facilitating scalable and organized state management.

- Performance Benefits: `useReducer` optimizes performance in components triggering deep updates and doesn't necessitate re-renders like `useState` when paired with `useContext`.

- State Logic Segregation: It allows for a clear segregation of state logic, which can be distributed across multiple reducers.

5. Practical Application and Setup

To effectively implement this state management pattern:

- Context Setup: Begin by creating a context using `React.createContext`.

- Reducer Function Creation: Devise a reducer function that dictates state transitions in response to actions.

- Context Provider Usage: Utilize the Context Provider to envelop your component tree, passing the state and dispatch function from `useReducer`.

- Context Consumption: Employ `useContext` in components to access and manipulate the global state and dispatch actions.

6. Applicability and Real-World Scenarios

This approach is particularly beneficial in:

- Global State Scenarios: Such as managing user preferences, themes, or authentication statuses.

- Inter-Component State Sharing: In applications where various components require complex and shared state interactions.

7. Testing and Debugging Strategies

With intricate state logic, effective testing and debugging are crucial:

- Reducer Testing: Reducers, being pure functions, can be easily unit tested.

- State Change Inspection: Leveraging tools like React DevTools for scrutinizing state alterations and understanding action impacts.

8. Optimal Practices

To ensure the efficacy of `useContext` and `useReducer`:

- Modularity in Reducers: Decompose reducers into smaller, focused functions for specific state segments.

237

- Judicious Use: Reserve this pattern for complex state scenarios; simpler states might be better served with `useState`.

- Clear Documentation: Thoroughly document the context and reducer structures and their intended usage for better long-term maintenance.

Conclusion

The amalgamation of `useContext` and `useReducer` in React furnishes developers with a robust framework for managing complex states. This combination not only ensures scalability and tidiness in state management but also aligns with React's functional programming ethos. As React applications expand in complexity, the adept use of these hooks can markedly enhance the efficiency and manageability of state management systems. Mastery of these tools empowers developers to construct sophisticated applications with intricate state requirements more effectively.

Best practices for using hooks effectively

In the dynamic realm of React development, hooks stand as pivotal tools, revolutionizing the way functional components are built and managed. Their introduction marked a substantial enhancement in handling state and life cycle features within applications. Utilizing hooks effectively, however, necessitates a disciplined approach to maintain code integrity and performance. This analysis focuses on the optimal practices for employing hooks in React projects.

1. Grasping the Role of Hooks

Hooks in React are designed to enable functionalities like state and life cycle features in functional components, traditionally confined to class components. Their primary aim is to streamline component logic, fostering enhanced reusability and composition.

- State Handling: Hooks such as `useState` facilitate local state management in functional components.

- Side Effects and Life Cycle: The `useEffect` hook is instrumental in managing side effects, similar to life cycle methods in class components.

- Advanced State Management: For more intricate scenarios, `useContext` and `useReducer` offer sophisticated state management solutions.

2. Adherence to Hooks' Fundamental Rules

React's documentation stipulates essential rules for hook usage:

- Top-Level Hook Calls: Hooks should always be called at the component's top level to ensure consistent execution across renders.

- Hook Usage in React Functions: Restricting hook calls to React functional components and custom hooks guarantees the proper functioning of the React component life cycle.

3. State Management Techniques

`useState` and `useReducer` cater to different state management needs:

- Simple State with useState: Ideal for straightforward and independent state variables.

- Complex State with useReducer: Offers more control for complex state interactions, particularly where the new state is dependent on the previous one.

4. Utilizing useEffect Wisely

`useEffect` is versatile but requires careful application:

- Effect Cleanup: Always provide a function for cleaning up side effects, crucial for subscriptions and event listeners.

- Dependency Array Management: Properly managing dependencies in the effect ensures it runs appropriately, avoiding unnecessary executions.

5. Creating Custom Hooks for Reusable Logic

Custom hooks are instrumental in extracting and reusing logic from components:

- Logic Extraction: Custom hooks are ideal for isolating complex or reusable logic, enhancing code organization.

- Naming Standards: Custom hooks should consistently begin with 'use' to indicate their nature.

6. Performance Optimization with useMemo and useCallback

These hooks, though critical for optimization, should be employed judiciously:

- **useMemo for Computation Intensive Calculations:** It should be used to memoize heavy computations.

- **useCallback for Functions:** Helps in preventing unnecessary re-renders due to functions' reference inequalities.

7. Testing Strategies for Hooks

Ensuring the reliability of hooks through testing is vital:

- **Testing Custom Hooks Individually:** Validate the logic of custom hooks through unit tests.

- **Component-Level Testing:** Verify the integration and functionality of hooks within components, particularly those with side effects.

8. Debugging with Enhanced Tools

React DevTools offer advanced capabilities for inspecting hooks:

- **Inspecting State and Effects:** Leverage DevTools to examine the state and effects in components, aiding in debugging.

9. Circumventing Common Hook Missteps

Awareness of frequent hook-related issues can prevent potential bugs:

- Prudent useEffect Use: Avoid employing `useEffect` for operations unrelated to side effects.

- Accurate Dependency Handling: Properly manage dependencies in `useEffect`, `useMemo`, and `useCallback` to avoid elusive bugs.

Conclusion

Hooks have reshaped the landscape of building and managing functional components in React, offering a more expressive and efficient way of coding. Adhering to best practices in hook usage is crucial for leveraging their full potential, leading to streamlined development processes and high-quality, scalable React applications. As React continues to evolve, these practices will remain fundamental for developers in crafting sophisticated and effective applications.

Chapter Four

Server-Side Rendering with React

Understanding server-side rendering (SSR)

Server-side rendering (SSR) stands as a pivotal technique in contemporary web application development, particularly valuable for enhancing performance and optimizing search engine optimization (SEO). SSR involves rendering web pages on the server instead of relying solely on client-side rendering (CSR), where the browser handles rendering. Grasping the nuances of SSR, including its advantages, inherent challenges, and implementation strategies, is essential for developers aiming to optimize web applications for both end-user experience and search engine visibility.

1. The Essence of Server-Side Rendering

SSR is a process where the server handles the initial rendering of a web page, sending a fully rendered HTML page to the client's browser.

- Historical Context: Traditional web development heavily relied on server-rendered applications. The emergence of single-page applications (SPAs) shifted focus towards CSR, necessitating a blend of both methodologies.

- Operational Flow: In SSR, server compiles the application into HTML, sends it to the browser, and then the browser executes JavaScript for interactivity.

2. Advantages of Server-Side Rendering

SSR brings forth several key benefits, making it an attractive option for web development:

- Enhanced Performance Metrics: SSR can improve critical performance metrics such as time to first paint (TTFP) and time to interactive (TTI).

- SEO Benefits: Pre-rendered content facilitates better SEO as search engines can index the content more effectively.

- Improved Initial Load Experience: Users perceive quicker content delivery, potentially reducing bounce rates.

3. Challenges with Server-Side Rendering

However, SSR comes with its challenges:

- Increased Server Demand: Every user request requires the server to render a new instance, increasing the server's workload.

- Development Complexity: Implementing SSR adds layers of complexity in handling API calls, state management, and aligning server and client environments.

- Infrastructure Needs: Robust server infrastructure and specific deployment strategies are often needed for SSR.

4. SSR-Enabled Technologies

Several frameworks and libraries support SSR:

- Node.js and Associated Frameworks: Essential for JavaScript-based SSR, with Express.js being a common choice for server-side logic.

- React Frameworks: Next.js, for instance, simplifies SSR in React by abstracting complex rendering processes.

- Other Libraries: Vue.js and Angular have their SSR solutions, such as Nuxt.js for Vue and Angular Universal for Angular.

5. Implementing Server-Side Rendering

Implementing SSR involves key considerations:

- Server Configuration: Setting up a server capable of rendering JavaScript.

- Application Design: Ensuring the application supports both server and client-side rendering.

- Client-side Hydration: JavaScript takes over the client side in a process known as hydration.

6. SEO Implications of SSR

SEO enhancement is a major driving force behind SSR:

- Effective Content Indexing: Pre-rendering content allows search engines to index it more efficiently.

- SSR for Dynamic Websites: Websites with frequently changing content, like e-commerce platforms or blogs, benefit significantly from SSR.

7. Optimizing SSR for Performance

To fully leverage SSR's performance benefits, certain optimizations are necessary:

- Server-Level Caching: Reducing the computational load for each request via caching.

- Load Management: Distributing server load can help accommodate higher user traffic.

8. Enhancing User Experience Through SSR

SSR can markedly improve user experience:

- Rapid Content Delivery: Quicker content visibility enhances perceived performance.

- Progressive Enhancement Strategy: Basic content is immediately available, with more complex functionalities loading subsequently.

Conclusion

Mastering server-side rendering is crucial for web developers focusing on balanced performance, enhanced SEO, and superior user experiences. While SSR offers significant benefits in speed and search engine visibility, it introduces complexities in development and server management. The decision to employ SSR, CSR, or a hybrid approach hinges on the specific requirements and objectives of the web application. In the evolving landscape of web development, SSR remains an integral strategy for creating competitive and high-performing web applications.

Configuring SSR with React

Integrating Server-Side Rendering (SSR) with React is a sophisticated endeavor, aimed at boosting performance and enhancing the search engine optimization (SEO) of web applications. React, primarily known for its client-side capabilities in creating single-page applications (SPAs), benefits significantly from SSR. This involves rendering React components on the server and sending the pre-rendered HTML to the client, improving both initial load time and search engine visibility. This guide details the necessary steps and considerations for effectively configuring SSR in a React environment.

1. Fundamentals of SSR with React

Traditionally, React applications render components in the client's browser. SSR shifts this dynamic by handling the rendering process on the server, sending the resultant HTML to the client.

- Enhanced Initial Loading: SSR ensures immediate content availability for users and search engines by sending a fully rendered page.

- SEO Improvements: Pre-rendering content with SSR enhances the application's visibility and ranking on search engine results.

2. Creating a Server Environment

Implementing SSR in React starts with establishing a Node.js server environment, as React components are JavaScript-based and require a Node.js server for execution.

- Need for Node.js: A Node.js environment is essential for executing JavaScript server-side.

- Utilizing Express.js: Often, Express.js, a Node.js framework, is employed for handling HTTP requests and rendering React components.

3. Server-Side Component Rendering

The essence of SSR in React is rendering components server-side:

- Utilizing ReactDOMServer: React's `ReactDOMServer` library, specifically `renderToString`, converts React elements into HTML strings.

- Consistent Routing: Aligning server-side routing with client-side routing is crucial, achievable with libraries like React Router.

4. Client-Side Hydration Process

After server-side rendering, the client-side of the React application undergoes "hydration" to become interactive.

- Hydration Mechanism: React's `hydrate` method attaches event listeners and sets up state to the server-rendered HTML.

5. Managing Data and API Interactions

SSR requires a distinct approach to data management and API interactions.

- Server-Side Data Fetching: Data for the initial render must be pre-fetched on the server.

- State Transfer: Data fetched server-side should be transferred to the client for consistent state management.

6. Adjusting Build Configurations

SSR with React often necessitates tailored build configurations.

- Webpack for Server and Client: Separate Webpack configurations may be needed for server and client builds.

- Server-Specific Babel Setup: Adjusting Babel configurations ensures server-side code is appropriately transpiled.

7. Addressing SSR Challenges

While SSR offers significant advantages, it introduces specific challenges:

- Resource Intensive Server Rendering: Rendering components per request can strain server resources, mitigated by caching strategies.

- Complex State Handling: Managing shared state between server and client can be intricate.

- Deployment Considerations: Server-side deployment demands additional considerations compared to static file hosting.

8. Streamlining SSR with Frameworks

Frameworks like Next.js can simplify the SSR process in React:

- **Advantages of Next.js:** Next.js abstracts complex aspects of SSR, providing simplified routing, data fetching, and build processes.

Conclusion

Configuring SSR in React applications can substantially improve both performance and SEO, ensuring immediate content availability. The implementation process, covering server setup, data handling, and configuration management, demands careful planning and execution. Utilizing frameworks like Next.js can ease this process, but a deep understanding of SSR's principles is vital for any React developer looking to optimize their web applications for performance and search engine rankings.

Benefits and challenges of SSR

Server-Side Rendering (SSR) has become a fundamental aspect of modern web development, offering significant improvements in user experience and search engine optimization (SEO). SSR involves the process of rendering web pages on the server as opposed to solely on the client's browser. While SSR brings notable advantages, it also introduces specific challenges that developers need to address.

This detailed discussion explores the various benefits and challenges associated with SSR.

1. Advantages of Server-Side Rendering

SSR offers a range of benefits that enhance the effectiveness of web applications:

- Performance Enhancement: SSR notably decreases the time it takes for users to see the first and full content of a web page (TTFP and TCP), especially beneficial for users with slower internet connections or devices with lower processing power.

- SEO Improvement: Since SSR delivers fully rendered content to the client, it's easier for search engines to crawl and index the site, enhancing the site's visibility in search results.

- User Experience: The immediate display of content with SSR contributes to a perceived quicker load time, potentially improving user engagement and reducing the likelihood of users leaving the site prematurely.

- Social Media Optimization: Content shared on social media platforms is properly displayed when pages are server-rendered, ensuring that the necessary metadata is present.

2. Challenges Presented by Server-Side Rendering

Despite its numerous benefits, implementing SSR can be complex:

- Architectural Complexity: SSR adds layers of complexity to web application architecture, necessitating considerations around server configuration, data handling, and state synchronization.

- Increased Server Demand: Rendering content server-side for each request can strain server resources, potentially leading to performance bottlenecks.

- SEO Specifics: While generally beneficial, SSR requires meticulous implementation to avoid potential SEO pitfalls, such as incorrectly rendered content.

- Development and Debugging Intricacies: Building and debugging SSR applications can be more complex, requiring environments that replicate server conditions and different error-handling approaches.

3. Optimizing SSR Performance

Optimizing actual performance in SSR requires strategic approaches:

- Server Caching: Employing caching mechanisms on the server can enhance response times and reduce server load, particularly for static content.

- Handling Traffic Spikes: Implementing load balancing can effectively distribute traffic across multiple servers, mitigating the impact of high traffic on server performance.

4. Integrating SSR and Client-Side Rendering

Many applications benefit from a hybrid approach, combining SSR and Client-Side Rendering (CSR):

- Hybrid Rendering Approaches: Using SSR for static content and CSR for dynamic, user-specific sections can optimize both performance and user experience.

- Progressive Web App Techniques: The app initially loads essential content through SSR and then enhances interactivity with additional client-side scripts.

5. Utilizing Frameworks for Simplified SSR Implementation

There are frameworks and tools designed to facilitate SSR in various JavaScript frameworks:

- React with Next.js: Next.js is a React framework that simplifies the complexities of implementing SSR.

- Angular Universal: This is a solution for Angular applications, enabling server rendering.

- Vue.js and Nuxt.js: Nuxt.js provides a structured approach to building server-rendered Vue.js applications.

Conclusion

SSR is an effective strategy for enhancing the performance, SEO, and user experience of web applications. While it offers significant advantages, it also brings challenges such as increased complexity, server load considerations, and intricate development processes. Employing a balanced approach between SSR and CSR, leveraging caching and load balancing, and using specialized frameworks can help overcome these challenges. Understanding the full spectrum of SSR's benefits and challenges is crucial for developers to effectively implement and optimize SSR in their web development projects.

Chapter Five

React and TypeScript

Integrating TypeScript with React

Incorporating TypeScript into React development is increasingly favored among developers for its ability to enhance application robustness and maintainability. TypeScript, a JavaScript superset, introduces static typing to JavaScript's dynamism, offering clear coding benefits. This integration is particularly valuable in large-scale or complex projects where code clarity and scalability are crucial. This exploration provides an insight into the process and benefits of integrating TypeScript with React.

1. The Role of TypeScript in React Development

TypeScript enriches JavaScript by adding static types, which describe the shape and function of an object, enhancing error detection and providing better editor support.

- Code Quality Improvement: TypeScript's ability to check for errors during coding reduces runtime errors.

- Developer Experience Enhancement: Auto-completion, interface checking, and refactoring tools in TypeScript significantly improve the development experience.

2. Initiating TypeScript in React Projects

Setting up TypeScript in a React project is straightforward with modern tools:

255

- Starting with Create React App: The easiest way to begin a new React project with TypeScript is by using Create React App's TypeScript template.

```
npx create-react-app my-app --template typescript
```

- Incorporating into Existing Projects: Adding TypeScript to existing projects involves installing TypeScript as a dev dependency and modifying the project configuration to include TypeScript files.

3. Utilizing TypeScript in React

Using TypeScript in React means defining components and their props using TypeScript interfaces or types.

- Defining Props and State: TypeScript interfaces are used to ensure type safety for component props and state.

```
interface AppProps {
  message: string;
}

const App: React.FC<AppProps> = ({ message }) => <div>{message}</div>;
```

- Typing JSX Event Handlers: Event handlers in JSX elements, such as onClick, can be typed for correct usage.

4. Exploiting TypeScript Features in React

TypeScript's unique features can be highly beneficial in React projects.

- Generics for Reusable Components: Generics in TypeScript can make React components reusable and type-safe.

- Enums and Utility Types Use: Enums and utility types in TypeScript aid in defining and manipulating types more effectively.

5. Managing Types in Third-Party Libraries

Handling types for third-party libraries is crucial in TypeScript-React integration.

- Type Declarations Availability: Many libraries come with their type declarations or have separate @types packages available.

- Writing Custom Types: For libraries lacking type declarations, creating custom type definitions might be necessary.

6. Implementing Advanced TypeScript Patterns

Advanced TypeScript patterns can further refine React development.

- Strongly Typed Higher-Order Components: TypeScript can be used to ensure strong typing in HOCs, maintaining correct prop passing.

- TypeScript with React Hooks: TypeScript is compatible with React hooks, enabling typing for useState, useContext, and custom hooks.

7. Testing TypeScript-React Applications

Testing is crucial in development, and TypeScript adds specific considerations.

- Using TypeScript-Aware Testing Frameworks: Select testing tools that support TypeScript to maintain type accuracy.

- Interface-Based Mocking: Utilize TypeScript interfaces for effective mocking and stubbing in tests.

8. Build and Deployment Considerations

Building and deploying a TypeScript-React app may involve additional steps.

- Transpiling TypeScript to JavaScript: Ensure the build process includes transpiling TypeScript into JavaScript.

- Type Checking in CI/CD Pipelines: Integrate type checking into continuous integration and deployment processes.

9. Challenges and Adjustments

Despite its advantages, TypeScript integration can present challenges:

- Adjustment Period: Teams new to TypeScript may experience a learning curve.

- Initial Development Pace: The pace of development might initially decrease as developers adapt to the TypeScript environment.

Conclusion

Incorporating TypeScript into React projects brings numerous advantages like improved code quality, enhanced developer experience, and greater maintainability, especially for complex or scalable applications. While it introduces a learning curve and some initial complexity, the long-term benefits of using TypeScript in React development—such as robust, error-resistant, and maintainable applications—are substantial. With TypeScript's growing popularity in the JavaScript community, its integration with frameworks like React signifies a significant advancement in web application development.

Benefits of using TypeScript in React applications

The adoption of TypeScript in React development has been increasingly recognized for its ability to tackle challenges commonly encountered in large and intricate JavaScript projects. As an extension of JavaScript, TypeScript augments its functionality by introducing static typing and a host of other potent features, offering a myriad of benefits to React application development.

1. Augmenting Code Quality and Dependability

TypeScript enhances the robustness and dependability of code in several significant ways:

- Static Typing: The introduction of static typing by TypeScript enables the early detection of errors during development, thereby minimizing runtime errors. Types offer a means to outline the structure of objects, providing better documentation and enabling the compiler to identify type-related mistakes.

- Code Predictability: Static typing leads to more predictable and stable code, simplifying the debugging and maintenance process. This is especially beneficial in extensive codebases, ensuring that props and state in React components are correctly utilized.

2. Elevating the Development Experience

Developers working with TypeScript in React applications enjoy an enhanced experience:

- Advanced Code Completion: TypeScript's integration with modern Integrated Development Environments (IDEs) offers sophisticated code completion, navigation, and automated refactoring, accelerating development and reducing bug introduction.

- Streamlined Team Collaboration: The self-descriptive nature of TypeScript makes the codebase more accessible, facilitating smoother collaboration among developers and easing the onboarding process for new team members.

3. Facilitating Safe Refactoring and Application Scalability

TypeScript's static typing system makes code refactoring safer and supports scalable application development:

- Secure Code Refactoring: The safety net provided by TypeScript's type system during refactoring helps in immediately identifying type-related issues that may emerge from code modifications.

- Scalability of Applications: TypeScript is particularly suited for growing applications due to its comprehensive handling of complex types and interfaces, allowing large teams to collaborate effectively with minimized risk.

4. Enhanced Prop and State Management in React

TypeScript significantly betters the management of props and state in React:

- Defined Prop Types: Explicitly defining prop types in TypeScript ensures that components receive and use data as expected, thereby lowering runtime errors.

- Handling Complex States: TypeScript's sophisticated type inference and interfaces enable precise modeling and control of intricate application states.

5. Boosting Code Maintainability

Maintaining large codebases over time is made more manageable with TypeScript:

- Structured Codebase: TypeScript encourages a well-organized and modular code structure, simplifying long-term maintenance and development.

- Documentation via Code: TypeScript's type annotations act as a form of documentation, enhancing the readability and navigability of the codebase.

6. Seamless Integration with Tools and Libraries

TypeScript smoothly integrates with a wide range of tools and libraries prevalent in React development:

- Build Tool Compatibility: TypeScript is compatible with major build tools like Webpack and Babel, allowing for straightforward integration into existing development processes.

- Third-Party Library Support: Most well-known third-party libraries in the React ecosystem are equipped with TypeScript type definitions, facilitating their use in TypeScript-based projects.

7. Embracing Modern JavaScript Features

TypeScript aligns with and supports the latest features of modern JavaScript, ensuring developers can utilize new advancements:

- Modern JavaScript Compliance: TypeScript stays updated with the latest ECMAScript standards, allowing developers to use new JavaScript features while benefiting from TypeScript's type system.

- Full JSX Support: TypeScript provides comprehensive support for JSX, enabling the complete use of React's JSX syntax within TypeScript files.

8. Enhancing Development-Phase Performance Optimization

Although TypeScript does not directly influence runtime performance, it aids in optimizing performance during development:

- Proactive Optimization: Early error detection with TypeScript's type checking helps avert performance issues that might result from incorrect data handling or type mismatches.

Conclusion

Integrating TypeScript into React projects brings a host of benefits, including heightened code reliability, an improved development experience, and superior maintainability and scalability. The addition of static typing and advanced type features makes TypeScript an invaluable tool in managing the complexities of modern web application development. While it introduces an initial learning curve and setup requirements, the long-term gains of employing TypeScript in React development significantly outweigh these early challenges. As TypeScript continues to grow in popularity within the JavaScript community, its integration with React cements its status as a fundamental tool for crafting robust, error-resistant, and maintainable web applications.

TypeScript best practices in React development

Incorporating TypeScript into React development has gained widespread popularity among developers for its ability to enhance application stability and maintainability. TypeScript, essentially an extension of JavaScript, adds static typing and other robust features, offering a range of advantages for complex project development. This overview highlights the best practices for effectively utilizing TypeScript in React projects.

1. Prioritizing Type Safety

The fundamental benefit of TypeScript lies in its static typing, which significantly diminishes runtime errors.

- Precise Type Definitions: It's crucial to define types accurately for variables, functions, props, and states, enhancing error detection and code clarity.

- Limited Use of `any` Type: The `any` type, while flexible, should be used sparingly to fully utilize TypeScript's type-checking capabilities.

2. Effective Use of Interface and Type Aliases

TypeScript's interfaces and type aliases are essential for organizing and reusing type definitions.

- Interfaces for Object Shapes: Use interfaces to outline shapes for objects, making them ideal for defining props and state in React components.

- Type Aliases for Complex Types: Employ type aliases for intricate type operations like union and intersection types.

3. Accurate Prop Typing in Components

Properly typing component props is vital for component functionality and reuse.

- Functional Components Typing: Utilize `**React.FC**` or `**React.FunctionComponent**` with TypeScript generics for functional components.

```
interface AppProps {
  message: string;
}

const App: React.FC<AppProps> = ({ message }) => <div>{message}</div>;
```

- Class Components Typing: For class components, use `**React.Component**` with generics for props and state.

4. Maximizing TypeScript's Utility Types

TypeScript's utility types offer advanced type manipulation capabilities.

- Using Utility Types: Types like `**Partial**`, `**Readonly**`, and `**Record**` are useful for modifying and creating new types, especially in state management contexts.

5. Effective Typing of Hooks

Hooks, integral to React, benefit significantly from TypeScript's typing.

- Typed useState: Ensure that state variables in `**useState**` are correctly typed.

- Typing useEffect and Custom Hooks: Properly type dependencies and return values in `**useEffect**` and custom hooks for optimal functionality.

265

6. Typing Forms and Event Handlers

Forms and event handlers are common in React applications and can be enhanced with TypeScript.

- Event Handler Typing: Apply appropriate types to event handlers like onClick and onChange.

- Form State Typing: Use TypeScript to accurately type form states and handlers.

7. Robust Testing with TypeScript

Testing plays a critical role in development, and TypeScript can make it more effective.

- Type Assertions in Testing: Employ type assertions to validate the conformity of mocks and test data.

- Component Testing: Test React components with correctly typed props and contexts.

8. Handling External Libraries

Many JavaScript libraries are compatible with TypeScript, but sometimes custom typing is required.

- Utilizing DefinitelyTyped: For libraries lacking TypeScript types, consult DefinitelyTyped, a repository of community-provided types.

- Creating Custom Types: When necessary, write custom types for third-party libraries to maintain type safety.

9. Fine-Tuning TypeScript Compiler Settings

Configuring the TypeScript compiler (tsc) is crucial for enhancing development experience and performance.

- Enabling Strict Mode: Activate strict mode in TypeScript settings for more rigorous type checking.

- Configuring File Inclusion: Manage which files are processed by TypeScript using `exclude` and `include` settings.

10. Integrating TypeScript into CI and Linting Processes

Incorporate TypeScript into continuous integration workflows and utilize linting tools for consistent code quality.

- TypeScript in CI Pipelines: Include TypeScript type checking in CI processes to identify type-related issues early.

- Linting with TypeScript: Apply ESLint with TypeScript-specific rules to uphold coding standards.

Conclusion

Adopting TypeScript in React development brings significant benefits, such as enhanced code reliability and developer efficiency. By adhering to these best practices, developers can capitalize on TypeScript's features to improve code quality and project maintainability. While introducing TypeScript adds a layer of complexity, especially for those new to static typing, its long-term advantages in code quality and error reduction make it a valuable asset in React development. As TypeScript continues to integrate with modern development practices, it remains an essential skill for React developers.

Chapter Six

Testing React Applications

Introduction to testing in React

Testing in the context of React development is a critical component that ensures the robustness and consistency of applications. React's architecture, centered around modular and reusable components, demands a strategic approach to testing. This introduction to testing in React encapsulates the essentials of the testing process, highlighting its significance, various methodologies, and tools.

1. The Significance of Testing in React

Testing is integral in React for several key reasons:

- Reliability Assurance: It confirms that components perform as expected in different scenarios.

- Code Quality Maintenance: Regular testing helps uphold high standards of code quality, minimizing bugs.

- Support for Refactoring: A well-tested application provides a reliable foundation for code refactoring or React version upgrades.

2. Testing Varieties in React

React testing encompasses several types:

- Unit Testing: Focuses on individual components in isolation, checking their independent functionality.

- Integration Testing: Evaluates the interaction between multiple components within an application.

- End-to-End (E2E) Testing: Simulates user interactions within the application in a browser, checking the entire application flow.

3. Tools for React Testing

The React ecosystem offers a variety of tools for effective testing:

- Jest: A comprehensive testing solution for unit and integration tests, developed by Facebook, featuring snapshot testing and more.

- React Testing Library: Provides utilities for testing React components with a user-centric approach.

- Enzyme: Allows detailed component testing, including shallow rendering, developed by Airbnb.

- Cypress: A tool for E2E testing, enabling testing in actual browser environments.

4. Crafting Effective Tests

Effective testing in React involves adhering to best practices:

- Behavioral Testing Over Implementation: Focus on the component's behavior rather than its internal workings.

- Mocking and Stubbing: Isolate components by mocking external dependencies and APIs.

- Gradual Test Development: Start simple and progressively cover more complex scenarios and edge cases.

5. Snapshot Testing Approach

Snapshot testing, unique to React, is facilitated mainly by Jest:

- Output Comparison: It captures and compares the rendered output of a component against a saved snapshot.

- Change Detection: Useful for identifying unintended rendering changes.

6. Managing Asynchronous Operations

Testing asynchronous behavior is a common requirement in React:

- Async/Await Handling: Employ async/await for managing asynchronous operations in tests.

- Mocking Async Calls: Tools and libraries can be used to mock asynchronous functions like API calls.

7. Testing React Hooks

With hooks becoming prevalent in React, testing them is essential:

- Isolated Hook Testing: Tools like the React Testing Library provide methods to test custom hooks independently.

8. Integrating Testing with CI

Incorporating testing into Continuous Integration (CI) workflows ensures consistency:

- Automated Test Execution: Configure CI tools to automatically run tests for every code commit or pull request.

9. React Testing Challenges

Testing React applications can present unique challenges:

- Complexity in Test Maintenance: The growing complexity of applications can make tests more intricate and harder to maintain.

- Keeping Tests Current: Ensuring that tests remain relevant with ongoing application development and React updates can be demanding.

Conclusion

In React development, testing is an indispensable part of the process, crucial for building reliable and high-quality applications. Embracing the appropriate tools and adhering to best practices enables developers to establish effective testing strategies tailored to React's specific needs. Whether it's through unit, integration, or E2E testing, a comprehensive approach is vital for developing resilient React applications. As

React continues to advance, keeping abreast of the latest in testing tools and practices remains imperative for developers aiming to deliver successful React-based projects.

Unit testing with Jest and React Testing Library

Unit testing holds a place of paramount importance in the development of React applications, with Jest and React Testing Library emerging as key tools in this domain. These tools are instrumental in ensuring that individual components operate as intended, harmonizing with React's component-centric architecture.

1. Jest: A Cornerstone for Testing in React

Developed by Facebook, Jest is a user-friendly JavaScript testing framework that offers a comprehensive suite of features for testing, including running tests, making assertions, and handling mocks.

- Effortless Setup: Jest's appeal lies in its minimal configuration requirement, making it both beginner-friendly and efficient for seasoned developers.

- Snapshot Testing Feature: A hallmark of Jest is its snapshot testing capability, which allows developers to store and compare the rendered output of components over time.

- Robust Mocking Capabilities: Jest provides extensive functionalities for mocking, enabling developers to simplify complex application parts during testing.

2. React Testing Library: Enhancing Testing Practices

React Testing Library complements Jest by offering utilities that emphasize better testing practices for React components.

- Focus on User Interaction: This library advocates for testing based on user interaction rather than component internals.

- Queries That Mimic User Behavior: It offers queries that mirror user actions, such as finding elements by text or role, which inadvertently promotes better accessibility.

- Seamless Jest Integration: React Testing Library integrates smoothly with Jest, creating a more rounded testing experience for React components.

3. Crafting Unit Tests Using Jest and React Testing Library

Together, Jest and React Testing Library enable comprehensive unit testing for React components.

- Organizing Test Suites: Test suites in Jest are usually organized into `describe` blocks containing several `test` or `it` blocks for individual test cases.

- Component Rendering: The `render` function from React Testing Library is used to render components within a test, providing various utilities to interact with them.

- Simulating User Interactions: Functions like `fireEvent` from React Testing Library allow for the simulation of user interactions in tests.

4. Utilizing Mocks in Jest

Effective unit testing may require mocking irrelevant parts of the application.

- Mock Functions: Jest's mock functions (`jest.fn()`) are used for tracking function calls and replacing their implementations.

- Module Mocking: Mocking entire modules, especially useful for external APIs or libraries, is a key feature in Jest.

5. Assertions in Jest

Jest's assertion syntax is user-friendly, with a wide array of matchers for various test conditions.

- Expect API: Jest's `expect` function is used with matchers like `toEqual`, `toBe`, and `toContain` to assert different conditions in tests.

6. Testing Asynchronous Behavior

Both Jest and React Testing Library are equipped to handle the testing of asynchronous operations, crucial in modern web applications.

- Async/Await Support: Jest accommodates async/await in tests for more straightforward asynchronous operation testing.

- Handling UI Asynchrony: `waitFor` and `findBy*` queries from React Testing Library manage asynchronous updates in the UI.

7. Unit Testing Best Practices in React

To ensure the effectiveness of unit tests in React:

- Behavior-Oriented Testing: Concentrate on testing the user-facing behavior of components rather than their internal details.

- Focused Test Cases: Develop concise tests that address specific functionalities.

- Integration with CI Processes: Integrate unit tests into continuous integration workflows for early detection of issues.

8. Overcoming Challenges in Testing

While Jest and React Testing Library offer comprehensive testing capabilities, certain challenges must be navigated:

- Initial Learning Process: There is a learning curve for new developers in understanding effective testing patterns.

- Test Maintenance: It's crucial to regularly update tests to align with changes in the application's codebase.

Conclusion

Employing Jest and React Testing Library for unit testing in React is an effective approach to ensure component quality and reliability. This combination provides a thorough testing framework that aligns with contemporary development practices, focusing on user experience and functionality.

Adhering to best practices and acknowledging potential challenges allows developers to leverage these tools effectively in crafting high-quality, resilient React applications. As the landscape of React evolves, maintaining proficiency in these testing methodologies is vital for the development of robust web applications.

Integration and end-to-end testing strategies

Integration and end-to-end (E2E) testing are pivotal elements in the software development lifecycle, particularly in ensuring that applications function cohesively and reliably. Unlike unit testing that focuses on individual components, these testing methodologies delve into the interactions between various parts of an application and validate the overall system behavior in realistic scenarios.

1. The Role of Integration Testing in Software Projects

Integration testing is centered on examining the interactions between different segments of an application, like inter-component communication or connection with external APIs.

- Objective and Significance: The main aim is to detect issues arising from the combination of individual units. This is vital in multifaceted applications with interconnected components.

- Methodology: This involves creating test cases for the interaction between multiple code units, testing integrations between different application layers or external systems.

- Utilized Tools: Common tools include Jest or Mocha, often paired with other libraries like Supertest for testing API integrations in Node.js environments.

2. Strategies for End-to-End Testing

E2E testing comprehensively tests an application from start to finish, mimicking real user interactions and processes.

- Mimicking User Behavior: E2E tests replicate actual user actions and interactions within the application, covering complete workflows.

- E2E Testing Tools: Tools such as Cypress, Selenium, and Puppeteer are widely used for E2E testing, automating browser actions to replicate a user-like environment.

- Incorporation in CI/CD: These tests are typically automated and integrated into CI/CD pipelines to ensure thorough testing in each deployment cycle.

3. Challenges in Comprehensive Testing Approaches

Integration and E2E testing, while crucial, come with their set of challenges:

- Complexity and Test Maintenance: The complexity of these tests can escalate, making them difficult to maintain as the application grows.

- Intermittent Test Results: E2E tests may exhibit flakiness, showing inconsistent results due to timing or external dependencies.

- Resource Intensity: Running these tests can be time-consuming and resource-intensive, requiring environments that mirror production setups.

4. Effective Practices in Integration and E2E Testing

Adopting best practices can help in navigating the challenges and maximizing the efficiency of these tests.

- Building Up Test Complexity: Start with simpler interaction tests and gradually progress to more comprehensive E2E scenarios.

- Mocking for Isolation: In integration tests, mock external services to focus on the specific interactions being tested.

- Focusing on Critical User Journeys: In E2E testing, prioritize scenarios that represent the most common user pathways.

- Creating Stable Testing Environments: Aim for stable and isolated environments to minimize test flakiness.

- Streamlining Test Execution: Where feasible, execute tests in parallel and seek ways to optimize them, reducing their impact on CI/CD timelines.

5. Ongoing Test Management and Refinement

Continuous monitoring and refinement are essential to ensure the relevance and effectiveness of integration and E2E tests.

- Routine Test Reviews and Updates: As the application evolves, consistently revisit and refine tests to maintain their effectiveness and relevance.

- Monitoring for Consistency: Regularly check test outcomes for irregularities or performance issues and address them promptly.

Conclusion

Integration and E2E testing form an integral part of a robust testing strategy, ensuring that applications not only work well in isolation but also perform seamlessly as a complete unit. These testing methodologies are key to delivering high-quality, reliable software. While they introduce additional layers of complexity and demand consistent maintenance, their role in verifying the overall health and functionality of software is indispensable. As software development continues to advance, the significance of comprehensive integration and E2E testing remains more pronounced, cementing their importance in the process of creating and maintaining effective software solutions.

Chapter Seven

GraphQL with React

Introduction to GraphQL

GraphQL, originating from Facebook in 2012 and made public in 2015, marks a substantial shift in data interaction within applications. As a query language for APIs, coupled with a runtime for executing queries based on a defined type system, GraphQL stands out for its adaptability and comprehensive features. It's not bound to any specific database or storage mechanism, making it a versatile choice adopted by various organizations and developers, revolutionizing data retrieval in contemporary applications.

1. Origins of GraphQL

GraphQL was conceived to address inefficiencies in client-server communication. Traditional REST APIs often led to excessive or insufficient data retrieval, necessitating multiple requests for complete data. GraphQL emerged as a remedy, allowing clients to request precisely what they need.

2. Distinguishing GraphQL from REST

GraphQL differs significantly from RESTful services in its approach to data management:

- Unified Endpoint: GraphQL operates through a single endpoint, unlike REST, which relies on multiple endpoints, streamlining data requests and updates.

- Selective Data Fetching: Clients define exactly what data they require, a stark contrast to REST's server-defined data return approach.

- Optimized Data Retrieval: GraphQL addresses over-fetching and under-fetching issues, ensuring more efficient data transfer.

3. Structure of GraphQL

At the heart of GraphQL lies a schema defining its type system and API capabilities. This schema acts as an agreement between server and client, detailing available queries and mutations.

- Defined Type System: GraphQL's robust type system, encompassing custom types, ensures structured and specific requests and responses.

- Distinct Queries and Mutations: Queries retrieve data in GraphQL, while mutations alter data, providing clear demarcation between reading and writing operations.

- Role of Resolvers: Resolvers in GraphQL are functions tasked with sourcing data for specific fields, allowing data retrieval from diverse sources.

4. Advantages of Adopting GraphQL

The use of GraphQL brings several benefits:

- Efficient Data Handling: Clients have the autonomy to dictate the exact data needed, optimizing network usage, particularly in complex systems.

- Enhanced Mobile Performance: The precise data fetching capabilities of GraphQL are beneficial for mobile applications, often constrained by slower network conditions.

- Strongly Typed Nature: GraphQL's typing system aids in better tooling, automated error detection, and API documentation.

- Subscriptions for Real-Time Data: GraphQL also supports real-time data through subscriptions, broadening its applicability to dynamic applications.

5. Implementing GraphQL

Incorporating GraphQL into an application involves establishing a GraphQL server capable of processing queries and mutations, with various libraries supporting this in different programming languages.

- Frontend Framework Compatibility: GraphQL seamlessly pairs with major frontend frameworks, utilizing libraries like Apollo or Relay.

- Database Flexibility: GraphQL's design focuses on data structure rather than the nature of data storage, making it database agnostic.

6. Challenges and Key Considerations

Despite its advantages, GraphQL implementation comes with its own set of challenges:

- Query Performance Optimization: The potential complexity of client-requested nested data necessitates advanced query optimization strategies.

- Caching Mechanisms: GraphQL's single endpoint structure requires alternative caching strategies compared to REST's HTTP caching.

- Security and Rate Limiting: Safeguarding a GraphQL API and implementing rate limiting can be more intricate than with REST APIs.

Conclusion

GraphQL has ushered in a new era in API design and data interaction, offering remarkable efficiency and control over data exchanges. Its growing adoption underscores its potential in building state-of-the-art, data-centric applications. While it introduces certain complexities, the strategic advantages of GraphQL, particularly in large or complex applications, make it an increasingly popular choice in the realm of API development. As the landscape of technology continues to evolve, GraphQL's influence in the development of web and mobile applications is poised to be significant and enduring.

Integrating GraphQL with React using Apollo Client

Merging GraphQL with React has been greatly enhanced by the adoption of Apollo Client, a comprehensive and efficient state management library that facilitates data fetching in a highly effective manner. This amalgamation empowers React developers to seamlessly harness the capabilities of GraphQL, thereby revolutionizing data management in React applications.

1. Exploring Apollo Client

Apollo Client stands as a powerful GraphQL client, celebrated for its straightforwardness, adaptability, and seamless integration with React. It equips developers with tools and functionalities for querying a GraphQL server and subsequently handling the data within a React application.

- Declarative Approach to Data Fetching: Apollo Client allows for fetching data via GraphQL in a declarative manner, directly within the components that require the data.

- Local and Remote Data Management: Besides facilitating remote data management, Apollo Client also manages local application data.

- Performance Boost with Caching: Built-in caching capabilities are a hallmark of Apollo Client, optimizing data fetching and reducing network load.

2. Implementing Apollo Client in React

Incorporating Apollo Client into a React project begins with establishing the Apollo setup.

- Easy Installation: Apollo Client can be swiftly integrated using package managers like npm or yarn, typically installing `@apollo/client` and the `graphql` library.

```
npm install @apollo/client graphql
```

- Configuring ApolloProvider: The `ApolloProvider` component, sourced from `@apollo/client`, wraps around the React application, making the Apollo Client instance available throughout.

3. Establishing Connection to GraphQL Server

Apollo Client requires configuration with the GraphQL server's URI to facilitate data fetching.

- Setting Up Apollo Client: This involves initializing an `ApolloClient` instance with the GraphQL server's URI.

```
import { ApolloClient, InMemoryCache } from '@apollo/client';

const client = new ApolloClient({
  uri: 'your-graphql-server-uri',
  cache: new InMemoryCache()
});
```

4. Querying Data from GraphQL Server

Data retrieval from a GraphQL server is simplified with Apollo Client.

- Creating GraphQL Queries: Queries are crafted in GraphQL and embedded within React components.

- Leveraging useQuery Hook: The `useQuery` hook from Apollo Client is employed to execute queries and handle the various states like loading, error, and data.

5. Handling Local State with Apollo Client

Apollo Client's capability to manage local state is particularly beneficial for complex applications.

- Merging Local and Server Data: It allows for the handling of both local and remote data using GraphQL.

- Local Data Manipulation: Local queries and mutations can be defined for interacting with the Apollo Client cache.

6. Caching for Enhanced Performance

Caching is a key aspect of Apollo Client, contributing to application performance.

- Utilizing InMemoryCache: Apollo Client uses `InMemoryCache` to cache query results, minimizing network requests for previously fetched data.

- Customizing Cache Behavior: The behavior of the cache, including storage and invalidation policies, can be tailored by developers.

7. Real-Time Updates with Subscriptions

Apollo Client also supports real-time data via GraphQL subscriptions.

- Real-Time Data Integration: By employing WebSocket protocols, Apollo Client keeps the user interface in sync with server-side updates.

8. Optimal Practices with Apollo Client and React

To fully harness Apollo Client's potential in React, certain best practices are recommended:

- Organizing Queries and Mutations: Maintain a structured approach to storing GraphQL queries and mutations, ensuring they are close to their respective components.

- Managing Loading and Error States: Apollo Client provides mechanisms to effectively handle loading and error states in the user interface.

- Monitoring Performance Impacts: Regularly assess the impact of Apollo Client on application performance, focusing on caching and state management.

Conclusion

The integration of GraphQL and React via Apollo Client presents a formidable approach to data fetching and state management in web applications. Apollo Client's comprehensive features, including declarative data fetching, combined local and remote data handling, and sophisticated caching, render it an exemplary choice for developers crafting React applications with GraphQL. As technological advancements continue, Apollo Client is poised to remain a significant tool in the development of dynamic, data-centric web applications, enabling developers to construct sophisticated applications with efficiency and accuracy.

Managing state and queries with GraphQL

GraphQL, a powerful query language developed by Facebook, has revolutionized state and query management in application development. Its unique approach, which allows clients to specify precisely what data they need, enhances the efficiency and simplicity of managing both application state and data retrieval.

1. GraphQL's Impact on State and Query Management

GraphQL offers a significant shift from the traditional REST API approach, providing a more streamlined and efficient method for handling data requests and state management.

- Unified Data Fetching Point: GraphQL uses a single endpoint for all data requests, unlike REST APIs that rely on multiple endpoints, simplifying the query process.

- Elimination of Data Over-fetching: It addresses the issue of over-fetching, prevalent in conventional API setups.

- Client-Specified Data Structure: With GraphQL, clients define the structure of the required data, leading to more predictable and manageable state handling.

2. State Management Dynamics with GraphQL

The use of GraphQL in managing application state offers a coherent and efficient strategy, particularly beneficial for data-rich applications.

- Handling Local Application State: GraphQL can effectively manage an application's local state, often achieved through the integration of client libraries like Apollo Client, which merges local and remote data handling.

- Synchronizing States: GraphQL ensures consistent local and remote state synchronization through its advanced query capabilities.

3. Formulating and Handling GraphQL Queries

Creating and managing GraphQL queries is a key component in its efficient operation within applications.

- Structured Query Language Design: The language structure of GraphQL facilitates clear, maintainable query formulation.

- Variable-Based Queries: The inclusion of variables in GraphQL queries enhances their flexibility and reusability.

- Real-time Data Updates: GraphQL's subscription model supports real-time data updates, crucial for interactive applications.

4. GraphQL Integration in Contemporary Applications

Incorporating GraphQL into modern application frameworks provides significant advantages.

- Integration with Front-end Frameworks: GraphQL integrates smoothly with leading front-end frameworks, using libraries like Apollo Client for React or Vue Apollo for Vue.js.

- Complex Data Structure Management: It excels in handling intricate data relationships, suitable for complex application models.

5. Optimizing Performance with GraphQL

Performance considerations are paramount in utilizing GraphQL, especially in data-intensive scenarios.

- Strategic Query Formulation: Crafting efficient GraphQL queries is vital to reduce server load and enhance application performance.

- Caching Mechanisms: Effective caching, either server-side or client-side, can significantly improve data retrieval times and application responsiveness.

6. Challenges in Implementing GraphQL

While GraphQL offers myriad benefits, it also presents challenges that need careful navigation.

- Managing Query Intricacies: The complexity of GraphQL queries, particularly for nested data, requires careful handling.

- Security Measures: Ensuring security through strategies like query depth limiting and authentication is essential in GraphQL implementations.

- Adaptation and Learning: Teams new to GraphQL may face a learning curve in grasping its syntax and optimal use cases.

7. Best Practices for GraphQL Use

Adhering to best practices in using GraphQL can maximize its efficiency in state and query management:

- Modular Query Design: Organize queries into smaller segments for better manageability and clarity.

- Robust Error Management: Implement comprehensive error handling mechanisms in GraphQL queries to maintain application stability.

- Regular Performance Reviews: Continuously monitor and refine GraphQL queries and state management strategies for optimal performance.

Conclusion

Employing GraphQL for managing state and queries marks an advanced and efficient approach in modern application development. Its precision in data fetching, compatibility with current development frameworks, and ability to optimize performance make it a formidable tool for today's developers. While it introduces certain complexities, effectively harnessing the power of GraphQL allows for the creation of streamlined, scalable, and robust applications. As the technological landscape evolves, GraphQL's role in the realm of state and query management is poised to become increasingly influential in developing complex, data-driven applications.

Chapter Eight

React and Progressive Web Apps

Building Progressive Web Apps (PWAs) with React

Developing Progressive Web Apps (PWAs) using React has become a prominent trend in modern web application design. React, renowned for its efficient UI rendering and component-based structure, aligns perfectly with the requirements of PWAs, which are designed to offer a seamless, app-like experience on the web.

1. The Essence of Progressive Web Apps

PWAs represent a hybrid between web and mobile app experiences, utilizing advanced web capabilities to deliver high performance, reliability, and user engagement.

- Speed and Efficiency: PWAs are designed to load swiftly and operate smoothly, mirroring native app behavior.

- Consistent Performance in Varied Network Conditions: They are built to function reliably, even in low or no-network scenarios.

- User-Centric Interface: PWAs aim to deliver an immersive, app-like user experience on the web.

2. Defining Characteristics of PWAs

Key features that set PWAs apart include:

- Service Workers for Background Operations: These scripts run separately from the web page, enabling offline support and background tasks.

- Web App Manifest for App-Like Feel: This JSON file allows customization of the app's appearance and launch behavior.

- Adaptability Across Devices: PWAs are responsive, fitting seamlessly across different devices and screen sizes.

- Mandatory HTTPS Usage: Secure contexts through HTTPS are a requirement for PWAs to ensure data safety.

3. React's Role in PWA Development

React's ecosystem offers tools and functionalities ideally suited for building PWAs.

- Starting with Create React App: This setup comes equipped with a service worker for offline caching, making it an excellent foundation for React-based PWAs.

- Service Worker Integration in React: Custom service workers can be added to a React PWA for more sophisticated offline capabilities.

- Setting Up the Web App Manifest in React: Including a manifest file in React's public directory customizes the PWA's launch and appearance.

4. Performance Optimization Techniques

Optimizing performance is crucial for PWAs, and React developers can employ various strategies to enhance it.

- Dynamic Code Loading: React supports code splitting, allowing the application to load only the necessary code chunks, improving load times.

- Asset Management: Efficient handling of assets like images through compression and lazy loading techniques can boost performance.

5. Offline Functionality Enhancement

One of the hallmarks of PWAs is their offline functionality.

- Advanced Service Worker Customization: Beyond the default setup, developers can craft custom service workers in React PWAs for tailored offline experiences.

- Browser Storage Utilization: LocalStorage and IndexDB can be used for data storage and handling in offline scenarios.

6. Implementing Push Notifications

Incorporating push notifications in React PWAs involves using service workers in tandem with the Push API to engage users effectively.

7. Testing and Debugging PWAs

Testing React-based PWAs, especially for their offline capabilities, is essential.

- Using Tools like Lighthouse: Google's Lighthouse can audit the PWA for performance and adherence to PWA standards.

- Employing Browser Developer Tools: These tools are useful for testing service worker behavior and offline functionality.

8. Deployment Considerations for React PWAs

Deploying a React PWA requires specific steps like ensuring HTTPS and correctly configuring the server for service workers.

- Hosting Solutions: Many hosting services offer easy deployment for React PWAs with built-in HTTPS support.

- Service Worker Update Management: Properly handling service worker updates and cache management is crucial during deployment.

9. Navigating Challenges and Adopting Best Practices

While React is conducive to PWA development, certain challenges need to be addressed.

- Managing Offline State: Ensuring the app functions effectively in offline or low-network situations can be challenging.

- Emphasizing Progressive Enhancement: Building the app with functionality across various browsers and conditions is key.

- Continuous Update and Maintenance: Regularly updating the PWA with new web standards and React features is essential.

Conclusion

React's integration into PWA development allows for the creation of web applications that are not only efficient and responsive but also provide a user experience on par with native apps. By capitalizing on React's strengths and following PWA best practices, developers can craft superior web experiences that are fast, reliable, and engaging. As web technologies continue to advance, React's significance in the realm of PWA development is expected to increase, cementing its role in shaping the future of web applications.

Service workers and offline capabilities

Service workers are integral to contemporary web development, offering a suite of features that markedly improve application performance and provide offline functionality, once solely the domain of native apps. As a type of web worker, service workers act as a bridge between the web browser and network, facilitating a variety of enhancements in web app performance.

1. Fundamental Aspects of Service Workers

Operating as background scripts in the browser, service workers enable functionalities like push notifications and background synchronization.

- Network Request Interception: A key role of service workers is to intercept and manage network requests, including effectively handling resource caching.

- Independent Operation: Their ability to function independently from the web application allows them to operate even when the app is not active.

2. Performance Benefits Brought by Service Workers

Service workers are instrumental in boosting the performance of web applications.

- Resource Caching: They cache assets and resources, reducing loading times and conserving data usage.

- Customized Caching Strategies: Developers have the flexibility to implement specific caching strategies that best suit their application's needs.

3. Offline Functionality Through Service Workers

Service workers are renowned for their capability to enable offline access in web applications.

- Access to Cached Content Offline: Users can access pages and apps offline, thanks to the caching capabilities of service workers.

- Data Synchronization in the Background: They can synchronize data in the background when the network becomes available.

4. Implementing Service Workers in Applications

The integration of service workers into web applications involves several key steps.

- Lifecycle Events: The implementation process includes registering, installing, and activating the service worker, managed through specific event listeners.

- Defining Scope and Influence: The scope of a service worker is crucial as it defines the extent of its control over the application, generally determined by its location.

5. Effective Caching Techniques

Developing effective caching strategies is essential for optimizing the utility of service workers.

- Diverse Caching Approaches: Various approaches like cache-first or network-first are employed based on the application's data requirements.

- Distinction Between Static and Dynamic Caching: This distinction allows for the caching of static resources during installation and dynamic resources upon fetching.

6. Challenges in Service Worker Implementation

Despite their advantages, service workers pose certain challenges.

- Complex Update Procedures: Managing updates and cache refreshes can be intricate, requiring a strategy to avoid serving outdated content.

- Browser Support Variabilities: Differences in browser support and implementation can impact the functionality of service workers.

7. Optimal Practices for Service Worker Deployment

Following best practices can enhance the reliability and functionality of service workers.

- Cache Version Control: Implementing versioning in cache management can mitigate conflicts and ensure the delivery of updated content.

- Comprehensive Testing: Rigorous testing across various network conditions is vital to ensure consistent behavior.

- Ensuring Basic Functionality Without Dependency: Service workers should augment an application, not be fundamental to its primary operations.

8. Advanced Functionalities Enabled by Service Workers

Service workers enable several advanced features beyond basic performance enhancements.

- User Engagement via Push Notifications: They allow apps to send notifications to re-engage users, even when the browser is inactive.

- Efficient Background Data Management: Service workers handle background data synchronization, aligning server and client data outside of active usage.

Conclusion

Service workers mark a notable evolution in web development, bringing enhanced capabilities such as improved performance and offline accessibility to web applications. By enabling efficient caching and network management, they unlock new possibilities for building robust, user-centric web applications. While integrating service workers adds complexity, the array of benefits they introduce to web applications is substantial. As web technologies progress, service workers continue to be an essential component in web development, significantly influencing the trajectory of future web application advancements.

Performance optimization for PWAs

Optimizing the performance of Progressive Web Apps (PWAs) is essential in the current landscape of web development. PWAs blend the functionalities of web and mobile apps, but without proper optimization, they can suffer from delayed load times and sluggish responsiveness, detracting from the overall user experience. Enhancing a PWA's performance involves a series of critical strategies and practices.

1. The Criticality of Performance in PWAs

Performance stands as a cornerstone in the user experience of PWAs. These apps should deliver quick load times and smooth interactions, akin to native apps, to meet user expectations and maintain engagement.

- **Expectations of Speed:** Users typically look for immediate loading and fluid operation in PWAs, akin to native applications.

- **Influence on User Engagement:** The speed and responsiveness of a PWA directly impact user engagement and retention, with slow-performing apps facing higher abandonment rates.

2. Leveraging Caching for Performance Improvement

Caching is a vital strategy for enhancing the performance of PWAs.

- **Caching with Service Workers:** Service workers in PWAs enable the caching of application resources, allowing faster loading times after the initial download.

- **Adaptive Caching Strategies:** Implementing various caching tactics, like cache-first or network-first, can be pivotal depending on the specific needs of the app.

3. Asset and Resource Optimization

Minimizing and refining assets and resources is key to boosting a PWA's performance.

- **Reduction and Compression Techniques:** Shrinking the size of CSS, JavaScript, and HTML files through minification and compression aids in speeding up load times.

- Streamlining Images: Image optimization through resizing, format conversion, and compression can drastically reduce data size.

4. Streamlining Data Fetching and API Interactions

The method of data retrieval in a PWA can significantly influence its performance.

- Optimizing API Requests: Limiting the number and size of API calls helps reduce data usage.

- Data Fetching with GraphQL: GraphQL can streamline data fetching compared to traditional REST APIs by requesting exactly what is needed in a single query.

5. Code Division and Deferred Loading

Dividing code into smaller sections and loading them as needed can markedly enhance performance.

- Segmented Code Loading: Modern JavaScript frameworks support breaking down code into segments, allowing for the loading of only necessary code segments for the current view.

- Deferred Loading of Resources: Postponing the loading of non-essential resources until they are needed can improve initial load times.

6. Employing Web Workers for Intensive Computations

Web Workers facilitate the execution of computationally heavy tasks on a separate thread, ensuring the UI remains responsive.

- Background Computation: Handling data-intensive operations in the background prevents interference with the user interface's responsiveness.

7. Utilizing Browser Caching and Enhanced Protocols

Effective use of browser caching and newer protocols like HTTP/2 can refine resource delivery.

- Effective Use of Browser Caching: Setting appropriate cache headers allows browsers to store static resources, reducing future load times.

- Advantages of HTTP/2: The HTTP/2 protocol provides improvements such as multiplexing, which can enhance the speed of resource delivery.

8. Rigorous Performance Assessments

Continual testing and monitoring are essential for sustaining and advancing a PWA's performance.

- Performance Evaluation Tools: Applications like Lighthouse and Chrome DevTools offer critical insights into performance and suggest optimization opportunities.

- Ongoing Performance Reviews: Regular monitoring is vital for identifying and addressing performance issues promptly.

9. Integrating Accessibility with Performance

Balancing accessibility with performance can yield beneficial results.

- **Efficient and Accessible Design:** Implementing accessible design principles can lead to more streamlined and effective code, indirectly enhancing performance.

Conclusion

Optimizing the performance of Progressive Web Apps is a vital aspect of their development. Effective caching, resource optimization, intelligent data fetching, and other strategies are key to making PWAs fast and responsive. Regular performance evaluations and adherence to best practices are essential in ensuring that PWAs offer an optimal user experience, rivaling that of native applications. As the popularity of PWAs grows, their performance will continue to be a critical focus area, essential to their success and user acceptance.

Chapter Nine

Advanced Styling Techniques

Advanced CSS and SASS in React

In contemporary web development, particularly within React applications, advanced CSS and SASS (Syntactically Awesome Style Sheets) are instrumental in elevating the aesthetic and functional aspects of user interfaces. While basic CSS is commonly used, advanced techniques and the incorporation of SASS can significantly enhance the capability to create more complex, maintainable, and efficient styling in React projects.

1. Advanced CSS in React Context

CSS, the foundational styling language for web applications, takes on an advanced role in React. It goes beyond mere aesthetics to augment user interaction and app efficiency.

- Complex Styling Methods: Utilizing advanced CSS involves employing sophisticated selectors, intricate animations, responsive design techniques, and leveraging CSS variables to craft interactive and dynamic UIs.

- Modular Styling Approach: Given React's component-centric nature, styling is often approached in a modular fashion, with CSS targeting specific components.

2. SASS Integration in React Applications

SASS, a CSS preprocessor, enhances the styling process with features like variables, nesting, mixins, and more, providing greater flexibility and power than standard CSS.

- Variables for Consistency: SASS variables facilitate the definition of common style elements, enhancing reusability and ease of updates.

- Nested Rules for Organized Styles: SASS's nesting capabilities align well with React's hierarchical structure, enhancing stylesheet readability and organization.

3. Leveraging SASS's Advanced Capabilities in React

SASS offers a range of sophisticated features beneficial for React development.

- Reusable Mixins and Functions: These SASS features allow for creating shareable style snippets, useful for consistent theming and cross-browser styling.

- Dynamic Style Creation: SASS's loops and conditional directives enable the dynamic generation of styles, suitable for complex design systems and theming.

4. Scoped Styling with CSS Modules

CSS Modules in React provide scoped styles, ensuring that CSS applies only to the component it's intended for.

- Local Style Encapsulation: CSS Modules default to local scoping, preventing style conflicts across components.

- Global Styling Options: They also offer mechanisms for defining and using global styles when needed.

5. Performance Considerations in Styling

Optimizing style performance is vital, especially for large React applications.

- Minimizing Style Load: Employing techniques like purging unused CSS and optimizing critical rendering paths can enhance performance.

- Selector Efficiency: Simple, direct selectors are preferred for performance over complex, deeply nested selectors.

6. Responsive Design Through CSS and SASS

Responsive design is a necessity in web development, and SASS aids in implementing it effectively.

- Adaptive Layouts: Utilizing responsive units and fluid measurements helps create layouts that adapt to various screen sizes.

- Responsive Mixins in SASS: These mixins provide a streamlined way to handle media queries across different components.

7. Implementing Theming Mechanisms

Theming in web applications can be efficiently managed using CSS custom properties and SASS variables.

- Dynamic Theme Switching: Combining SASS variables with CSS custom properties allows for flexible, runtime theme changes.

8. Styling Best Practices in React

When applying advanced CSS and SASS in React, certain best practices can enhance the scalability and maintainability of styles.

- Component-Level Styling Focus: Styles should be tailored to individual components, aligning with React's modular design.

- Scalability and Maintenance of Styles: Organizing styles in a scalable and maintainable manner is essential, particularly for larger projects.

- Consistent Styling Across Components: Shared styles or SASS mixins can help maintain a uniform look and feel across different components.

Conclusion

Advanced CSS and SASS are pivotal in refining the styling of React applications, enabling developers to create more sophisticated, responsive, and maintainable designs. By harnessing the advanced features of CSS and SASS, developers are equipped to build visually appealing and functionally rich user interfaces. As the field of web development continues to evolve, the importance of advanced styling techniques in React will increasingly become more prominent, necessitating ongoing skill development and adaptation to new best practices.

CSS Modules and CSS-in-JS libraries

In today's web development arena, effectively managing CSS is key to building scalable and maintainable web applications. Two approaches have risen to prominence in addressing CSS-related challenges: CSS Modules and CSS-in-JS libraries. These methodologies offer distinct strategies for handling CSS, resolving common issues such as conflicts in the global namespace and enhancing styling practices in web development.

1. CSS Modules: Encapsulating Style Locally

CSS Modules address the global scope issue inherent in traditional CSS. Typically, CSS's global scope can lead to unintended conflicts across an application. CSS Modules solve this by scoping styles locally by default.

- Automatic Local Scope: CSS Modules automatically confine styles to the local scope, preventing accidental style overlaps between different parts of an application.

- Unique Class Name Generation: They automatically generate unique class names for each style during the build process, ensuring uniqueness across the application.

- Deliberate Global Styles: While local scoping is the default, CSS Modules also allow for intentional global styling when required.

2. CSS-in-JS Libraries: Merging Styles with JavaScript

CSS-in-JS represents an approach where CSS is embedded within JavaScript, marrying styles closely with their respective components and leveraging JavaScript's capabilities for dynamic styling.

- Responsive and Dynamic Styles: This methodology allows styles to change dynamically in response to component states or props, useful for adaptive designs or theme variations.

- Focused Component Styling: CSS-in-JS aligns with component-based frameworks like React, encouraging a more modular styling approach.

- Diverse Library Options: Several CSS-in-JS libraries are available, each offering unique features and syntax, such as Styled-Components, Emotion, and JSS.

3. CSS Modules vs. CSS-in-JS: A Comparative Overview

CSS Modules and CSS-in-JS both address the global scope issue but in different manners, each bringing its own set of advantages.

- Styling Philosophy: CSS Modules remain closer to traditional CSS, with styles in separate files, whereas CSS-in-JS integrates styles directly within JavaScript files.

- Performance Dynamics: CSS Modules have no runtime impact since styles are processed during build time, whereas CSS-in-JS may incur slight runtime overhead due to JavaScript-based style processing.

312

- Ecosystem and Tools: CSS-in-JS benefits from JavaScript's features for styling, while CSS Modules are more aligned with traditional CSS practices.

4. Optimal Practices for Employing CSS Modules and CSS-in-JS

Adopting best practices is crucial in effectively utilizing CSS Modules and CSS-in-JS.

- Uniform Naming Practices: Maintaining consistent naming conventions is essential in both approaches for clarity and maintenance.

- Dynamic Style Optimization: In CSS-in-JS, it's important to optimize dynamically changing styles to avoid performance bottlenecks.

- Organized and Simplified Styles: Styles should be kept organized and straightforward to avoid complexity, whether using CSS Modules or CSS-in-JS.

5. Prioritizing Performance

Performance considerations are especially pertinent when utilizing CSS-in-JS, as the JavaScript processing involved can impact application performance.

- Restrained Use of Inline Styles: Minimizing the use of inline styles in CSS-in-JS can help reduce JavaScript bundle size and avoid render-blocking issues.

- Efficient Application of CSS Modules: Ensuring that CSS Modules are loaded efficiently and without unnecessary replication is vital for performance optimization.

Conclusion

CSS Modules and CSS-in-JS libraries provide powerful solutions for contemporary CSS management challenges in web development. They facilitate the creation of maintainable, conflict-free, and scalable styling solutions. The choice between these two approaches often hinges on the specific needs of a project and the preferences of the development team. As the field of web development evolves, both CSS Modules and CSS-in-JS continue to be invaluable in the toolkit of web developers for creating aesthetically pleasing, user-centric web applications.

Theming and dynamic styles

Theming and dynamic styling are essential facets of contemporary web development, enabling the creation of versatile and engaging user interfaces. These techniques allow for the customization of applications to suit various user preferences, branding guidelines, and context-specific requirements, thereby enhancing user interaction and experience.

1. The Significance of Theming in Web Development

Theming involves designing a cohesive set of design elements, like colors, fonts, and layouts, that can be consistently applied throughout an application. This approach is pivotal for several reasons:

- Upholding Brand Image: Theming ensures that an application's aesthetic is in line with its brand identity, providing a consistent visual experience.

- Facilitating User Customization: It allows users to select their preferred themes, which can significantly boost user satisfaction and engagement.

- Enhancing Accessibility: Effective theming can improve accessibility, making web applications more inclusive.

2. The Concept of Dynamic Styling

Dynamic styling takes theming a step further by enabling styles to adapt in real-time based on user interactions, environmental factors, or other dynamic variables.

- Adaptability in Design: It is crucial for responsive designs where styles must adjust to various screen sizes and orientations.

- Interaction-Based Feedback: Dynamic styling can be used to provide immediate visual feedback based on user actions, enhancing the interactive experience.

- Context-Sensitive Styling: Styles can change in response to external conditions, like time or location, to offer a more immersive and relevant user experience.

3. Techniques for Implementing Theming and Dynamic Styles

Various technologies and methods are employed to achieve theming and dynamic styling in web applications.

- Utilization of CSS Custom Properties: CSS variables are commonly used for defining a set of easily modifiable style properties.

- CSS-in-JS Libraries Usage: Tools such as Styled-Components in React enable the integration of styles within JavaScript, facilitating dynamic styling based on component states.

- SASS/SCSS Preprocessors: These tools offer enhanced capabilities like variables and mixins for creating comprehensive theming mechanisms.

4. Best Practices in Theming and Dynamic Styling

Implementing theming and dynamic styling effectively involves adhering to certain best practices.

- Development of Modular Styles: Creating styles that are modular and reusable across various components enhances efficiency and maintainability.

- Optimization of Performance: Dynamic style alterations should be managed to ensure they don't hinder the application's performance.

- Consistency Across Themes: Regardless of the theme, the user experience should remain consistent, with a focus on usability and accessibility.

5. Challenges in Implementing Theming and Dynamic Styling

Despite their advantages, theming and dynamic styling come with their set of challenges.

- Achieving Stylistic Coherence: Ensuring uniform styling across different themes can be complex, particularly in extensive applications.

- Complexity in Theming Systems: Developing an intricate theming system requires thoughtful planning, considering factors like color schemes and API design for theming.

- Ensuring Compatibility: It's crucial that themes and dynamic styles are consistent across various browsers and devices.

6. Real-World Applications and Scenarios

Theming and dynamic styling are utilized in diverse scenarios, adding value to the functionality and aesthetics of web applications.

- E-commerce and Retail Websites: These platforms can offer theme-based personalization for an enhanced shopping experience.

- Analytical Dashboards: Dynamic styling can be employed to tailor styles based on data insights or specific user roles.

- Content-Driven Sites: Providing options like light and dark modes can make reading more comfortable and adaptable to user preferences.

Conclusion

Theming and dynamic styling are pivotal in crafting responsive, user-focused, and visually appealing web applications. Utilizing CSS custom properties, CSS-in-JS libraries, and SASS/SCSS, developers can create adaptable and easily maintainable styling solutions. As the expectations and preferences of users evolve, the role of theming and dynamic styling in delivering personalized and engaging user experiences becomes increasingly vital in the world of web development.

Chapter Ten

Animation in React

Integrating animations in React applications

Incorporating animations into React applications is a crucial aspect of modern web interface design, significantly enhancing the user experience and the interactive nature of the application. React's component-driven structure offers a robust platform for embedding animations, which can range from subtle, nuanced interactions to more elaborate motion sequences. Properly executed animations can greatly amplify the visual engagement and user interaction of a React application.

1. The Role of Animations in React Interfaces

Animations serve multiple purposes in web applications, transcending mere aesthetic enhancement. They can direct user focus, provide interactive feedback, and facilitate smooth transitions between different application states.

- Improving User Interaction: Thoughtfully implemented animations can make applications more intuitive and engaging, clarifying user interaction paths.

- Interactive Feedback Mechanism: Animations offer instant feedback on user actions, indicating processes like loading, completion, or errors, thereby elevating interactivity.

2. Animation Varieties in React

React supports diverse animation types, from straightforward CSS transitions to intricate animated sequences.

- Simple CSS-based Animations: Basic animations like hover effects and state transitions can be efficiently handled with CSS.

- Advanced JavaScript-Driven Animations: For more complex and controlled animation sequences, JavaScript animation libraries are often employed.

3. CSS Animation Integration in React

Integrating CSS animations in React components is a seamless process. They can be defined in external CSS files or inline and triggered via class name changes or inline styling.

- Utilizing CSS Modules or Styled-Components: These approaches help encapsulate CSS animations within React components, ensuring modularity.

- React Lifecycle for Animation Triggers: React's lifecycle methods can effectively manage class additions or removals to trigger animations.

4. Utilizing JavaScript Animation Libraries

There are several JavaScript libraries designed for intricate animations in React, each offering distinct features:

- React-Spring for Natural Motions: A library based on spring physics, ideal for creating fluid and lifelike movements.

- Framer Motion for Simplified Complex Animations: This tool provides an easy-to-use solution for elaborate animations and interactive gestures.

- React-Motion for Physics-Based Dynamics: Offers a comprehensive API for crafting animations based on physics principles.

5. Animation Control via State and Props

React's state management and props system can be leveraged to govern animations:

- State-Driven Animation Control: Using React state, animations can adapt to user interactions or application state changes.

- Dynamic Animation with Props: Passing different props to components can modify animations dynamically, responding to user choices or data variations.

6. Addressing Performance in Animations

Animations, while enhancing experience, can impact application performance, especially if they are complex or numerous.

- Ensuring Smooth Animations: It's vital to optimize animations to maintain fluid motion and avoid performance bottlenecks.

- Minimizing Component Rerenders: Preventing unnecessary rerenders of components involved in animations is crucial to avoid performance issues.

7. Prioritizing Accessibility in Animated Interfaces

When integrating animations, accessibility considerations are imperative. Some users may prefer or require reduced motion settings.

- Adhering to Reduced Motion Preferences: Utilize media queries like `**prefers-reduced-motion**` to tailor or disable animations for users who opt for reduced motion.

- Maintaining Accessibility Standards: Animated elements must remain accessible, ensuring they are navigable via keyboard and visibly focused.

8. Recommended Practices for React Animations

Effectively embedding animations in React apps involves following certain guidelines:

- Intentionality in Animation Design: Each animation should have a defined purpose, such as guiding user focus or enriching the visual narrative.

- Coherent Integration with UI Design: Animations should complement the overall design, enhancing rather than overwhelming the user interface.

- Comprehensive Testing on Various Platforms: Ensuring animations perform consistently across different devices and browsers is key to maintaining uniform user experience.

Conclusion

Embedding animations in React applications is a strategy that significantly improves user interaction and interface dynamism. Whether through simple CSS animations for basic effects or through sophisticated JavaScript libraries for complex motion, developers have a range of tools to create responsive, animated UIs. However, it's important to balance aesthetic appeal with considerations for performance and accessibility to ensure that animations contribute positively to the user experience. As React remains a popular framework for web development, integrating animations is an essential skill for developers aiming to craft advanced and engaging web applications.

Using libraries like Framer Motion and React Spring

In the arena of web development, especially within React environments, animation libraries such as Framer Motion and React Spring play a pivotal role in enriching user interfaces. These tools, tailored for React, offer a broad spectrum of features that simplify the integration of sophisticated animations, thereby elevating the interactivity and visual allure of interfaces.

1. Framer Motion: Streamlined Animation Tool for React

Framer Motion stands out as a preferred animation library for React developers, renowned for its user-friendly API that facilitates the crafting of intricate animations effortlessly.

- **User-Friendly API for Complex Animations:** Framer Motion's API eases the creation of detailed animations, enabling developers to animate diverse component properties with minimal coding.

- **In-built Gesture and Hover Animations:** This library offers innate support for interactive animations responsive to user gestures, such as dragging and hover effects.

- **Rich Feature Set:** Framer Motion encompasses advanced capabilities including path animations and shared element transitions, suitable for creating detailed animation sequences.

2. React Spring: Simulating Real-World Motion

React Spring is lauded for its physics-based approach to animations, rendering movements that mirror natural dynamics, thereby adding a realistic touch to animations.

- **Realistic Motion with Physics-based System:** The library's focus on simulating real-world physics results in fluid, lifelike animations.

- **Broad Range of Animation Applications:** React Spring is adept at handling everything from basic transitions to more intricate chained and trail animations.

- Performance Efficiency: It is optimized for high performance, ensuring that even complex animations are rendered smoothly.

3. Distinctive Features of Framer Motion and React Spring

Each of these libraries brings unique strengths to the table in React-based animation.

- Simplicity vs. Realism: Framer Motion is often preferred for its straightforward implementation and extensive documentation, ideal for quickly adding complex animations. In contrast, React Spring is chosen for animations that demand a more natural and realistic flow.

- Diverse Functionalities: Framer Motion excels in providing interactive animations like gestures, while React Spring specializes in creating animations that follow physical behaviors.

4. Practical Applications

The choice between Framer Motion and React Spring can be influenced by specific animation requirements and project goals.

- Interactive UI Elements: Framer Motion is typically chosen for elements requiring interactive animations, such as buttons or modals, due to its gesture and hover capabilities.

- Animations Mimicking Physical Forces: For components needing animations that emulate natural forces, like expansion or collapse, React Spring is more apt.

5. Implementation Techniques in React

Incorporating these libraries into React projects involves understanding their APIs and leveraging them to create and manage animations.

- Component-Based Animation Integration: Both libraries adopt a component-centric approach, aligning animations closely with UI elements.

- Utilizing React's State and Props: These libraries can be used in conjunction with React's state and props to control animations dynamically based on user interactions or changes within the application.

6. Prioritizing Performance in Animations

Ensuring animations are performant is crucial, particularly for intricate or resource-intensive animations.

- Animation Optimization: Both libraries provide mechanisms to fine-tune animations for optimal performance, avoiding any negative impact on the app's responsiveness.

- Balancing Visual Appeal and Application Efficiency: It is essential to strike a balance between creating visually engaging animations and maintaining application efficiency.

7. Considering Accessibility in Animated Interfaces

When implementing animations, accessibility considerations are essential, particularly for users with specific preferences or sensitivities to motion.

- Adapting to Reduced Motion Settings: Both Framer Motion and React Spring can be configured to respect user preferences for reduced motion, modifying or omitting animations accordingly.

- Maintaining Accessibility in Animated Elements: It's important to ensure that animations do not hinder the accessibility of interactive elements, preserving keyboard functionality and focus visibility.

Conclusion

Framer Motion and React Spring serve as essential tools for React developers aiming to incorporate animations into their web applications. Whether it's for designing detailed, interactive animations with Framer Motion or creating animations that emulate natural motion with React Spring, these libraries offer necessary functionalities to enhance user interfaces through animation. The choice between them typically depends on the specific needs of the project and the desired animation effects. As the trend towards dynamic and interactive web applications continues to rise, proficiency in these animation libraries is increasingly important for developers seeking to create state-of-the-art web experiences.

Principles of UI animation

In contemporary interface design, particularly in web and app development, the integration of UI animations is a key factor in augmenting user engagement. Understanding and applying the fundamental principles of UI animation is essential, ensuring that animations contribute positively to the user experience rather than detracting from it.

1. Intentionality in Animation

Every animation integrated into a UI should have a definitive purpose. Animations serve to direct user attention, indicate processes, or enhance the narrative of the interface.

- Directing User Attention: Strategic animations can steer users towards important elements or features.

- Interactive Feedback: Animations are effective in providing responses to user interactions, affirming the interactive nature of the UI.

2. Subtlety and Refinement

UI animations should be refined and not overpower the core content. Excessive animations can be distracting and potentially annoying to users.

- Minimalistic Approach: The most effective animations are those that integrate seamlessly and are almost imperceptible.

- Fluid State Transitions: Aim for animations that offer smooth transitions between states or pages, enhancing the user flow.

3. Consideration of Timing

The effectiveness of animations heavily depends on their timing and duration. Too quick animations can be disorienting, while overly slow animations can make the interface appear sluggish.

- Balanced Animation Speed: Achieving an optimal speed for animations is key, ensuring they are noticeable yet not obstructive.

- Uniform Duration: Similar animations should have consistent timing to maintain a rhythmic flow in the interface.

4. Responsiveness in Animation

Animations need to be responsive and react swiftly to user inputs, creating a perception of direct manipulation.

- Prompt Feedback: Animations should initiate instantly upon interaction to provide timely feedback.

- User-Driven Animations: Animations that adapt to the user's input speed and direction offer a more engaging experience.

5. Realism and Physics in Motion

Incorporating real-world physics principles can make animations more intuitive and relatable.

- Natural Movement: Emulating real-world physics, such as acceleration and deceleration, adds realism to animations.

- Contextual Relevance: Ensure that animations follow a logical and natural progression, appropriate to their context.

6. Function-Oriented Animation

Animations should enhance the functionality of the UI, not just act as ornamental elements.

- Navigational Clarity: Utilize animations to clarify transitions and navigational changes.

- Instructional Cues: Use animations as visual guides to demonstrate how to interact with the interface.

7. Accessibility in Animation Design

Design animations with a focus on accessibility, catering to users with various needs and sensitivities.

- Options for Motion Sensitivity: Implement settings for reduced motion to accommodate users with motion sensitivity.

- Non-Distracting Animations: Avoid animations that flash or distract, which can be problematic for users with certain neurological conditions.

8. Complementing Overall Design

Ensure that animations are an integral part of the overall design ethos of the application.

- Stylistic Harmony: Animations should align with the application's design language, whether minimalist or elaborate.

- Contribution to Experience: Each animation should add value to the overall design and user experience.

9. Impact on Performance

Be mindful of the impact animations can have on an application's performance.

- Performance Optimization: Animations should be optimized to prevent any negative impact on loading times or responsiveness.

- Cross-Device Testing: Verify that animations maintain smooth performance across different devices and platforms.

Conclusion

Ultimately, the core principles of UI animation revolve around crafting animations that are purposeful, subtle, and contribute to an enhanced user experience. They should be crafted with a focus on timing, interactivity, realism, functionality, and accessibility. Seamlessly integrating with the overall design while being optimized for performance, these animations serve as a crucial tool in elevating the usability and attractiveness of applications. As the field of UI design continues to progress, the strategic use of well-executed animations remains vital in creating engaging and user-friendly digital interfaces.

Chapter Eleven

React and WebAssembly

Introduction to WebAssembly

WebAssembly, commonly known as Wasm, stands as a groundbreaking innovation in web technology, offering a new approach to building web applications. It is a binary instruction format enabling code written in multiple programming languages to be executed on the web at speeds comparable to native applications, representing a significant evolution in browser capabilities.

1. Origins of WebAssembly

WebAssembly was developed through a collaboration of major tech giants like Mozilla, Microsoft, Google, and Apple under the World Wide Web Consortium (W3C). Its inception addressed the need for enhanced performance in web applications, particularly for computation-intensive tasks such as gaming, image processing, and handling large data sets.

- A Standardized Binary Format: WebAssembly is a low-level binary format, compiled from languages like C, C++, and Rust, and is executed within a web browser.

- Harmonious with the Web Ecosystem: Designed to work alongside, not replace, JavaScript, WebAssembly integrates smoothly with the existing web ecosystem.

2. The Rationale for WebAssembly

WebAssembly aims to supplement JavaScript by addressing performance-related challenges where JavaScript may fall short.

- Boosting Performance: It offers significant performance improvements for web applications, especially those requiring extensive computational power.

- Expanding Language Choice: WebAssembly allows developers to build web applications in languages other than JavaScript, diversifying web development options.

3. WebAssembly's Mechanism

WebAssembly operates within the same security sandbox as JavaScript, ensuring safe execution in web environments.

- From High-Level to Binary Code: Languages like C++ and Rust are compiled into WebAssembly's binary code, which is then run in the browser.

- Browser Execution: Modern web browsers are equipped to support WebAssembly, enabling the binary code to be executed alongside JavaScript.

4. Synergy between WebAssembly and JavaScript

WebAssembly and JavaScript are designed as complementary technologies.

- Web API Accessibility: WebAssembly can access the same web APIs as JavaScript and can be called from JavaScript, allowing fluid interaction between the two.

- Optimal Use Cases for Both: While JavaScript remains ideal for tasks like DOM manipulations, WebAssembly excels in CPU-intensive processes.

5. Advantages of Adopting WebAssembly

WebAssembly introduces several benefits to the realm of web development:

- Near-Native Speed: WebAssembly allows code to run at near-native speeds, outperforming conventional JavaScript, especially in CPU-heavy tasks.

- Portability and Compactness: As a low-level language, WebAssembly is both portable and compact, making it well-suited for web applications.

- Programming Language Flexibility: Developers can utilize familiar languages like C++ or Rust for web application development.

6. Challenges with WebAssembly

Despite its advantages, WebAssembly also brings certain challenges:

- Understanding Low-Level Concepts: Developers used to high-level programming may find WebAssembly's low-level nature challenging.

- Web API Access Limitations: Currently, WebAssembly has limited direct interaction with Web APIs, often depending on JavaScript for such tasks.

7. Practical Applications of WebAssembly

WebAssembly has been applied in various sectors, showcasing its versatility:

- Gaming: High-performance games now run in browsers thanks to WebAssembly.

- Image and Video Editing: Resource-intensive applications like image and video editing software benefit from the performance enhancements WebAssembly offers.

- Immersive Web Experiences: WebAssembly is apt for demanding applications like VR and AR on the web.

8. WebAssembly's Prospective Future

The future trajectory of WebAssembly is promising, with continuous improvements and growing adoption.

- Expanding Developer Tools and Community: The ecosystem around WebAssembly is rapidly developing, making it increasingly accessible for developers.

- Anticipated Feature Enhancements: Future improvements in WebAssembly, such as enhanced memory management and direct Web API integrations, are likely to broaden its use cases.

Conclusion

WebAssembly marks a pivotal shift in web application development, offering a methodology for executing high-performance applications in a web browser. It opens doors for using various programming languages on the web, pushing the boundaries of browser-based applications. As it continues to develop, WebAssembly is poised to significantly influence the future landscape of web development, enabling faster, more powerful, and versatile web applications. With its growing support and community, WebAssembly presents an exciting opportunity for developers to explore advanced web application possibilities.

Use cases for WebAssembly in React applications

WebAssembly, commonly abbreviated as Wasm, stands as a pivotal innovation in web development, offering new avenues for enhancing React applications. React, recognized for its efficient component-based architecture, greatly benefits from the incorporation of WebAssembly, particularly in scenarios demanding high performance and advanced functionality.

1. Handling Computationally Intensive Tasks

A key application of WebAssembly in React is managing tasks that require intensive computation. WebAssembly's capability to execute code at speeds akin to native applications makes it perfectly suited for operations that are too demanding for JavaScript in React apps.

- Complex Data Operations: Tasks like intricate data sorting and mathematical computations can be offloaded to WebAssembly, alleviating the load on JavaScript.

- Processing of Images and Videos: For React apps involved in image or video manipulation, WebAssembly can efficiently handle processes like real-time editing, compression, and format conversions.

2. Advancements in Web-Based Gaming

WebAssembly's integration in React enhances the development of web games, especially those with elaborate graphics and intensive physics simulations.

- Enhanced Graphics Rendering: WebAssembly can manage the heavy lifting of graphics computation, facilitating smoother gameplay and graphics in React-based games.

- Physics Simulation Handling: Incorporating physics engines through WebAssembly can significantly boost the performance and responsiveness of gaming applications.

3. Cryptographic Operations

WebAssembly can significantly enhance the speed and security of cryptographic operations in React applications, making it a vital tool for applications that prioritize data security.

- Efficient Encryption Processes: Encryption and decryption routines run faster and more securely in WebAssembly within React applications, crucial for protecting data.

- Secure Hashing and Signature Verification: Implementing secure hashing algorithms via WebAssembly can bolster the security measures in a React application.

4. Audio and Video Manipulation

React applications that engage in audio and video processing can immensely benefit from WebAssembly's ability to handle demanding computational tasks.

- Real-Time Audio Processing: Tasks such as audio synthesis and effects processing can be efficiently executed by WebAssembly, ensuring minimal delay.

- Optimized Video Processing: For applications like video streaming services or editing tools, WebAssembly can expedite video encoding and decoding processes.

5. Scientific and Simulation Applications

React applications designed for scientific computations or simulations can leverage WebAssembly for enhanced performance and accuracy.

- Advanced Scientific Simulations: WebAssembly aids in running complex simulations for scientific or engineering purposes efficiently.

- Optimized Data Visualization: Handling large-scale data visualization becomes more efficient with WebAssembly, especially when dealing with extensive datasets.

6. Machine Learning and Artificial Intelligence

The integration of machine learning and AI within web applications is another area where WebAssembly can enhance React applications.

- **Model Training and Execution:** Running machine learning models or conducting predictive analysis can be accelerated with WebAssembly.

- **Real-Time AI Interactions:** Applications requiring instantaneous AI responses can benefit from the improved performance that WebAssembly offers.

7. Integrating Legacy Systems

WebAssembly also provides a pathway to incorporate existing legacy code into modern React applications, expanding the possibilities in web app development.

- **Legacy Code Reutilization:** Existing codebases, particularly those in languages like C/C++, can be compiled to WebAssembly for use in React, circumventing the need for complete rewrites.

- **Facilitating Multi-Language Integration:** The multi-language compatibility of WebAssembly allows for a smooth transition of various codebases into React applications.

8. Challenges and Key Points

Integrating WebAssembly with React, while beneficial, comes with its set of challenges and considerations.

- Adaptation Challenges: Developers might face hurdles in adapting to WebAssembly, especially those more familiar with high-level programming languages.

- Ensuring Cross-Browser Performance: It's crucial to guarantee that WebAssembly modules are consistently performant across different web browsers.

Conclusion

WebAssembly opens a spectrum of applications for React, from boosting performance in computation-heavy tasks to enabling complex functionalities like gaming and AI. By shifting intensive processes to WebAssembly, React applications can achieve heightened efficiency and offer richer experiences. As WebAssembly continues to develop, its integration with React is set to expand further, enabling the creation of sophisticated, high-performance web applications. This combination of React's UI prowess and WebAssembly's computational strength forms a formidable platform for the next generation of web applications.

Integrating WebAssembly modules

WebAssembly, abbreviated as Wasm, is a revolutionary development in the web technology landscape, offering an innovative approach to enhancing web applications. As a binary instruction format, it allows code written in various programming languages to execute within web browsers at speeds close to native applications, marking a significant advancement in browser functionality.

1. Fundamentals of WebAssembly Modules

WebAssembly modules, compiled from languages like C, C++, or Rust, are binary codes that can be run in a browser. These modules consist of functions callable from JavaScript, resembling typical JavaScript function calls.

- Binary Code Compilation: WebAssembly modules are essentially low-level binary codes, efficiently executable by browsers.

- Language Independence: WebAssembly's design allows for the utilization of multiple programming languages, extending beyond the confines of JavaScript.

2. Advantages of WebAssembly Modules Integration

Incorporating WebAssembly modules into web applications offers key benefits, particularly in enhancing performance and broadening development options.

- Performance Improvements: WebAssembly significantly boosts performance, especially for compute-intensive tasks, outpacing traditional JavaScript execution.

- Expanded Development Language Options: It opens the door for developers to use a range of programming languages for web development, breaking the monopoly of JavaScript.

3. Incorporating WebAssembly Modules

The process of integrating WebAssembly modules into a web application is multifaceted, involving the compilation of source code and its subsequent execution within JavaScript.

- Source Code Compilation: Source code in languages like C++ is compiled into WebAssembly using compilers such as Emscripten.

- Module Loading and Instantiation: The compiled module is loaded into the web application, usually via JavaScript's fetch API, and then instantiated for interaction with JavaScript.

4. Function Invocation from WebAssembly Modules

WebAssembly modules, once instantiated, allow their functions to be invoked from JavaScript.

- Exported Function Accessibility: Functions intended for JavaScript interaction are exported from the WebAssembly module.

- Seamless JavaScript Integration: These functions are accessible in JavaScript, allowing data exchange between JavaScript and WebAssembly.

5. Managing Memory Between WebAssembly and JavaScript

WebAssembly maintains its separate linear memory space, distinct from JavaScript's memory, necessitating careful memory management.

- Shared Memory Utilization: WebAssembly and JavaScript can share memory space for efficient data handling.

- Attention to Memory Allocation: Proper memory allocation and deallocation in WebAssembly are crucial to prevent memory leaks and excessive resource usage.

6. Assessing Performance Impacts

While WebAssembly provides performance advantages, it's essential to consider the specific benefits and any associated overhead.

- Appropriate Performance Use Cases: WebAssembly is best suited for CPU-intensive tasks, with its overhead being justifiable in such scenarios.

- Balanced Use with JavaScript: Combining WebAssembly and JavaScript effectively can leverage the strengths of both technologies.

7. Debugging and Evolving Tooling

Debugging WebAssembly modules poses unique challenges, although the tooling landscape is evolving to address these.

- Source Map Support for Debugging: Tools and browsers supporting source maps for WebAssembly enable debugging in the original programming language.

- Advancements in Development Tools: The development ecosystem around WebAssembly is growing, with enhancements in compilers, debuggers, and IDEs.

8. Ensuring Security

Security is a paramount consideration in WebAssembly, especially given its capability to run code from various languages within a secure browser environment.

- Adherence to Web Security Protocols: WebAssembly follows the same-origin policy and requires appropriate CORS settings for secure module fetching.

- Secure Coding Practices: Employing secure coding standards is essential to mitigate vulnerabilities, particularly when dealing with low-level languages.

9. Integration Best Practices

Effectively integrating WebAssembly modules into web applications necessitates following certain best practices.

- Judicious Application: Utilize WebAssembly for specific tasks where its performance benefits are most pronounced.

- Optimized Data Exchange: Enhance the efficiency of data transfer between JavaScript and WebAssembly to reduce performance overhead.

- Modular Code Design: Approach WebAssembly code structuring with modularity in mind for better maintainability and reusability.

Conclusion

The integration of WebAssembly modules into web applications heralds new possibilities for performance optimization and leveraging a wider array of programming languages in web development. Thoughtful implementation of these modules can lead to significant enhancements in application efficiency and capability. With WebAssembly's ongoing development and expanding support, it is increasingly becoming a vital and accessible tool for web developers aiming to extend the capabilities of web browsers.

Chapter Twelve

Optimizing React Applications

Performance analysis and optimization techniques

Performance analysis and optimization play an indispensable role in modern software engineering, essential for crafting efficient, responsive, and user-centric applications. In an era where swift and seamless functionality is a baseline expectation, the deployment of strategic performance optimization methods is crucial for the success of any application, whether it's web-based, mobile, or desktop software.

1. Fundamentals of Performance Analysis

Performance analysis is the process of scrutinizing various components of an application to pinpoint inefficiencies and performance issues. This evaluation encompasses multiple aspects, ranging from the speed of code execution to resource utilization, and database query efficiency.

- Usage of Profiling Tools: Leveraging profiling tools is a standard practice in performance analysis. These tools track and document application execution, shedding light on resource-intensive code segments.

- Setting Benchmarks and Monitoring Metrics: Establishing performance benchmarks and keeping tabs on key performance indicators are instrumental in

346

quantifying performance and highlighting optimization needs.

2. Optimizing Front-End Performance

In web applications, enhancing front-end performance is critical for ensuring a swift and interactive user interface.

- Reducing HTTP Requests: Lessening the number of HTTP requests through file bundling and sprite sheets usage can significantly quicken loading times.

- Asset Optimization: Compressing images, minifying CSS and JavaScript, and adopting formats like WebP for images and ES6 for JavaScript can lead to notable performance improvements.

- Non-Blocking Resource Loading: Implementing non-blocking loading for resources such as JavaScript and CSS enhances perceived load speed.

3. Enhancing Back-End Performance

Back-end optimization focuses on refining server-side processes and database transactions.

- Database Efficiency: Streamlining database queries, effective indexing, and normalization can drastically quicken data retrieval.

- Implementing Caching Mechanisms: Caching frequently requested data reduces database load and expedites data access.

- Back-End Code Refinement: Optimizing server-side code, including the adoption of efficient algorithms and data structures, is key to improving overall performance.

4. Performance in Mobile Applications

For mobile apps, optimization also involves addressing device-specific limitations like CPU and memory constraints.

- Efficient Resource Utilization: Managing resources adeptly, including optimizing for memory and battery usage, is vital in mobile apps.

- Adaptive Design and Layouts: Ensuring mobile apps are adaptable to various screen sizes and orientations is key to a superior user experience.

5. Network Performance Enhancements

Applications reliant on network interactions must optimize their network performance.

- Data Transfer Compression: Compressing data for network interactions reduces data transfer volume, enhancing communication speed.

- Streamlining API Interactions: Reducing and optimizing API calls, and employing data fetching methods like GraphQL, can lessen network strain and improve response times.

6. Memory Management and Leak Mitigation

Effective memory handling is critical in averting performance decline, especially in applications with prolonged runtimes.

- Detecting Memory Leaks: Regularly checking for memory leaks, using tools like Valgrind or memory profiling tools, aids in identifying and addressing memory issues.

- Optimizing Garbage Collection: For languages that employ garbage collection, refining this process can enhance memory handling and application performance.

7. Load and Stress Testing

Conducting load and stress tests is essential for assessing an application's performance under varying user load levels.

- User Load Simulation: Tools that simulate user traffic provide insights into application behavior under heavy usage, revealing scalability challenges.

- Performance Under Extreme Conditions: Stress testing helps in determining the application's limits, revealing how it copes under strenuous conditions.

8. Ongoing Monitoring and Progressive Enhancement

Performance optimization is a continuous endeavor, necessitating ongoing monitoring and progressive refinements.

- Monitoring Performance in Real-Time: Employing real-time performance monitoring tools offers continuous insights into application performance.

- Iterative Enhancements: Regular performance data-driven updates and optimizations ensure steady improvement in application performance.

Conclusion

Performance analysis and optimization are crucial elements of the software development lifecycle, ensuring that applications meet the high performance and efficiency standards expected by today's users. Through a variety of techniques, from optimizing front-end assets to refining back-end code, and by maintaining a cycle of continuous monitoring and enhancement, developers can ensure their applications deliver optimal performance. As technologies and user expectations evolve, so too must strategies for performance optimization, presenting an ongoing challenge for software developers to adapt and innovate.

Code splitting and lazy loading

Code splitting and lazy loading are essential methodologies in contemporary web development, crucial for boosting the efficiency and user experience of web applications. As web applications become more extensive and intricate, leveraging these techniques is key to optimizing load times and effective resource utilization.

1. Fundamentals of Code Splitting

Code splitting involves segmenting a web application's code into smaller, manageable chunks loaded as needed. Traditional approaches load the entire JavaScript bundle at the first visit, often leading to prolonged load times for substantial applications.

- **Strategic Segmentation:** Code is divided at logical junctures, such as per route or component, ensuring only relevant code loads for specific functionalities or views.

- **Dynamic Imports:** Modern tools and frameworks facilitate dynamic importing, allowing developers to designate specific code sections for loading on demand.

2. Concept of Lazy Loading

Lazy loading is a tactic that delays the loading of non-essential resources during the initial page load. Instead, these resources are loaded when required, typically triggered by user interactions.

- **Minimizing Initial Load Time:** By delaying the loading of certain images, scripts, and modules, the initial loading duration can be substantially decreased.

- **User Experience Enhancement:** This approach contributes to a smoother browsing experience by not overburdening the user with unnecessary resource loading upfront.

3. Integration Techniques

Incorporating code splitting and lazy loading typically involves a blend of build tools and specific framework functionalities.

- Build Tools and Bundlers: Tools such as Webpack offer inherent support for code splitting, enabling developers to configure their application's code division and loading strategy.

- Framework-Specific Features: Frameworks like React, Angular, and Vue.js provide simple methods for implementing these techniques, often requiring minimal setup.

4. Application Scenarios and Advantages

Code splitting and lazy loading are especially beneficial in contexts where performance and user experience are paramount.

- Large Applications: For applications with numerous routes and components, code splitting ensures only the necessary code is loaded per user interaction.

- Performance-Critical Environments: Applications where load time is crucial benefit from lazy loading, as it reduces the initial data transfer and processing load.

5. Challenges and Optimal Practices

Implementing these techniques presents challenges and necessitates adherence to certain best practices.

- Identifying Split Points: Determining the most effective locations for code splitting requires analysis of usage patterns and component interdependencies.

- Dependency Handling: Accurate management of dependencies is essential in code-split environments to avoid execution errors.

- Handling of Lazy Loading Content: Providing placeholders for content that is being lazy-loaded ensures a user-friendly interface during loading periods.

6. SEO and Accessibility Implications

The use of code splitting and lazy loading can impact SEO and accessibility, which needs careful consideration.

- SEO Strategies: Ensuring that search engines can effectively index lazy-loaded content might require techniques like server-side rendering.

- Accessibility Measures: Lazy-loaded content should be fully accessible to all users, including those using assistive technologies like screen readers.

7. Regular Performance Assessment

Ongoing evaluation and refinement are vital for maximizing the benefits of these methodologies.

- Monitoring Key Performance Metrics: Continuous tracking of performance indicators can highlight further opportunities for code splitting and lazy loading.

- Progressive Refinement: Based on performance data and user feedback, the application's performance should be regularly enhanced.

Conclusion

Code splitting and lazy loading are crucial strategies in the toolkit of modern web developers, directly addressing the challenges posed by large-scale and complex web applications. By strategically dividing code and postponing the loading of non-critical resources, these methods significantly improve loading times and user interaction quality. While their implementation requires thoughtful planning and attention to potential impacts on SEO and accessibility, the performance and efficiency gains they offer make them invaluable in web development. As web technologies continue to advance, the importance of code splitting and lazy loading in optimizing web application performance remains a key area of focus.

Optimizing React for production

Optimizing React applications for production deployment is a crucial phase in the development lifecycle, aimed at ensuring the application operates efficiently, rapidly, and reliably once it goes live. React, renowned for its effectiveness in building user interfaces, demands specific optimization strategies to realize its full potential in a production setting.

1. Bundle Size Reduction

A primary consideration in React optimization is to minimize the JavaScript bundle's size, which directly impacts load times.

- Code Splitting Application: Breaking down the app's code into smaller, on-demand loadable segments can significantly accelerate initial loading.

- Implementing Tree Shaking: Employing tree shaking, which eliminates unused code from the bundle, contributes to a lighter application.

- Code Minification: Minifying the code by removing superfluous characters without altering its functionality effectively reduces the bundle size.

2. Rendering Optimization of Components

The efficiency of how components render in React significantly influences overall performance.

- Utilizing ShouldComponentUpdate and React.memo: These functions are instrumental in preventing unnecessary re-renders.

- Employment of Pure Components: Leveraging pure components minimizes redundant rendering by updating only with state or prop changes.

- Component Lazy Loading: Delaying the loading of non-critical components until necessary can enhance the app's initial load speed.

3. State Management Efficiency

Robust state management is vital for high-performing React applications.

- Effective Global State Management: Efficient use of libraries like Redux or Context API is crucial for managing global state without triggering excessive re-renders.

- Adoption of Immutable Data Structures: Immutable data structures facilitate optimized state updates and comparisons.

4. Prudent Use of Third-Party Libraries

Third-party libraries, while adding functionality, can increase the bundle size and affect performance.

- Assessing Library Necessity: It's important to critically evaluate the need for each library and consider native React features as alternatives.

- Selection of Lightweight Libraries: Opt for lighter libraries that offer the required functionality without a significant performance cost.

5. Server-Side Rendering (SSR) Implementation

Server-side rendering can markedly improve both load times and SEO for a React application.

- Enhanced Initial Load: SSR allows the server to send a pre-rendered page to the client, making content visible more quickly.

- SEO Advantages: Server-rendered content is more efficiently crawled and indexed by search engines, enhancing the app's online visibility.

6. Optimizing API Interactions

The way a React app interacts with APIs and fetches data is key to its performance.

- Response Caching: Implement caching to minimize repetitive API calls.

- Data Structure Optimization: Employ efficient data structures for storing and handling API response data.

7. Image Optimization Strategies

Considering that images typically form a significant portion of web content, their optimization is crucial.

- Image Compression and Format Selection: Compressing images and using formats like WebP reduces file size without compromising quality.

- Image Lazy Loading: Loading images as they enter the viewport, rather than all at once, can significantly improve load times.

8. Leveraging Web Workers

Web Workers in React can handle complex tasks in the background, ensuring the UI remains responsive.

- Task Offloading: Assign data processing and intensive calculations to Web Workers to maintain a smooth UI.

9. Performance Monitoring and Analysis

Continual monitoring and analysis are essential for identifying and addressing performance issues.

- Using Profiling Tools: Browser-based and React-specific profiling tools can pinpoint performance bottlenecks.

- Tracking Performance Metrics: Regularly measuring key performance indicators helps gauge the effectiveness of optimization efforts.

10. Focus on Accessibility and Responsive Design

An optimized React app should be accessible and responsive, catering to all users and devices.

- Ensuring Device Responsiveness: The app should adapt seamlessly to different screen sizes and orientations.

- Accessibility Compliance: Regular accessibility evaluations ensure the app remains usable for individuals with various disabilities.

Conclusion

Optimizing a React application for production encompasses a broad range of strategies, from reducing the bundle size and enhancing component rendering to effective state management and third-party library usage. Techniques such as server-side rendering, API optimization, image management, and the use of Web Workers further contribute to performance improvement. Ongoing performance monitoring, combined with a commitment to accessibility and responsive design, ensures that the application delivers a superior user experience across all platforms. Mastery of these optimization techniques is crucial for developers aiming to create React applications that are not only fast and efficient but also robust and user-friendly in the production environment.

Chapter Thirteen

Building Mobile Apps with React Native

Overview of React Native

React Native is a prominent framework for developing mobile applications, offering a harmonious blend of adaptability, efficiency, and compatibility across platforms. Initiated and sustained by Facebook, React Native enables the creation of mobile apps utilizing JavaScript and React, providing an alternative to conventional mobile development methodologies.

1. Origins and Development of React Native

Launched by Facebook in 2015, React Native was envisioned as a means to leverage web development principles and technologies in mobile app creation. It was born from the necessity to transcend the constraints of web-centric apps and the intricacies inherent in native mobile app development.

- Bridging Web and Mobile Development Worlds: React Native serves as a conduit between web and mobile app development, employing familiar web technologies for mobile app creation.

- Community Growth and Ecosystem Expansion: Since its inception, React Native has witnessed rapid growth, buoyed by an active community and a burgeoning ecosystem of libraries and tools.

2. Fundamental Principles of React Native

React Native operates on several foundational principles that define its functionality and allure.

- Learn Once, Apply Anywhere Philosophy: This approach emphasizes acquiring a set of skills applicable to both iOS and Android development, diverging from the "write once, run anywhere" philosophy.

- Native-Level Performance: React Native compiles into native code, ensuring performance parity with traditional native apps on both iOS and Android.

3. React Native's Architectural Design

The architecture of React Native is crafted to harness React's power for mobile app development while maintaining performance and native capabilities.

- The Bridge Mechanism: A "bridge" facilitates communication between JavaScript code and the native platform, enabling smooth integration of native components.

- Component-Centric Architecture: Mirroring React's structure, React Native adopts a component-based approach, streamlining development and enhancing component reusability.

4. Development Approach in React Native

React Native's approach to development offers several advantages over traditional mobile development practices.

- Shared Code Across Platforms: A significant portion of code can be used for both iOS and Android, curtailing development time and resources.

- Instantaneous Reload Capability: The hot reloading feature allows immediate visibility of changes without the need for a complete app rebuild.

5. Crafting User Interfaces with React Native

Building user interfaces in React Native is both intuitive and efficient, thanks to its declarative UI style and the integration of JavaScript and React.

- Declarative UI Composition: The framework employs a declarative style for UI construction, enhancing predictability and simplifying debugging.

- Utilization of React Components: React Native capitalizes on React components, known for their reusability and ease of management.

6. Native Functionality Access

A key strength of React Native is its proficiency in tapping into native device functionalities.

- Inclusion of Native Modules: A variety of native modules in React Native grant access to device features like cameras, GPS, and accelerometers.

- Creation of Custom Native Modules: Developers have the liberty to craft bespoke native modules, broadening the functional scope of their applications.

7. Performance Optimization Strategies

Achieving optimal performance in React Native requires attention to certain specific factors.

- Bridge Optimization: Enhancing the efficiency of the bridge that links JavaScript with native code is pivotal for performance.

- Resource Management: The judicious management of resources like memory and CPU is critical, especially for intricate or resource-intensive apps.

8. Community Resources and Support

The strength of React Native lies in its vibrant community and a rich ecosystem of resources.

- Diverse Libraries and Tools: The framework is supported by an extensive array of third-party libraries, tools, and plugins, expanding its capabilities.

- Active Community Engagement: A robust community provides invaluable support through forums, tutorials, and comprehensive documentation, facilitating problem-solving and knowledge dissemination.

9. Comparative Analysis with Other Frameworks

React Native is often contrasted with other cross-platform frameworks like Flutter or Xamarin.

- Preference for JavaScript: The use of JavaScript in React Native sets it apart, making it accessible to a wide array of web developers.

- Native Component Integration: Compared to other frameworks, React Native's method of integrating with native components typically offers a more authentic native user experience.

Conclusion

React Native marks a significant evolution in the domain of mobile application development, blending the simplicity and accessibility of web development with the robustness and functionality of native apps. Its component-based structure, combined with the ability to integrate with native device functions, renders it an appealing choice for developers aiming to build versatile cross-platform mobile applications. As it continues to develop and garner support from an enthusiastic community, React Native solidifies its status as a frontrunner in the mobile development arena.

Differences and similarities between React and React Native

React and React Native, both creations of Facebook, have become staples in the realms of web and mobile application development. Despite sharing foundational principles and design approaches, they are distinctively tailored to suit their respective platforms of web and mobile.

1. Fundamental Commonalities

Both React and React Native are grounded in similar fundamental concepts that have contributed to React's success in web development.

- Component-Based Structure: They both adopt a component-based approach, enabling developers to construct applications using reusable and isolated components.

- Shared React Libraries and Ecosystem: Access to a wide array of React libraries and tools is a common advantage, including state management tools and HTTP utilities.

- Utilization of JSX Syntax: JSX, a syntax that combines JavaScript with a markup-like syntax, is a key feature in both, facilitating UI component creation.

- JavaScript Centricity: Central to both frameworks is the use of JavaScript, easing the transition for developers between web and mobile development domains.

2. Differences in Rendering UI

The way React and React Native render user interfaces marks one of their fundamental differences.

- React for Web: React is employed for web applications and uses the browser's DOM to render HTML elements.

- React Native for Mobile: In contrast, React Native bypasses the DOM, using native components to render user interfaces on mobile devices.

3. Approaches to Styling

Styling in React and React Native varies to cater to different platform needs.

- CSS Styling in React: React developers use CSS for styling, which can be implemented through external stylesheets or styled-components.

- JavaScript-Based Styling in React Native: React Native, on the other hand, uses a JavaScript-based Stylesheet API, with Flexbox for layout, ensuring consistency across mobile platforms.

4. Platform-Specific Code Usage

React Native uniquely caters to platform-specific code requirements, a feature not needed in React for web.

- Platform Module in React Native: It includes a Platform module that allows different code to be executed depending on the operating system.

- OS-Specific File Extensions: Developers can write separate files for iOS and Android, and React Native will automatically select the appropriate file.

5. Hardware and API Interaction

Direct interaction with mobile device hardware and APIs is a specific capability of React Native.

- Native Modules Availability: React Native directly accesses device functionalities like cameras and GPS, a feature absent in React for web development.

6. Navigation Mechanisms

Navigation in React and React Native is tailored to the nature of web and mobile apps.

- Web-Based Navigation in React: React often employs libraries like React Router for managing web app navigation.

- Native Navigation in React Native: For mobile apps, React Native utilizes native navigation libraries that offer a mobile-centric user experience.

7. Development and Debugging Environments

The development and debugging environments for React and React Native are distinct due to their platform-specific nature.

- Web Dev Tools for React: React development typically involves standard web development tools and browser extensions.

- Mobile Dev Environment for React Native: React Native requires a mobile development setup and often uses specialized debugging tools.

8. Ecosystem and Community Dynamics

While both technologies benefit from strong communities, their ecosystems have different focal points.

- Wider Web Community for React: React's community is more extensive, reflecting its widespread use in web development.

- Mobile-Focused Community for React Native: The React Native community is centered around mobile development, with growing contributions to mobile-specific libraries and tools.

9. Performance Optimization Aspects

Performance considerations for React and React Native are distinct, owing to their platform-specific characteristics.

- DOM Management in React: Performance optimization in React often involves strategies around efficient DOM handling.

- Native Interactions in React Native: For React Native, performance is closely linked to how effectively it interacts with native elements and manages the bridge between JavaScript and native code.

Conclusion

React and React Native, while based on React's foundational concepts, are individually specialized for web and mobile application development. Their shared principles facilitate a smoother transition for developers moving between web and mobile projects. However, understanding their differences is key to maximizing each framework's capabilities in their respective areas. React excels in creating dynamic web interfaces, whereas React Native's forte is in developing mobile applications that offer a native-like experience using familiar React paradigms. As the domains of web and mobile development evolve, both React and React Native continue to be robust and adaptable choices for contemporary application development.

Building and deploying a simple mobile app

Creating and launching a straightforward mobile application is a multifaceted process that encompasses various stages, from initial conception and meticulous planning to the final deployment and ongoing maintenance. In today's digital era, mobile apps serve as crucial tools for both businesses and individual users. This journey can be segmented into distinct phases for clarity and effectiveness.

1. Initial Concept and Strategy Formation

The genesis of a mobile app begins with its conceptualization and strategic planning.

- Purpose Definition: Clearly define what issue or need the app aims to address.

- Identifying the Audience: Pinpoint who will be using the app, guiding the design and functionality.

- Feature Planning: List the essential features for the initial launch of the app.

- Market Analysis: Evaluate similar apps for insights and to carve out a unique niche.

2. Selecting a Development Approach

Different methodologies exist for mobile app development, each with its set of pros and cons.

- Native App Development: Creating apps specifically for iOS or Android using native languages like Swift or Kotlin provides the best performance but requires distinct codebases.

- Cross-Platform Development Options: Tools like React Native or Flutter enable the use of a single codebase for both iOS and Android, though there may be compromises in performance or native functionality.

- Hybrid App Development: This approach uses web technologies wrapped in a native container for quicker development but may lack in providing a high-quality user experience.

3. Design Phase

Design is a critical phase to ensure the app is both visually appealing and easy to navigate.

- UI/UX Focus: Develop initial designs and prototypes, emphasizing a user-friendly interface and experience.

- Navigation Mapping: Design the app's navigation flow to be intuitive and logical.

- Iterative Design Feedback: Use feedback to refine the designs iteratively.

4. The Development Process

This stage involves the actual coding and creation of the app.

- Environment Setup: Prepare the necessary development tools for the chosen platforms.

- Building the Front-End: Develop the visual and interactive elements of the app.

- Constructing the Back-End: If required, develop the server-side aspects, including databases and APIs.

5. Testing for Quality Assurance

Testing is crucial to ensure the app's reliability and functionality.

- Component Testing: Conduct tests on individual parts of the app for functionality.

- Comprehensive System Testing: Ensure all components work together seamlessly.

- Beta Testing: Test the app with a sample of the target audience for feedback on usability and experience.

6. Launching the App

Deploying the app involves making it available to users through app stores.

- Adhering to App Store Standards: Ensure compliance with the standards of platforms like the Apple App Store and Google Play Store.

- Submission and Launch: Prepare and submit the app with the necessary metadata and monitor its performance upon launch.

7. Post-Launch Activities

Post-launch, the app requires ongoing attention and updates.

- Feedback Integration: Regularly incorporate user feedback for improvements.

- Routine Updates: Update the app to fix issues, enhance performance, and add new features.

- Optimization for App Stores: Continuously optimize the app's presence in app stores for better visibility.

8. Marketing the App

A crucial aspect often overlooked is the marketing and promotional strategies for the app.

- Strategizing Marketing Efforts: Develop and implement a marketing plan to promote the app.

- Initiating a Launch Campaign: Create a buzz around the launch to encourage downloads.

- Persistent Promotion: Maintain a steady effort in marketing to grow and sustain the user base.

Conclusion

The development and deployment of a simple mobile app encompass a series of well-orchestrated steps, from its inception to ongoing post-launch maintenance. The chosen development path, be it native, cross-platform, or hybrid, should align with the app's intended purpose and target audience. After launch, the focus shifts to regular updates and leveraging user feedback for continual improvement. With a strategic approach and consistent engagement, even a straightforward mobile app can achieve substantial reach and success.

Chapter Fourteen

React and Micro-Frontends

Understanding micro-frontends

Micro-frontends represent an innovative approach in web application development, mirroring the principles of microservices but applied to the frontend. This methodology involves segmenting the frontend architecture into smaller, independently manageable units, each typically overseen by separate teams. This approach is particularly beneficial for enhancing the scalability and flexibility of large-scale web projects.

1. The Essence of Micro-frontends

At its core, micro-frontends are about splitting the frontend of a web application into smaller, self-sufficient segments.

- Modular Breakdown: Similar to how microservices dissect the backend, micro-frontends disassemble the user interface into distinct features or components.

- Team Autonomy: Each segment of a micro-frontend is usually managed by a dedicated team, overseeing everything from database interactions to the user interface for that segment.

2. Advantages of Micro-frontends

Implementing a micro-frontend structure offers several key benefits, particularly for complex and sizable web applications.

- Concentrated Development Efforts: Teams can concentrate on specific aspects of the application, potentially enhancing quality and development speed.

- Freedom in Technology Selection: Micro-frontends allow teams to choose their preferred technology stacks, fostering innovation and tailored solutions.

- Simultaneous Development Streams: Multiple teams can concurrently develop different features, accelerating the overall development timeline.

- Easier Testing and Deployment: Smaller, more focused codebases simplify the processes of testing and deployment, reducing the risks associated with large-scale updates.

3. Micro-frontends Challenges

Despite their benefits, micro-frontends also present unique challenges that need careful management.

- Integration Intricacies: Seamlessly integrating various components into a cohesive whole can be complex.

- Management Overhead: The burden of managing numerous codebases and deployment processes can be considerable.

- Uniformity in User Experience: Ensuring a consistent user interface and experience across diverse micro-frontends, especially when varied technologies are involved, can be challenging.

4. Architectural Approaches in Micro-frontends

There are various architectural models for implementing micro-frontends, each with its specific considerations.

- **Build-Time Integration:** This approach involves combining different micro-frontends into a single package during the build process.

- **Dynamic Server-Side Composition:** Servers dynamically assemble web pages from various micro-frontends.

- **Client-Side Composition:** Here, micro-frontends are independently loaded in the client's browser, utilizing methods like iframes or JavaScript frameworks for integration.

5. Inter-Micro-frontend Communication

Effective communication and data sharing between micro-frontends are crucial for maintaining application integrity.

- **State Sharing Mechanisms:** Utilizing state management tools or bespoke solutions to share state data between micro-frontends.

- **Event-Driven Interactions:** Micro-frontends can interact through an event-driven model, minimizing tight coupling between components.

6. Micro-frontends Development Best Practices

To fully capitalize on the micro-frontends architecture, adherence to certain best practices is recommended.

- Independence Principle: Each micro-frontend should function independently for ease of development and deployment.

- Design System Consistency: Employing a unified design system ensures a cohesive look and feel across the application.

- Attention to Performance: Given that multiple micro-frontends can lead to additional resource loading, performance considerations are crucial.

7. Ideal Scenarios for Micro-frontends

Micro-frontends are particularly advantageous in specific development contexts.

- Extensive Applications: In large-scale applications with multiple development teams, micro-frontends offer manageable and scalable development processes.

- Technologically Diverse Environments: For applications requiring varied technologies or frameworks, micro-frontends provide the necessary flexibility for each segment of the application.

8. Alignment with Contemporary Web Development Trends

Micro-frontends are well-suited to current trends in web development.

- Compatibility with Agile and DevOps: This architectural style integrates seamlessly with Agile workflows and DevOps practices, facilitating rapid development and continuous delivery.

- Symbiosis with Backend Microservices: Micro-frontends complement backend microservices, offering a harmonious full-stack development approach.

Conclusion

Grasping the concept of micro-frontends is essential for developers and organizations working on complex, large-scale web applications. This architectural style brings significant advantages in development agility, technological diversity, and team autonomy. However, it also introduces complexities in terms of component integration, maintaining a consistent user experience, and management overhead. By following established best practices and making thoughtful architectural decisions, development teams can effectively utilize micro-frontends to construct scalable, maintainable, and high-quality web applications. As the field of web development progresses, micro-frontends emerge as a pivotal innovation towards more modular and adaptable web architectures.

Architecting a micro-frontend landscape with React

Developing a micro-frontend architecture using React represents a modern approach to constructing web applications, emphasizing the principles of segmentation and decentralized management. This method entails dividing a large-scale front-end project into smaller, independently manageable units, each encapsulating distinct features or business logic, and typically managed by separate teams.

React's component-based architecture plays a key role in this strategy, enhancing both scalability and maintainability of applications.

1. Micro-frontends with React: Core Principles

In a React-based micro-frontend setup, the UI is segmented into individual units, each responsible for a distinct aspect of the application.

- Self-Contained Components: Each micro-frontend is comprised of React components that manage specific functionalities.

- Decentralized Team Management: Diverse teams can independently develop, test, and deploy their segments, leading to more efficient workflows.

- Utilization of React's Capabilities: Teams can leverage React's comprehensive ecosystem, including various state management tools and hooks, to efficiently handle state and side-effects.

2. Architectural Models for Micro-frontends

Several architectural approaches can be employed for micro-frontends in React, each tailored to specific application needs.

- Build-Time Integration Model: This model involves amalgamating components from various micro-frontends during the build process into a single application bundle.

- Dynamic Run-Time Loading: Micro-frontends are loaded dynamically during runtime, often through JavaScript frameworks or Web Components.

- Server-Side Assembly: Servers dynamically assemble pages by combining different micro-frontends.

3. Design Strategies in React Micro-frontends

Designing micro-frontends in React demands thoughtful planning to ensure both modularity and design uniformity.

- Modularity in Design: Craft each micro-frontend as an independent entity with its own dependencies and isolated state.

- Common UI Elements: Use a shared component library for frequently used UI elements to ensure a consistent design across the application.

- Inter-Team Collaboration: Regular interaction between teams is crucial to align strategies and prevent duplicated efforts.

4. State and Data Management

Effectively managing state and data flow is vital in a micro-frontend architecture, especially for maintaining a unified application state.

- Local and Global State: Differentiate between state managed locally within a micro-frontend and global state shared across multiple segments.

- Global State Tools: Consider global state management solutions like Redux or the Context API for managing shared application state.

5. Inter-Component Communication

Seamless communication between individual micro-frontends is essential for ensuring a cohesive application experience.

- Event-Based Interaction Model: Implement an event-driven communication model to facilitate interactions between micro-frontends without creating tight dependencies.

- Defined API Interactions: Establish clear API guidelines for data exchange and interactions between different micro-frontends.

6. Navigation and Routing

Routing in a micro-frontend architecture can become complex and requires careful planning.

- Centralized vs. Distributed Routing: Choose between a central routing system controlled by the main application or independent routing managed within each micro-frontend.

- Routing Solutions: Leverage React-compatible routing libraries, such as React Router, for managing navigation within each micro-frontend.

7. Deployment Strategies and Scalability

Effective deployment strategies in a micro-frontend setup should support both independent deployment and scalability.

- Independent CI/CD Processes: Set up distinct continuous integration and continuous deployment processes for each micro-frontend, allowing for independent updates and releases.

- Scalability Focus: Ensure that each micro-frontend is scalable, with considerations for load balancing and efficient resource use.

8. Overcoming Challenges and Implementing Best Practices

Micro-frontends offer numerous benefits but also pose specific challenges that need to be tactically addressed.

- Managing Complexity and Overhead: Be aware of the increased complexity in managing multiple codebases and deployment strategies.

- Focus on Performance: Prioritize performance, especially regarding bundle sizes and load times. Techniques like code splitting and lazy loading can be highly effective.

- Uniform User Experience: Aim to maintain a consistent user experience throughout all micro-frontends.

Conclusion

Employing a micro-frontend landscape using React provides a flexible and scalable solution for developing contemporary web applications. By breaking down a large application into smaller parts, organizations can enhance development agility, promote team autonomy, and ensure better maintainability of the overall application. This approach requires meticulous planning in aspects such as design, state management, communication, and deployment. By embracing best practices and addressing the challenges proactively, development teams can fully exploit the potential of micro-frontends, building robust, scalable, and user-centric web applications. As technological advancements continue, micro-frontends in React stand as a testament to the industry's ongoing evolution towards more modular and efficient web development methodologies.

Best practices and potential pitfalls

In software development, adhering to established best practices and being cognizant of common pitfalls is crucial for project success. Best practices are essentially guidelines validated through consistent use and success. They offer a framework for developers to ensure code quality, maintainability, and operational efficiency. However, each project comes with its unique set of challenges, and awareness of potential pitfalls can significantly aid in navigating these complexities.

1. Established Best Practices in Software Development

a. Clarity and Simplicity in Code: Writing code that is clear, understandable, and well-commented is fundamental for maintenance and knowledge sharing. Tools like linters can help in maintaining code consistency.

b. Effective Version Control Usage: Proficient use of version control systems like Git is essential for tracking changes, facilitating team collaboration, and preserving code integrity.

c. Conducting Regular Code Reviews: Regular reviews or pair programming sessions are crucial for quality assurance, early bug detection, and fostering team collaboration.

d. Emphasis on Automated Testing: A robust testing framework, including different types of tests, is vital for ensuring the application's reliability and stability.

e. Streamlined CI/CD Processes: Automating the testing and deployment processes through CI/CD pipelines helps in reducing manual errors and accelerates deployment.

f. Comprehensive Documentation: Up-to-date documentation covering both the codebase and operational procedures is key for ongoing project management.

g. Prioritizing Security Measures: Ensuring regular updates, adopting secure coding practices, and performing security audits are critical for application security.

2. Common Pitfalls in Software Development

a. Complexity in Solutions: Overcomplicating solutions can lead to unnecessary complexity and should be avoided in favor of simplicity.

b. Overlooking Performance: Not adequately addressing performance issues can result in slow and inefficient applications, especially as they grow.

c. Dependency Management Issues: An over-dependence on external libraries can pose maintenance challenges. Regular updates and audits of dependencies are necessary.

d. Incomplete Testing Coverage: Failing to comprehensively test an application can lead to instability and frequent post-release fixes.

e. Accumulating Technical Debt: Ignoring technical debt can lead to compounded problems and hinder future development efforts.

f. Scalability Neglect: Not designing systems with scalability in mind can pose significant challenges as the user base and data volume grow.

g. Underestimating UX/UI Design: Overlooking the importance of user experience and interface design can negatively impact user adoption and satisfaction.

3. Real-World Application of Best Practices

Applying best practices in software development should be balanced with the specific demands and context of each project.

a. Adaptability: Adapt best practices to suit the project's specific needs and circumstances.

b. Prioritization and Applicability: Recognize that not all best practices may be relevant in every situation and prioritize accordingly.

c. Staying Informed and Adaptable: Keeping abreast of the latest developments in software development practices and technologies is crucial.

Conclusion

In software development, following established best practices is integral to delivering robust, efficient, and maintainable applications. Equally important is recognizing and skillfully navigating potential pitfalls. Balancing these practices with the unique requirements of each project, while staying flexible and committed to continuous learning, is key to successful software development. As the technological landscape evolves, so must the strategies and methodologies employed, always with the aim of creating impactful and reliable software solutions.

Conclusion

Reviewing the journey of integrating React with modern web technologies

The fusion of React with contemporary web technologies marks a pivotal chapter in web development history. Since Facebook unveiled React in 2013, it has transformed into a linchpin for crafting user interfaces in web applications. This journey reflects a significant shift in development practices, particularly in constructing dynamic, interactive user interfaces.

1. The Inception of React and Its Initial Impact

React's introduction revolutionized UI development with its unique approaches, notably the virtual DOM for performance enhancement and a component-centric architecture promoting code reusability and maintainability.

- Virtual DOM Approach: React's adoption of a virtual DOM allowed efficient UI updates, minimizing direct manipulation of the actual DOM.

- Component-Based Model: This model empowered developers to create isolated, state-managed components, fostering scalable and manageable codebases.

2. Expansion of the React Ecosystem

React's growing popularity led to its integration with a variety of modern web tools and technologies.

- Advanced State Management: The inclusion of libraries like Redux and the Context API addressed complex state management in large applications.

- Dynamic Routing: Tools like React Router emerged as integral components, enabling dynamic routing in single-page applications.

- Simplified Build Tools: The emergence of tools such as Webpack and Create React App streamlined the build process, enhancing developer accessibility to React.

3. Introduction of Hooks and Embracing Functional Programming

React's version 16.8 introduced hooks, steering development towards functional programming, allowing state and side-effect management in functional components.

- Fundamental Hooks: Hooks like useState and useEffect became instrumental in functional components for managing state and lifecycle.

- Innovation with Custom Hooks: The ability to create custom hooks opened doors for reusing stateful logic across components.

4. Integration with Server-Side Rendering and Next.js

React's adaptation to server-side rendering, particularly with frameworks like Next.js, marked an improvement in performance and SEO for React applications.

- Enhanced SEO: Server-side rendering in React ameliorated SEO challenges typically associated with client-side rendered applications.

- Performance Gains: Frameworks like Next.js facilitated server-side rendering of React components, delivering faster initial page loads.

5. React's Role in the JAMstack Architecture

React became pivotal in JAMstack, an architecture emphasizing JavaScript, APIs, and prebuilt Markup, for building modern web applications.

- Adoption in Static Site Generation: Integrating with static site generators like Gatsby, React was employed in developing speedy, SEO-optimized static sites.

- Combination with Headless CMS: React's compatibility with headless CMSs and APIs reinforced its utility in building dynamic, content-driven web applications.

6. Convergence with TypeScript for Enhanced Development

The integration of TypeScript brought type safety to React applications, addressing the need for more predictable and error-resistant code in large-scale projects.

- Improved Code Reliability: TypeScript's static typing brought an additional layer of reliability and enhanced the overall developer experience with React.

7. Extending React's Principles to Mobile with React Native

React Native extended React's principles to mobile app development, enabling the creation of mobile applications for iOS and Android using React.

- Unified Code for Web and Mobile: React Native bridged the gap between web and mobile development, allowing shared codebases and logic.

8. React's Ongoing Evolution with Modern Web Technologies

React's journey in integrating with modern web technologies continues, with new features and enhancements shaping its future.

- Adopting Modern UI Patterns: Future developments in React aim to refine user experiences with more efficient rendering and data fetching techniques.

- Server Components Innovation: React is exploring server components to optimize performance by rendering more components server-side.

Conclusion

React's integration with modern web technologies has been a journey of continuous adaptation and innovation. It has not only redefined UI development but also seamlessly aligned with various advancements in the web tech arena. Its ongoing evolution and integration with diverse technologies highlight its vital role in the evolving landscape of web development. As web technologies advance, React's journey is expected to set new standards in web application construction and user experience.

Preparing for advanced-level React development

Advancing in React development, a popular JavaScript library for constructing user interfaces, demands a deep understanding of its complex features and integration with contemporary web technologies. For developers aiming to excel in complex project management, performance tuning, and applying industry best practices in scalable applications, advanced proficiency in React is essential.

1. Solidifying React Core Principles

Advanced-level proficiency begins with a robust foundation in React's basic concepts.

- Lifecycle Methods Expertise: A comprehensive understanding of component lifecycle methods is crucial for effective component management.

- Advanced State and Props Handling: Expertise in handling internal component states and external data via props is vital.

- Utilizing Hooks Effectively: Mastery over hooks and their application in functional components is necessary for state and lifecycle management.

2. Complex State Management Techniques

Handling state in large-scale applications requires advanced state management strategies.

- Utilizing Global State Tools: Mastery in tools like Redux, MobX, or the Context API is necessary for managing state across components.

- Applying Immutable Data Concepts: Knowledge of immutability principles is important for optimizing state management and application performance.

- Developing Custom Hooks: Creating custom hooks to encapsulate complex state logic can streamline state management processes.

3. Enhancing Application Performance

Optimizing an application's performance is a critical skill for advanced React developers.

- Performance Profiling and Tuning: Using React's profiling tools to identify and optimize performance bottlenecks.

- Implementing Efficient Loading Strategies: Applying code splitting and lazy loading techniques to improve initial load performance.

- Adopting Memoization: Employing memoization to minimize unnecessary re-renders and computations.

4. Advanced React Design Patterns

Familiarity with advanced React design patterns is essential for building scalable applications.

- Leveraging Higher-Order Components: Understanding the use of HOCs to augment component functionality.

- Utilizing Render Props: Employing render props patterns to share logic between components.

- Working with Compound Components: Handling complex component relationships using compound components.

5. Integrating with Modern Web Ecosystem

Advanced React development includes the ability to integrate React with a wide array of modern web technologies.

- Incorporating TypeScript: Employing TypeScript in React projects for added type safety.

- Server-Side Rendering Techniques: Applying SSR, particularly with frameworks like Next.js, for improved performance and SEO.

- Data Fetching from APIs: Mastery in using GraphQL or REST APIs for backend data retrieval.

6. Comprehensive Testing Approaches

Robust testing is paramount in advanced React development.

- Detailed Unit and Integration Testing: Conducting thorough testing using tools like Jest and React Testing Library.

393

- End-to-End Testing Implementation: Utilizing tools like Cypress for comprehensive user flow testing.

7. Navigating the React Ecosystem

A thorough understanding of the React ecosystem enhances development capabilities.

- React Router Mastery: Proficient use of React Router for effective navigation management.

- Familiarity with Build Tools: In-depth knowledge of tools like Webpack and Babel for efficient project builds.

- Utilizing Third-Party Libraries: Knowledge of popular libraries for functionalities like form handling and animations.

8. Adhering to Project and Code Management Best Practices

Following best practices in code organization and project management is crucial.

- Effective Code Structuring: Organizing code into readable, maintainable modules and components.

- Version Control and Workflow Management: Skilled use of version control and implementing CI/CD pipelines for streamlined development.

- Team Collaboration and Review Processes: Effective team collaboration and conducting rigorous code reviews to maintain code quality.

9. Embracing Continuous Learning

Staying current with the evolving landscape of React and web development is essential for continuous growth.

- Keeping Up-to-Date: Regularly updating knowledge with the latest React advancements and community practices.

- Active Experimentation: Experimenting with emerging patterns, libraries, and tools to enhance development techniques.

Conclusion

Preparation for advanced-level React development encompasses a deep understanding of React's fundamentals, sophisticated state management, performance tuning, and a broad knowledge of integrating with modern web technologies and testing methodologies. It also involves mastering complex React patterns, continuous learning, and adherence to best practices in project and code management. This preparation forms a strong foundation for handling intricate projects, optimizing application performance, and contributing effectively to the development of scalable, maintainable React applications. As web development continues to progress, advanced React developers play a pivotal role in driving innovation and shaping the future of web application development.

Resources for continuous learning and growth

In today's fast-paced technological landscape, continuous learning and professional growth are imperative for staying ahead in the tech industry. This is especially true for fields like software development, data analytics, and digital marketing. The path to continual skill enhancement involves a diverse array of resources and methodologies.

1. Leveraging Online Educational Resources

The digital age has ushered in a plethora of online learning platforms that offer a wide range of courses across various subjects.

- MOOCs Platforms: Coursera, edX, and Udacity are examples of platforms providing courses from universities and leading companies.

- Tech-Focused Learning Sites: Platforms such as Pluralsight, Udemy, and Codecademy specialize in technical and coding skills.

- Subscription Learning Services: Skillshare and LinkedIn Learning offer a wide range of courses under a subscription model, catering to diverse educational needs.

2. Pursuing Professional Certifications

Professional certifications are a strategic way to validate expertise and dedication to ongoing education.

- Company-Specific Certifications: Google, Microsoft, and Amazon offer certifications in their respective technologies and platforms.

- Industry-Wide Certifications: Recognized certifications like PMP or CISSP are valued across various industries.

3. Formal Education and Specialized Training

For more comprehensive knowledge, formal education and specialized training play a vital role.

- Online and Part-Time Degrees: Many institutions offer online or part-time programs in specialized fields.

- Focused Learning Programs: Postgraduate certificates and targeted programs offer specialized training in areas like cybersecurity or AI.

4. Reading Books and Industry Publications

Books, both in physical and digital formats, are a timeless resource for in-depth learning.

- Keeping Up with Current Literature: Reading the latest publications in one's field can provide valuable insights.

- Digital Libraries: Platforms like Amazon Kindle and Google Books provide easy access to a wide range of educational material.

5. Engaging in Webinars and Online Seminars

Participating in webinars and online seminars offers insights from industry experts and keeps one updated with current trends.

- Expert-Led Webinars: These are excellent sources for delving into specific technologies or industry updates.

- Interactive Online Workshops: They provide practical, hands-on experiences in various fields.

6. Podcasts and Educational Videos

For learning on the move, podcasts and educational videos are invaluable resources.

- Informative Podcasts: Many podcasts focus on technology trends, professional development, and interviews with industry leaders.

- Educational YouTube Channels: Various experts and educators offer free tutorials and lectures on tech-related topics.

7. Networking and Joining Professional Communities

Engaging with professional communities and networking can lead to new learning opportunities and insights.

- Professional Organizations: Membership in relevant professional bodies can offer access to exclusive resources and networking opportunities.

- Industry Conferences and Meetups: Attending these events, either virtually or in-person, is beneficial for learning and professional networking.

8. Participating in Forums and Online Discussions

Active participation in online forums and discussions can enhance problem-solving skills and keep one updated.

- Platforms like Stack Overflow and GitHub: These are not just for troubleshooting but also for learning new methodologies.

- Online Tech Forums and Groups: Engaging in discussions on platforms like LinkedIn can offer insights into industry practices and trends.

9. Learning through Mentorship and Peer Groups

Mentorship and learning in group settings can offer practical insights and knowledge sharing.

- Seeking Mentorship: A mentor in your field can provide valuable advice and career guidance.

- Joining Peer Learning Groups: Collaborative learning in groups can be a mutually beneficial way to acquire new skills.

10. Personal Projects and Hands-On Practice

Applying skills to real-world projects or experiments is an effective way to consolidate learning.

- Personal Project Development: Using new skills in personal projects can be both educational and fulfilling.

- Hackathons and Coding Challenges: These events provide a platform for applying and testing skills in a competitive, practical environment.

Conclusion

Continuous learning and development in the tech sector require embracing various educational methods, including online courses, formal education, certifications, and practical experiences. A combination of these resources ensures comprehensive professional development. In a sector characterized by rapid advancements and innovation, commitment to ongoing learning is crucial for career advancement and personal growth.

Introduction

Setting the stage for advanced React JS development

Embarking on advanced React JS development necessitates a deep dive into the more intricate aspects of this widely-used JavaScript library. This advanced journey is crucial for developers seeking to tackle complex web applications, optimize app performance, and adhere to the highest standards of code scalability and maintenance.

1. Solid Foundation in React Basics

Before progressing to advanced topics, a robust understanding of React's fundamental concepts is imperative.

- In-depth Component Lifecycle Knowledge: A thorough grasp of React's lifecycle methods is essential for effective component management.

- Advanced Handling of State and Props: Proficiency in managing the state within components and manipulating data through props is critical.

- Expertise in Hooks: A solid understanding of React hooks is necessary for managing state and side effects in functional components.

2. Sophisticated State Management Approaches

Managing application state in complex projects requires nuanced and advanced strategies.

- Utilization of State Management Tools: Familiarity with tools like Redux and the Context API is important for handling widespread state across components.

- Immutable Data Techniques: Applying immutable data principles is key to optimizing state management and enhancing performance.

- Creation of Custom Hooks: Crafting custom hooks can streamline complex state logic, improving code manageability.

3. Focus on Performance Enhancement

Optimizing application performance is a significant aspect of advanced React development.

- Profiling and Performance Tuning: Using React's profiling tools to diagnose and optimize rendering performance is crucial.

- Strategies for Efficient Loading: Implementing code splitting and lazy loading techniques can significantly enhance application load times and user experience.

- Application of Memoization: Using memoization to avert unnecessary re-renders and computations can boost performance.

4. Implementing Advanced React Patterns

Familiarity with complex React patterns and techniques is essential for building scalable applications.

- Employing Higher-Order Components: Understanding the use of HOCs to extend component capabilities is vital.

- Applying Render Props Pattern: Using the render props pattern allows for flexible code sharing and composition.

- Managing Complex Component Structures: Utilizing the Context API to address the challenge of prop drilling in deep component trees.

5. Integrating Cutting-Edge Web Technologies

Integrating React with modern web technologies is foundational for advanced development.

- Combining React with TypeScript: Integrating TypeScript with React brings enhanced developer experience and code robustness.

- Server-Side Rendering with Next.js: Implementing SSR, especially with frameworks like Next.js, is key for improved SEO and loading times.

- Modern Styling Practices: Leveraging CSS-in-JS libraries for styling enhances both maintainability and scalability.

6. Extensive Testing and Quality Assurance

Advanced React development demands a comprehensive approach to testing.

- In-depth Testing with Frameworks: Mastery in frameworks like Jest and React Testing Library for thorough unit and integration testing is essential.

- End-to-End Testing Proficiency: Implementing end-to-end testing ensures the overall functionality of the application.

7. Navigating the React Ecosystem

An in-depth understanding of the React ecosystem is crucial for advanced developers.

- Advanced Use of React Router: Proficient handling of React Router is necessary for effective navigation in applications.

- Build Tools Expertise: A thorough understanding of tools like Webpack and Babel is important for efficient development.

- Integrating Third-Party Libraries: Skill in incorporating third-party libraries for additional functionalities is beneficial.

8. Adherence to Best Practices in Development

Maintaining best practices in coding and project management is key.

- Effective Code Structuring: Organizing code into clear, modular components and sections is essential for large applications.

- Version Control and CI/CD Mastery: Proficient use of version control and CI/CD pipelines is crucial for streamlined development processes.

- Collaborative Development and Code Reviews: Effective teamwork and rigorous code reviews are important for maintaining high code quality.

9. Commitment to Continuous Learning

Staying updated with the latest in React and web development trends is vital for ongoing professional development.

- Keeping Current with Trends: Regularly updating one's knowledge of React and participating in community forums is crucial.

- Hands-On Experimentation: Actively applying new concepts in personal projects or experiments is an effective way to solidify learning and explore new ideas.

Conclusion

Preparing for advanced React JS development involves not just a deep understanding of React's core principles and advanced state management techniques, but also a commitment to optimizing application performance, mastering complex patterns, and integrating with the latest web technologies. Comprehensive testing, a thorough grasp of the React ecosystem, and adherence to best practices in code management are equally important. Continuous learning and staying abreast of the latest developments in React and web technology are crucial for developers looking to excel in sophisticated web application development. As the field of web development continues to advance, those skilled in advanced React development are well-positioned to lead and innovate in this dynamic arena.

The evolution of front-end development with React JS

React JS's introduction by Facebook in 2013 marked a transformative era in front-end web development. This JavaScript library brought a novel perspective to user interface construction, emphasizing declarative programming and component-based architecture, significantly diverging from the then-dominant imperative and DOM-focused approaches.

1. React's Introduction: A Paradigm Shift in UI Development

React's arrival heralded a new methodology in building user interfaces, pivoting towards modularity and efficient rendering techniques.

- Modular Component Structure: React championed the concept of encapsulating UI elements in self-sufficient, reusable components, streamlining the development of complex interfaces.

- Virtual DOM Implementation: The introduction of the Virtual DOM, an abstract representation of the actual DOM, marked an innovation in optimizing rendering processes, enhancing application performance.

2. Single-Page Applications (SPAs) and React

React has been instrumental in popularizing SPAs, offering dynamic updates within a single HTML page, thus elevating the user experience.

- Seamless User Interactions: React-driven SPAs deliver fluid and native-like user experiences.

- Advanced State Management: The complexity of state management in SPAs led to the creation of specialized libraries like Redux, further integrating with React's architecture.

3. The Evolving Ecosystem and Community of React

React's adaptability and efficiency have catalyzed the growth of a comprehensive ecosystem and a robust community.

- Diverse Libraries and Tools: The React ecosystem encompasses a variety of tools for routing, state management, and UI components.

- Community Engagement and Open Source Contributions: React's open-source nature has fostered a dynamic community actively contributing to its evolution.

4. React's Continuous Evolution

React has consistently evolved, introducing features that reinforce its pivotal role in front-end development.

- Hooks Introduction: The launch of hooks in React 16.8 marked a significant stride, enabling state and effects management in functional components.

- Enhanced Server-Side Rendering: React's improved SSR capabilities, coupled with frameworks like Next.js, have bolstered performance and SEO for React applications.

5. The Influence of React on Functional Programming

React has steered the JavaScript community towards embracing functional programming principles.

- Emphasis on Immutability and Purity: React's design aligns with functional programming tenets, advocating for immutable data structures and pure functions, contributing to more predictable and manageable code.

6. Expansion to Mobile Development with React Native

React Native extended React's principles to the mobile app development domain, facilitating cross-platform mobile app development.

- **Shared Web and Mobile App Logic:** React Native enables the sharing of logic and even components between web and mobile platforms, streamlining development efforts.

7. Modern Development Practices Influenced by React

React's rise has shaped modern development practices, making the development process more efficient.

- **Real-Time Code Updating:** Tools like Webpack introduced HMR, enabling real-time reflection of code changes.

- **Enhanced Development and Debugging Tools:** The advent of tools tailored for React has simplified the debugging process, improving the overall developer experience.

8. React's Prospects in Front-End Development

React continues to progress, with forthcoming features indicating its future trajectory in front-end development.

- **Introduction of Concurrent Mode:** React's concurrent mode is anticipated to offer improved rendering performance and enhanced data fetching capabilities.

- Data Fetching with Suspense: The suspense feature in React is set to simplify asynchronous code management, streamlining data fetching and state handling.

Conclusion

React JS has indubitably redefined the front-end development landscape. Its approach to building user interfaces through modular components and efficient rendering practices has set new benchmarks in UI development. As React evolves, it maintains its status as a leader in front-end innovation, influencing not just technological adoption but also fostering a collaborative and progressive developer community. React's ongoing development promises to continue its influential role in shaping modern web development practices, adapting to emerging challenges and innovations in the dynamic world of web technology.

Preparing for cutting-edge techniques and best practices

Staying ahead in the fast-paced world of technology requires a proactive approach to learning and adapting to new techniques and best practices. This necessity spans across various sectors, including software engineering, data science, and digital marketing, where the rapid evolution of technology dictates a continual enhancement of skills.

1. Commitment to Ongoing Education

Central to keeping up with cutting-edge techniques is an unwavering commitment to ongoing education.

- Utilization of Digital Learning Platforms: Platforms like Coursera, edX, and Udacity offer a range of courses that cover emerging technologies and advanced methodologies.

- Pursuing Specialized Training: Targeted training programs and certifications from recognized bodies or industry leaders can solidify and certify your expertise.

- Engagement in Formal Education: Enroll in part-time, online degree programs or targeted workshops to gain comprehensive insights into specialized fields.

2. Staying Informed on Industry Developments

Awareness of the latest industry trends and technological advancements is critical.

- Regular Industry Literature Review: Stay updated by reading reputable journals, online tech news portals, and industry publications.

- Active Participation in Conferences: Attend industry conferences, webinars, and seminars to gather insights from experts and connect with peers.

- Networking with Professionals: Engage in professional groups and online communities for knowledge exchange and staying abreast of industry movements.

3. Application and Experimentation

Practical application of newly acquired skills is key to understanding and mastery.

- Project Involvement: Apply new skills in real-world projects, either in professional settings or through personal initiatives.

- Explorative Prototyping: Experiment with new tools and techniques to gauge their real-world applicability and effectiveness.

4. Collaborative Learning and Knowledge Exchange

Collaboration and sharing knowledge with peers are instrumental in deepening understanding.

- Mentorship Programs: Participate in mentorship as a mentor or mentee, and join peer learning groups to share experiences and insights.

- Team Projects: Collaborate on diverse projects to benefit from different perspectives and skillsets.

5. Fostering an Innovative Mindset

Adopting a mindset that is receptive to change and innovation is essential for leveraging new techniques.

- Openness to New Ideas: Be receptive to experimenting with novel approaches and adapting to technological shifts.

- Creative Problem-Solving: Cultivate creative thinking to tackle challenges in unique and innovative ways.

6. Mastery of Modern Tools

Staying proficient in the latest tools and technologies is critical for implementing cutting-edge methods.

- Staying Updated with Software Tools: Regularly update your knowledge and skills in the latest industry-standard software and platforms.

- Monitoring Emerging Tech Trends: Keep an eye on developing technologies like AI and blockchain that could revolutionize your industry.

7. Adherence to Industry Best Practices

Implementing recognized best practices ensures your work is efficient, high-quality, and consistent.

- Upholding Quality and Methodologies: Follow recognized industry standards and methodologies in your work.

- Continuous Process Optimization: Regularly evaluate and refine your workflows for better efficiency and output quality.

8. Balancing Professional and Personal Growth

Both personal and professional growth are crucial for a balanced and sustainable career trajectory.

- Enhancing Interpersonal Skills: Develop essential soft skills such as communication, leadership, and teamwork.

- Maintaining Work-Life Harmony: Strive for a healthy balance between professional responsibilities and personal well-being.

Conclusion

Preparing for cutting-edge techniques and best practices in the tech realm involves a comprehensive strategy encompassing continuous learning, practical application, staying current with industry trends, and fostering a mindset geared towards innovation and adaptability. Embracing these practices not only furthers individual skill development but also contributes significantly to the broader field. As technology continues to advance at a rapid pace, this readiness to evolve and expand one's skill set becomes increasingly crucial for maintaining relevance and excellence in the tech industry.

Chapter One

Advanced State Management

Exploring complex state management patterns

Navigating the complexities of state management in contemporary web development is a critical skill, particularly as applications become more intricate and data-driven. Effective management of application state – the data maintained and manipulated during an application's life cycle – is essential for creating scalable, maintainable, and efficient web applications.

1. The Criticality of State Management in Web Applications

Effective state management is a cornerstone of web application development, dictating how data is stored, accessed, and transformed.

- Balancing Centralized and Decentralized State: Understanding the interplay between a centralized state, managed in one location, versus a decentralized state, managed across components, is fundamental.

- Challenges with Scaling State Management: With application growth come challenges such as ensuring state consistency, managing asynchronous operations, and optimizing performance.

2. Exploring Diverse State Management Patterns

A range of state management patterns have been devised to tackle the complexities in large-scale web applications.

- Global State Management Solutions: Tools like Redux and MobX offer global solutions for managing state across applications, enhancing consistency and predictability.

- Differentiating Component State from Shared State: Recognizing the distinction between state local to a component and state shared across an application is crucial.

- Principles of Immutable State Management: Employing immutable data structures is a key strategy for preventing direct state mutation, leading to more predictable state changes.

3. Leveraging Context API in React for Complex State

React's Context API provides a potent solution for managing state in complex applications, eliminating the need for external libraries.

- Context API Against Prop Drilling: The Context API allows for passing data through the component tree without manually handling props at each level.

- Synergy with Hooks in React: Using Context in tandem with React Hooks like useState or useReducer offers robust state management within React.

4. Handling Asynchronous State Changes

Managing asynchronous operations, such as data fetching or API calls, is an integral part of state management.

- Asynchronous Handling with Redux Thunk or Saga: Libraries like Redux Thunk or Redux Saga aid in managing side effects and asynchronous actions in Redux.

- Streamlining Async Operations with Async/Await: Utilizing async/await in JavaScript enhances the readability and maintainability of asynchronous state management.

5. Adopting Reactive State Management with RxJS

Using reactive programming patterns, especially with libraries like RxJS, introduces a novel approach to complex state management.

- Employing Observables for State Monitoring: RxJS's observables offer a dynamic way to handle asynchronous data streams and state changes.

- Integrating RxJS in Modern Frameworks: RxJS can be integrated with frameworks like React and Angular to achieve a reactive and scalable state management system.

6. Framework-Specific State Management Approaches

Different front-end frameworks offer unique philosophies and tools for state management.

- State Management in Vue and Angular: Vue's Vuex and Angular's NgRx are examples of framework-specific libraries, employing reactive programming and Flux architecture for state management.

- Framework-Centric State Management Tools: Utilizing framework-specific hooks or functions designed for efficient state management within these ecosystems.

7. Middleware's Functionality in State Management

Middleware serves an essential function in state management, particularly in global state management systems.

- Using Middleware for Operations and Logging: Middleware is used for diverse purposes like logging state transitions, handling asynchronous operations, or implementing custom logic during state changes.

- Middleware and Development Tools Synergy: Middleware often works in conjunction with development tools to provide enhanced debugging capabilities and insights into application flow.

8. Prioritizing Performance in State Management

It's vital to ensure state management approaches do not adversely affect application performance.

- Strategies for State Normalization: Normalizing state to minimize redundancy and enhance data retrieval efficiency.

- Leveraging Memoization and Selectors: Implementing memoization and using selector libraries like Reselect with Redux to calculate derived data, reducing unnecessary re-renders.

Conclusion

Mastering complex state management patterns is indispensable in modern web development. From embracing global state management systems to reactive programming approaches and specific solutions for various frameworks, each method offers distinct advantages. Understanding these approaches, their applications, and how they integrate with contemporary web development practices is crucial for crafting scalable, effective, and maintainable web applications. As the landscape of web technology evolves, so too will state management strategies, necessitating a continuous learning and adaptation approach from developers.

Advanced Redux, MobX, and Recoil use cases

In today's dynamic web development landscape, mastering state management in JavaScript applications, particularly with libraries like Redux, MobX, and Recoil, is essential for developers. Each of these libraries provides unique mechanisms for handling application state, catering to different complexities and requirements in web development.

1. Redux: A Mainstay for Complex State Management

Renowned for its structured approach, Redux is a staple in handling state in sizable applications.

- Ideal for Extensive Applications: Redux shines in large-scale projects where a unified approach to state management is key. Its single-store architecture ensures consistency across the application.

- Handling Complex Interactions and Asynchronous Actions: Redux's middleware, such as Thunk and Saga, is invaluable for managing complex interactions and asynchronous operations.

- Enhanced Debugging Capabilities: The Redux DevTools extension offers powerful debugging features, including time-travel debugging, crucial for tracing state changes over time.

2. MobX: A Flexible, Reactive Approach

MobX offers an alternative paradigm with its reactive and object-oriented nature.

- Efficient for Projects with Intricate State Relations: MobX is adept at managing applications where state relationships and computations are complex, offering automatic dependency tracking.

- Suitable for Quick Development Cycles: For projects that require speed and less boilerplate, MobX provides a more direct and less verbose approach than Redux.

- Compatibility with Object-Oriented Programming: MobX aligns well with object-oriented programming styles, making it a preferred choice in such environments.

3. Recoil: Tailored State Management for React

As a relatively new player, Recoil is designed to complement React's features and offer a more granular state management approach.

- Atomic State Management in React Applications: Recoil's concept of 'atoms' as fundamental state units is effective for complex React applications with intertwined state requirements.

- Handling Derived State and Asynchronous Operations: Recoil's selectors are adept at managing derived state and handling asynchronous operations, suitable for data-intensive scenarios.

- Integration with React's Concurrent Mode: Recoil works harmoniously with React's advanced features like concurrent mode and Suspense, addressing modern asynchronous UI challenges.

4. Selecting the Appropriate Library

Choosing between Redux, MobX, and Recoil depends on various project-specific factors.

- Redux for Scalable Enterprise Solutions: Redux remains the preferred choice for enterprise-level applications due to its scalability and extensive ecosystem.

- MobX for Agile Development and OOP-Driven Projects: MobX is ideal for projects that require rapid development and favor an object-oriented approach.

- Recoil for Applications Leveraging Latest React Features: Recoil suits applications that make full use of the latest React capabilities, offering a state management style that complements React's modern features.

5. Harmonizing with Contemporary Development Practices

Effectively integrating these state management libraries with current development practices is key to building efficient and maintainable applications.

- Ensuring Testability: Whether it's Redux, MobX, or Recoil, ensuring the state management approach allows for effective testing is paramount.

- Modular Architecture: Adopting a modular approach to state management, whether through Redux's reducers, MobX's stores, or Recoil's atoms and selectors, aids in maintaining scalable applications.

- Performance Optimization: Being mindful of the impact of state management on application performance is critical, with strategies like memoization and selector usage being instrumental in performance tuning.

Conclusion

Advanced use cases of Redux, MobX, and Recoil present a range of solutions for managing application state in JavaScript-based projects. Redux offers a structured and predictable environment ideal for large-scale applications, MobX provides a more dynamic and less boilerplate-intensive approach suitable for applications with complex state relationships, and Recoil offers a modern, atom-based approach perfectly aligned with React's latest features. The choice among these tools should be made based on specific project needs, team expertise, and the project's scale and complexity. As web development continues to evolve, keeping abreast of these state management options and effectively integrating them into development workflows remains crucial for developing sophisticated and user-friendly web applications.

State management in large-scale applications

In large-scale web applications, managing the application state – the data and user interactions – is a pivotal component of software design, significantly impacting the system's performance, scalability, and maintainability. As the complexity of applications escalates, the challenge of maintaining an effective, efficient, and coherent state management system becomes more pronounced.

1. Navigating State Management Complexities in Large Applications

Large applications pose unique challenges in state management due to their scale and complexity:

- Diverse Data Sources Management: Such applications typically draw data from multiple origins, necessitating a synchronized and cohesive state management approach.

- Managing Complex User Interactions: With an increase in user interface elements, efficiently handling their states without compromising performance becomes critical.

- Scalability of State Management Systems: Ensuring that the chosen state management framework can efficiently scale with the application is essential.

2. Effective Patterns in State Management

Several approaches have evolved to address state management in complex systems:

- Centralized Global State Management: Techniques like Redux or MobX offer centralized solutions, ideal for managing global application state in a consistent manner.

- Local State Management in Components: Managing state locally within components for specific functionalities can help reduce overall complexity.

- Adopting Immutable Data Practices: Immutable data structures are crucial in ensuring predictable state changes and simplifying the debugging process.

3. Selecting an Appropriate State Management Solution

The choice of a state management tool is a decision that hinges on multiple factors:

- Complexity and Size of the Application: The size and complexity of the application often dictate whether a more comprehensive solution like Redux is needed, or if simpler solutions would suffice.

- Team's Expertise and Tool Ecosystem: The development team's familiarity with the tool and the supporting ecosystem, including available middleware and community support, is also a determining factor.

- Impact on Application Performance: The chosen state management solution should not adversely affect the application's performance.

4. Middleware's Integral Role

Middleware in state management frameworks provides essential functionalities for complex operations:

- Asynchronous Actions Handling: Middleware like Redux Thunk or Saga is crucial for managing asynchronous processes such as API calls.

- State Change Logging and Debugging: Middleware also aids in logging state changes and integrating with development tools for enhanced debugging.

5. Asynchronous State Management Strategies

Handling asynchronous state, especially in large-scale applications, is a critical aspect of state management:

- Update Frequency Management: Implementing techniques like throttling and debouncing is important to manage state update frequency effectively.

- Implementing Caching Mechanisms: Caching strategies can optimize performance by minimizing redundant data fetching.

6. State Normalization and Efficient Data Structuring

Proper structuring and normalization of the application state are vital in large-scale applications for maintaining efficiency and consistency:

- Normalization Approaches: Normalizing state structure helps in reducing data duplication and simplifying data updates.

- Strategic Data Modeling: Carefully designing the state structure to align with the application's data model enhances maintainability.

7. Advanced State Management Techniques and Trends

Keeping pace with advanced techniques and new trends is essential for managing state in complex scenarios:

- Server-Side State Management: Approaches like server-side rendering and state hydration are increasingly relevant for performance and SEO considerations.

- Adopting Reactive State Management: Reactive programming models, as seen in RxJS or MobX, provide dynamic state management suitable for intricate applications.

8. Ensuring Robust Testing and Quality Assurance

Effective testing regimes are critical for the reliability of state management systems:

- Comprehensive Unit and Integration Testing: Testing all facets of state management, including actions and middleware, ensures the system's reliability.

- Holistic End-to-End Testing: Testing the integration of the state management system with user interfaces and external systems validates the overall functionality of the application.

Conclusion

State management in large-scale applications is a complex yet crucial aspect of web development, requiring a well-thought-out strategy encompassing tool selection, best practices in data structuring, and ensuring scalability. With the evolution of application architectures, the complexity of managing state also increases, emphasizing the need for scalable, maintainable, and efficient state management solutions.

Adopting the right blend of state management strategies, along with staying updated on the latest trends and methodologies, is fundamental to the success of large and complex web applications.

Chapter Two

React Hooks - Deep Dive

Advanced use cases of standard hooks

In the realm of React development, standard hooks play a pivotal role in enhancing the capabilities of functional components, especially as application complexity increases. Introduced in React 16.8, hooks like `useState`, `useEffect`, `useContext`, `useReducer`, and `useRef` have revolutionized the way developers handle state and side effects, offering more streamlined and efficient approaches compared to traditional class component patterns.

1. `useState` in Complex State Scenarios

The `useState` hook is a fundamental tool for managing state within functional components and can adeptly handle scenarios that were once the domain of class components.

- Multi-State Variables Management: `useState` can effectively manage several state variables within a single component, each representing a different aspect of the component's state.

- Creating Custom Hooks for State Logic: Using `useState` within custom hooks allows for the encapsulation of intricate state logic, aiding in component simplification and enhancing code reusability.

2. `useEffect` for Managing Side Effects

The `useEffect` hook is versatile in dealing with side effects, encompassing API calls, subscriptions, or manual DOM manipulations.

- Advanced Dependency Handling: Skillful use of `useEffect` includes managing intricate dependencies to optimize performance by reducing unnecessary component updates.

- Cleanup Mechanisms: Utilizing the cleanup function in `useEffect` is essential in complex applications for tasks like unsubscribing from services or clearing intervals to prevent memory leaks.

3. useContext for Efficient State Distribution

The `useContext` hook enables sharing states and functionalities across multiple components, offering a simpler and more efficient solution than prop drilling.

- Managing Global States: When combined with `useState` or `useReducer`, `useContext` can manage global application states, posing as an alternative to complex state management libraries.

- Propagating Themes and Configurations: It's especially useful for distributing themes, configurations, and localization settings across several components.

4. `useReducer` in Complex State Structures

For scenarios where state management is intricate, `useReducer` provides a more structured approach compared to `useState`.

- Managing Complex State Changes: `useReducer` is ideal for situations where the next state is dependent on the previous one, requiring intricate logic to determine the state transition.

- Pairing with Context API: Integrating `useReducer` with `useContext` forms a robust pattern for handling and distributing complex application states.

5. `useRef` for DOM Interactions and Mutable References

`useRef` is commonly employed for direct interactions with DOM elements and maintaining mutable data that doesn't trigger re-renders on updates.

- Direct DOM Manipulations: `useRef` can access DOM elements for tasks like managing focus, reading values, or initiating animations.

- Tracking Previous Values: It's also beneficial for tracking previous states or props across renders, useful for comparing changes or implementing custom logic based on past values.

6. Crafting Advanced Custom Hooks

Developing sophisticated custom hooks allows for the consolidation of complex component logic and state handling, fostering reusability and clean code.

- API Interactions and Data Management: Custom hooks can streamline API interactions, manage data fetching, response caching, and error handling.

- Streamlining Forms and Validations: Custom hooks that handle form states, validation logic, and submission handling can simplify form implementations.

7. Hooks for Performance Enhancements

In React applications, performance optimization often involves strategic use of hooks.

- Memoization Techniques: Utilizing `useMemo` and `useCallback` for memoizing computationally heavy functions and callbacks aids in reducing the load on rendering-intensive components.

- Optimizing Context Consumption: Applying context selectors or combining `useContext` with `useMemo` helps in minimizing unnecessary re-renders for context consumers.

Conclusion

Standard hooks in React, such as `useState`, `useEffect`, `useContext`, `useReducer`, and `useRef`, provide developers with a versatile toolkit for managing state and side effects in functional components. Their advanced application enables handling of complex component logic and state with greater efficiency and less code compared to traditional methods. The development of custom hooks and optimization strategies further enhances the power and flexibility of these standard hooks, making them indispensable in the toolkit of modern React developers. As React continues to evolve, these hooks remain central to building reactive, dynamic, and complex web applications.

Building and managing custom hooks

In React development, the creation and management of custom hooks have emerged as a transformative approach to streamlining and reusing functionality across components. Custom hooks, leveraging React's core hooks, enable developers to encapsulate complex operations into standalone, reusable functions, enhancing code organization and maintainability.

1. Understanding Custom Hooks in React

Custom hooks are JavaScript functions that use React's native hooks to encapsulate and modularize logic.

- Encapsulating Logic for Reuse: They allow for the abstraction of intricate logic from components, promoting reuse and cleaner code.

- Managing Specific Functionalities: Custom hooks handle specific, stateful logic or side effects, applicable across various components.

2. Developing Custom Hooks for Various Needs

Custom hooks can be tailored for a wide range of functionalities, from handling API interactions to managing form states.

- Data Retrieval and State Management: Hooks can manage fetching data, state updates following API responses, and efficient caching.

- Forms and Validation Logic: They simplify form handling, ensuring consistent validation across different forms.

- Interacting with Global States: Custom hooks also facilitate interactions with global state management systems, offering a more intuitive way to manage state in components.

3. Principles for Crafting Custom Hooks

Certain key principles ensure the effectiveness and maintainability of custom hooks.

- Focused Functionality: Each hook should address a single concern or functionality.

- Composability: Hooks should be designed to be used within other hooks, enabling complex functionality construction.

- Clear Naming Practices: Consistent and descriptive naming for hooks helps in clearly conveying their purpose and usage.

4. Managing Lifecycle and State in Hooks

Custom hooks effectively manage state and lifecycle events using foundational hooks like `useState` and `useEffect`.

- State Handling: `useState` within custom hooks is used to maintain state pertinent to the hook's function.

- Lifecycle and Side Effect Management: `useEffect` handles side effects, subscriptions, and cleanup, akin to its usage in functional components.

5. Addressing Side Effects and Asynchronous Operations

Handling side effects and asynchronous tasks is a core functionality of many custom hooks.

- Async Operations for Data Fetching: Custom hooks often encapsulate the logic for making asynchronous API calls and handling state updates based on responses.

- Optimizing Input Handling: Implementing techniques like debouncing in custom hooks optimizes performance for operations such as search inputs.

6. Testing Strategies for Custom Hooks

Ensuring the reliability of custom hooks through rigorous testing is vital.

- Isolated Unit Testing: Custom hooks should be subjected to unit testing to ensure their functionality works as intended in isolation.

- Component Integration Testing: Testing how these hooks perform when integrated within components verifies their effectiveness in actual application scenarios.

7. Reusability and Distribution of Custom Hooks

One of the main advantages of custom hooks is their potential for reuse across different components and projects.

- Building a Repository of Hooks: Developing an internal collection of custom hooks can facilitate sharing and reuse within an organization.

- Contributing to Open Source: Sharing custom hooks with the broader development community can provide solutions for commonly faced challenges.

8. Adherence to Best Practices

Following best practices in the creation and application of custom hooks is essential for high-quality React development.

- Thorough Documentation: Detailed documentation, including descriptions, parameters, and returns, is critical for the effective use of custom hooks.

- Prudent Dependency Management: Managing dependencies within hooks, particularly in `useEffect`, is crucial to prevent unnecessary executions and maintain optimal performance.

Conclusion

Custom hooks in React represent a significant advancement in how developers handle reusable, stateful logic across components. By abstracting complex operations into custom hooks, developers can achieve a higher level of code reusability and simplicity in their React applications. Adhering to best practices in building, documenting, and testing these hooks is key to creating efficient, maintainable, and scalable solutions within the React ecosystem. As React continues to evolve, custom hooks remain a fundamental tool for developers, driving towards more modular and manageable codebases.

Hooks for performance optimization

In React's ecosystem, hooks play a pivotal role in enhancing the performance of applications, particularly in scenarios where efficient state management and minimal re-renders are crucial. Hooks such as `useMemo`, `useCallback`, `useReducer`, and `useRef` have become essential tools in the optimization arsenal, allowing developers to write more efficient, cleaner, and optimized code.

1. The Role of Hooks in Performance Optimization in React

Performance optimization hooks in React are designed to address specific challenges like unnecessary re-renders and complex computations.

- Reducing Redundant Rendering: A key goal of performance optimization in React is to minimize

437

unnecessary component re-renders, which can drain resources and degrade user experience.

- Managing Computations and State Efficiently: These hooks aid in managing state transitions and computations in a way that ensures components update only when absolutely necessary.

2. `useMemo` for Computation Memoization

`useMemo` is crucial for memoizing the output of expensive function calls, preventing needless recalculations.

- Caching Computation Results: `useMemo` stores the results of heavy computations and only re-computes when its dependencies change, thereby conserving computational resources.

- Enhancing Render Performance: This hook is particularly useful in optimizing components that rely on data-intensive operations or calculations.

3. `useCallback` for Callback Memorization

`useCallback` is employed to memorize callback functions, ensuring their stability across renders unless dependencies change.

- Stabilizing Functions in Renders: `useCallback` helps prevent the recreation of functions on each render, which is critical for functions passed as props to child components.

- Minimizing Child Component Rerenders: By memoizing callback functions, `useCallback` plays a vital role in reducing unnecessary re-renders of child components.

4. `useReducer` for Complex State Handling

`useReducer` is particularly suited for components with complex state logic, offering a more structured approach compared to `useState`.

- Streamlining State Transitions: It provides a clear mechanism for state updates, especially when the next state depends on the previous one in complex ways.

- Suitable for Large Components: `useReducer` is especially beneficial in large components or those with intricate state interactions.

5. `useRef` for Mutable References and DOM Access

`useRef` is valuable for accessing DOM elements directly and for storing mutable data that doesn't trigger re-renders.

- Direct DOM Manipulation: It enables direct interaction with DOM elements, useful for managing focus, measurements, or integrating with external DOM libraries.

- Holding Mutable Data: `useRef` is also used for storing data that persists across renders but does not necessitate a render when changed.

6. Utilizing `useContext` for Optimized State Sharing

Although not exclusively for performance, `useContext` can be leveraged to enhance performance, particularly in large component trees.

- Streamlining State Propagation: `useContext` simplifies state sharing across components, reducing the need for prop drilling and potentially improving performance.

7. Developing Custom Hooks for Performance Logic

Custom hooks can encapsulate specific performance-related logic, making it easier to apply optimizations consistently across components.

- Custom Data Fetching and Caching Hooks: Creating hooks for handling data fetching processes, including response caching and error management, can lead to significant performance improvements.

- Abstracting Common Performance Logic: Custom hooks can abstract and standardize frequently used performance optimization logic, promoting consistency and reducing redundancy.

8. Adherence to Performance Best Practices Using Hooks

Using hooks for performance optimization requires adherence to certain best practices to fully harness their potential.

- Managing Dependencies Correctly: Properly handling dependencies in hooks like useMemo and useCallback is critical for their effective functioning.

- Balancing Optimization with Code Clarity: While optimization is important, it's also crucial to avoid overusing these hooks to prevent code complexity. They should be applied judiciously, focusing on areas that are critical for performance.

Conclusion

Hooks in React, specifically `useMemo`, `useCallback`, `useReducer`, and `useRef`, offer significant capabilities in optimizing application performance, particularly in managing state and reducing unnecessary re-renders. Understanding the appropriate application of these hooks is essential in crafting high-performing React applications. Additionally, the development of custom hooks for reusable performance logic can greatly enhance the efficiency of development processes. Following best practices in dependency management and judicious use of these hooks ensures their effectiveness, contributing to React applications that are both performant and user-friendly.

Chapter Three

React and the Jamstack

Introduction to the Jamstack architecture

Jamstack architecture, an innovative approach in the web development domain, emphasizes enhanced performance, security, and scalability. This architecture, denoting JavaScript, API, and Markup, diverges from conventional web development practices by separating the frontend from the backend, thus fostering a more dynamic and efficient method of creating web applications.

1. Fundamentals of Jamstack Architecture

At its core, Jamstack revolves around three key components:

- JavaScript: This is utilized for all dynamic functions during the request/response cycle, executed entirely in the client's browser.

- APIs: Backend operations or database actions are abstracted into reusable APIs, which are called from JavaScript over HTTPS.

- Markup: This is prebuilt at deployment time using a static site generator, which contributes to faster page load speeds.

2. Benefits of Adopting Jamstack

Jamstack's approach offers several key advantages over traditional web development architectures:

- Performance Enhancement: The use of pre-rendered markup significantly improves website loading times.

- Security Improvements: Decoupling the frontend from the backend minimizes server-side vulnerabilities.

- Ease of Scalability: Separating frontend and backend simplifies the process of scaling applications.

- Developer Productivity: Jamstack promotes a more organized development workflow, enhancing productivity.

3. Utilization of Static Site Generators

Static site generators are pivotal in Jamstack architecture, converting source files into static HTML, CSS, and JavaScript.

- Popular Static Site Generators: Gatsby, Jekyll, and Hugo are among the widely used generators, each suitable for different project types.

- SEO and Performance Optimization: These generators enhance SEO and performance by serving pre-built files, eliminating the need for server-side rendering.

4. Integration with Headless CMS

In Jamstack, headless CMS systems play a crucial role in content management, providing backend content management capabilities and delivering content via APIs.

- Enhanced Content Management Flexibility: Headless CMS allows for the independent management of content, separate from its presentation.

- API-Driven Content Delivery: Content is delivered through APIs and rendered using JavaScript, aligning with the static nature of Jamstack sites.

5. Hosting Solutions for Jamstack Sites

Jamstack sites are ideally hosted on platforms that specialize in serving static files, like Netlify, Vercel, or Amazon S3.

- Streamlined Build and Deployment Processes: These platforms typically offer automated deployment from version control systems, simplifying the build process.

- CDN Usage for Global Reach: Utilizing CDNs ensures faster content delivery across the globe, enhancing the application's overall performance.

6. Embracing Serverless Functions in Jamstack

Serverless functions complement the Jamstack architecture by enabling backend functionalities without the need to manage server infrastructure.

- Dynamic Features in Static Sites: Serverless functions facilitate the execution of backend code in response to events, thus introducing dynamic capabilities to otherwise static sites.

- Cost-Efficiency and Scalability: This approach aligns with Jamstack's principles, as it utilizes resources only when the functions are executed.

7. Challenges in Jamstack Implementation

Despite its numerous advantages, certain challenges in Jamstack implementation must be considered:

- Project Suitability: Jamstack may not be the optimal choice for projects requiring intense server-side processing or highly dynamic content.

- Reliance on External Services: The architecture's dependence on external APIs and services means that their performance and availability can directly impact the application.

Conclusion

Jamstack architecture is revolutionizing web development by offering an approach that is more efficient, secure, and scalable than traditional methodologies. It is particularly effective for enhancing load times, ensuring security, and simplifying the development process. Through the integration of static site generators, headless CMS, serverless functions, and specialized hosting services, Jamstack enables the creation of robust, high-performing web applications. As the digital landscape continually evolves, Jamstack stands as a progressive architectural choice, suitable for a wide range of modern web applications, provided its applicability aligns with the project requirements.

React in static site generators like Gatsby and Next.js

React's integration with static site generators like Gatsby and Next.js marks a significant evolution in web development practices, blending React's interactive UI capabilities with the efficiency and security of static site generation. These frameworks leverage React to build dynamic web experiences while benefiting from the performance gains of static content.

1. React's Integration in Modern Static Site Frameworks

In static site generators, React plays a pivotal role in building UI components, offering a dynamic user experience which is then compiled into static HTML at build time.

- Component-Driven Development: React's structure, based on reusable components, is ideal for developing scalable web interfaces.

- JSX as a Templating Language: React's JSX allows developers to write HTML structures directly within JavaScript, enhancing the developer experience in static site frameworks.

2. Gatsby: A React-Based Static Site Powerhouse

Gatsby stands out as a static site generator that fully harnesses React's potential, providing an ecosystem that extends React's capabilities for static generation.

- Performance Optimization: Gatsby automatically optimizes site performance, splitting code into smaller bundles.

- Data Layer with GraphQL: Gatsby's integration with GraphQL offers a streamlined way to pull data from various sources, which is then rendered into React components.

- Extensive Plugin Library: Gatsby's extensive range of plugins offers functionalities for SEO, image optimization, and more, enriching the React development experience.

3. Next.js: Bridging Static Generation and Server-Side Rendering

Next.js, built atop React, is recognized for server-side rendering but also supports static site generation, offering a versatile development approach.

- Mixed Rendering Modes: Next.js allows developers to choose between static generation and server-side rendering on a per-page basis, offering flexibility in how pages are rendered.

- Serverless API Routes: It includes serverless API route support, simplifying the creation of server-side logic within a React application.

- Optimized Page Loading: Next.js implements automatic code splitting, ensuring efficient page loading.

4. SEO and Performance Benefits

Both Gatsby and Next.js leverage React to enhance SEO and website performance, crucial factors in modern web development.

447

- Quick Load Times: The static nature of Gatsby sites and the SSR/SSG capabilities of Next.js lead to improved loading times, benefiting both SEO and user experience.

- Asset Optimization: These frameworks optimize the delivery of assets, improving overall site performance.

5. Dynamic Features in Static Sites

Despite generating static content, Gatsby and Next.js enable dynamic functionalities, showcasing React's flexibility.

- Interactive Client-Side Features: Post-load, React enables interactive elements and state management akin to a traditional SPA.

- Dynamic Hydration in Next.js: Server-rendered pages in Next.js become dynamic through client-side JavaScript hydration.

6. Streamlined Deployment and Hosting

Hosting and deployment of static sites created with Gatsby or Next.js are simplified, supported by modern hosting solutions.

- CDN-Based Hosting: Platforms like Netlify, Vercel, and AWS Amplify, optimized for static content, offer global distribution.

- Automated Build Processes: These services typically offer continuous deployment from version control, automating the build and deployment cycle.

7. Considerations and Challenges

While offering numerous benefits, there are certain challenges in adopting these React-based static site generators.

- Initial Learning Phase: Understanding React, along with Gatsby or Next.js, can be challenging for newcomers.

- Build Time Considerations: For large sites, build times can be considerable, though this is being mitigated with incremental build features.

Conclusion

The incorporation of React into static site generators like Gatsby and Next.js exemplifies the synergy of dynamic UI development with the advantages of static site generation. Gatsby enriches the React experience with optimized performance and a rich plugin ecosystem, while Next.js offers flexibility with its combined static and server-side rendering approaches. These frameworks expand React's applicability, enabling the creation of web applications that are both performant and interactive, fitting the diverse needs of modern web development. As the digital landscape evolves, React's role in these static site frameworks underscores its adaptability and strength as a front-end development tool.

Optimizing React apps for Jamstack

Optimizing React applications for the Jamstack framework is an essential practice for developers aiming to harness modern web technologies effectively. Jamstack, known for its emphasis on performance, security, and scalability, complements React's component-based structure, creating a robust platform for developing high-performing web applications.

1. Aligning React Development with Jamstack Principles

To effectively optimize React apps for Jamstack, developers should align with its core principles, including separation of concerns, pre-rendering, and leveraging client-side JavaScript with serverless backends.

- Adopting a Decoupled Approach: Structuring React applications to clearly separate front-end interfaces from back-end logic enhances both security and scalability.

- Emphasizing Pre-rendering: Employing tools like Gatsby or Next.js for pre-rendering improves performance, with static files served rapidly from CDNs, benefiting SEO.

2. Utilizing React with Static Site Generators

In the Jamstack approach, using static site generators (SSGs) with React is crucial for optimal performance and efficiency.

- Gatsby for Static React Sites: Gatsby is tailored for building static React websites, pre-loading resources for swift navigation.

- Next.js for Versatile Rendering: Next.js offers flexibility, supporting both static generation and server-side rendering, ideal for React apps requiring dynamic content alongside Jamstack benefits.

3. Enhancing React App Performance

Performance optimization is a key aspect of Jamstack applications, and several strategies can enhance React app efficiency.

- Implementing Code Splitting: Breaking down code into smaller chunks ensures that only necessary code is loaded per page.

- Applying Lazy Loading: React's lazy loading capabilities for components and images can significantly boost load times.

- Streamlining Data Retrieval: Efficiently fetching data using GraphQL or REST APIs, either at build time or on the server, aligns with static generation and server-side rendering principles.

4. State Management and API Interactions

In React apps designed for Jamstack, state management and API integrations should reflect the architecture's ethos.

- Handling Dynamic Data on the Client-Side: Dynamic data and user-specific content should be managed via client-side API calls to maintain the static integrity of the site.

- Incorporating Serverless Functions: Serverless functions are ideal for backend processes, such as handling form submissions or database interactions, keeping the architecture decoupled.

5. Optimizing React Apps for SEO

SEO optimization is vital for web application visibility and success, especially in React applications built on Jamstack.

- Leveraging Server-Side Rendering for SEO: Utilizing server-side rendering in Next.js ensures that dynamic content is searchable and indexable by search engines.

- Dynamic Meta Tags Management: Tools like React Helmet can dynamically manage meta tags and structured data to enhance SEO.

6. Focusing on Security Measures

Given Jamstack's decoupled nature and API reliance, security is a significant focus.

- Implementing Robust Content Security Policies: These policies are essential to guard against XSS attacks.

- Securing API Endpoints: All API endpoints should have stringent security measures, including proper authentication and authorization.

7. Streamlining Build and Deployment Processes

Efficient build and deployment processes are crucial for maintaining productive development workflows.

- Automating Builds and Deployments: Automated tools and CI/CD pipelines facilitate seamless deployment processes.

- Utilizing Incremental Builds: Leveraging incremental build features in SSGs can significantly reduce build times for extensive applications.

8. Monitoring Performance and User Engagement

Ongoing monitoring of application performance and user behavior is key to continuous improvement.

- Incorporating Performance Monitoring: Utilizing tools to track load times and user interactions aids in identifying and rectifying performance bottlenecks.

- Integrating Analytical Tools: Analytics help in understanding user engagement and refining application features based on user behavior.

Conclusion

Optimizing React applications for the Jamstack architecture entails a comprehensive approach that includes enhancing performance, managing data efficiently, ensuring SEO optimization, and maintaining robust security. By leveraging static site generators and adhering to the principles of Jamstack, developers can create React applications that are not only quick and scalable but also secure and user-centric. Incorporating modern development practices like serverless computing and automated deployments further amplifies the potential of React apps within this architecture. As the web development landscape evolves, this optimization strategy represents a progressive alignment with the needs of contemporary web users and the broader digital environment.

Chapter Four

Real-Time Applications with React

Building real-time features with WebSockets and Socket.IO

In the landscape of modern web development, incorporating real-time functionalities has become increasingly essential. Technologies like WebSockets and Socket.IO are at the forefront of enabling such features, providing the necessary infrastructure for live, bidirectional communication between clients and servers. This capability is pivotal for applications requiring instant data updates, like live chat systems, real-time notifications, or collaborative tools.

1. The Role of WebSockets in Real-Time Communication

WebSockets establish a continuous two-way communication channel, offering a significant advancement over the traditional HTTP request-response model.

- Continuous Connection: WebSockets maintain an open connection, allowing for ongoing data exchange without needing new HTTP requests for each interaction.

- Minimizing Latency: By avoiding the overhead of repeated HTTP handshakes, WebSockets reduce latency, making them ideal for applications where quick data transfer is crucial.

2. Socket.IO: Enhancing WebSocket Interactions

Socket.IO is a widely-used JavaScript library that simplifies working with WebSockets, providing enhanced functionality and broader compatibility across various environments.

- Facilitating Real-Time Features: Socket.IO is designed for building real-time applications, enabling instant communication between web clients and servers.

- Compatibility and Reliability: It provides fallback mechanisms for environments where WebSockets aren't supported and offers a more user-friendly API for handling real-time data.

3. Developing Real-Time Applications

The choice between using raw WebSockets and Socket.IO largely depends on the specific requirements and context of the application.

- Using Raw WebSockets: For scenarios where ultra-low latency is paramount and the environment is controlled, using raw WebSockets may be appropriate.

- Preferring Socket.IO: In cases where ease of use, reliability, and cross-platform compatibility are key, Socket.IO often becomes the preferred choice.

4. Real-Time Chat Applications

One of the most common real-time features is a chat application, where WebSockets or Socket.IO can be employed for immediate message delivery.

- Seamless Messaging Experience: Users can send and receive messages instantaneously, emulating the feel of a natural conversation.

- Managing Online Statuses and Broadcasts: Real-time connectivity also allows for tracking user presence and broadcasting messages to multiple users.

5. Implementing Live Notifications

Real-time notifications, similar to those in social media or email applications, are another application of these technologies.

- Pushing Updates Instantly: Users receive notifications about new activities or messages without needing to refresh the page.

- Scalability in High-Traffic Applications: Handling a multitude of connections simultaneously requires a scalable architecture to manage WebSocket connections.

6. Collaborative Online Tools

Collaborative environments like document editing or live drawing applications benefit significantly from real-time features.

- Managing Concurrent Edits: Real-time communication is key in allowing multiple users to see and respond to each other's changes instantly.

- Synchronizing User Actions: Ensuring that all participants' actions are reflected in real-time is crucial for the integrity of collaborative work.

7. Ensuring Robust Connections and Scalability

Maintaining stable connections and scalability is essential in real-time applications.

- Stability of Connections: Strategies for handling connection drops and maintaining active communication are necessary for a seamless user experience.

- Scaling WebSockets: Considering server capacity and implementing efficient load distribution are critical for applications with high user volumes.

8. Securing WebSocket Communications

Security is a paramount concern when dealing with WebSockets, as they are susceptible to similar threats as standard web traffic.

- Secured Connections: Utilizing WSS (WebSocket Secure) ensures encrypted data transmission, and appropriate authentication methods should be integrated.

- Mitigating Security Risks: Awareness of vulnerabilities like CSWSH (Cross-Site WebSocket Hijacking) and implementing countermeasures are crucial for secure real-time communication.

Conclusion

WebSockets and Socket.IO have significantly changed the dynamics of web application development, enabling an array of real-time features that offer users interactive and immediate experiences. Whether it's through the direct use of WebSockets for their low-latency benefits or through Socket.IO for its ease of use and compatibility, these technologies empower developers to create responsive, engaging, and live features in web applications. As the web continues to progress, the ability to implement real-time communication efficiently is becoming increasingly vital, making WebSockets and Socket.IO key tools in the modern developer's toolkit.

Integrating with Firebase for real-time updates

Incorporating Firebase into web and mobile applications for real-time functionality is a strategy widely embraced in the contemporary development landscape. Firebase, a robust platform by Google, brings a suite of development tools, including a real-time database and cloud-based functions, which are instrumental in enabling instant data synchronization and facilitating serverless backend processes.

1. Firebase Realtime Database for Instantaneous Data Synchronization

Firebase's Realtime Database stands at the forefront of its real-time capabilities. This cloud-hosted database allows for the immediate synchronization of data across all connected clients.

- Instant Data Sync: The database ensures that any changes in data are promptly reflected across all client interfaces, a critical feature for applications like collaborative platforms or chat systems.

- Offline Data Handling: It also offers offline support, where data changes are locally saved and later synced with the server when online connectivity is re-established.

2. Implementing Real-Time Updates with Firebase

To integrate Firebase for real-time updates, a series of steps are involved:

- Firebase Initialization: This process involves setting up a Firebase project, integrating Firebase into the application, and configuring it with the necessary credentials.

- Listening to Data Updates: Firebase allows the setting up of listeners to database references, which enables the application UI to react in real-time to any data changes.

3. Firebase Cloud Functions for Backend Operations

Firebase Cloud Functions allow for the execution of server-side logic in response to events triggered in the Firebase ecosystem, enhancing the application's serverless architecture.

- Reactive Backend Logic: These functions can be configured to react to changes in the Realtime Database, facilitating automated backend responses to real-time events.

- Scalable Backend Solutions: This serverless framework eliminates the need for dedicated server maintenance, scaling automatically with the application's demand.

4. Security and User Authentication

Firebase also offers comprehensive security and authentication solutions to safeguard data and user access.

- Robust Authentication System: Firebase Authentication supports various authentication methods, including social media accounts, email/password, and phone authentication.

- Configurable Security Rules: Security rules in the Firebase Realtime Database ensure that data access and modifications are properly authenticated and authorized.

5. Real-Time Application Scenarios for Firebase

Firebase's real-time features are particularly effective in several types of applications:

- Chat Applications: Real-time chat functionalities are streamlined with Firebase, enabling live messaging interactions.

- Collaborative Platforms: Firebase facilitates the development of applications where multiple users can interact and modify shared content simultaneously.

- Dynamic Content Feeds: Creating social media-like feeds with live updates becomes more manageable with Firebase's real-time data capabilities.

6. Managing Large-Scale Firebase Applications

For applications with extensive user bases and data, strategic data structuring and query optimization are key.

- Efficient Data Queries: Structuring the database to ensure queries are performant and data-fetching is optimized is vital in large applications.

- Denormalizing Data: Firebase's performance is maximized with denormalized data structures, differing from traditional relational database structures.

7. Firebase Integration with Modern Frontend Frameworks

Firebase complements various frontend frameworks, enhancing the development of real-time applications.

- React Integration: Tools like ReactFire provide custom hooks and utilities for seamlessly integrating Firebase with React applications.

- Angular Compatibility: AngularFire, designed for Firebase and Angular integration, offers reactive bindings and observables for real-time interactions.

8. Analytics and Performance Monitoring

Beyond real-time features, Firebase provides tools for monitoring user interactions and application performance.

- User Behavior Insights: Firebase Analytics offers valuable insights into how users interact with the application.

- Performance Analysis: The Firebase Performance Monitoring tool helps identify and rectify performance-related issues, ensuring a smooth user experience.

Conclusion

Leveraging Firebase for real-time updates in applications delivers a powerful, efficient, and scalable solution, ideal for scenarios that demand quick data synchronization. With its straightforward database setup, serverless backend capabilities, comprehensive security measures, and integration with various frontend frameworks, Firebase stands as a preferred choice for developers crafting modern, interactive applications. As the domain of web and mobile application development evolves, Firebase's role in driving real-time interactions and efficient backend processes becomes increasingly indispensable.

Design patterns for real-time data flow

Designing for real-time data flow is increasingly critical in contemporary application development, especially for platforms requiring instant data updates like messaging apps, live event tracking, or financial trading systems. These design patterns not only ensure efficient data management but also contribute to the scalability, maintainability, and responsiveness of such applications.

1. Fundamentals of Real-Time Data Flow

Real-time data flow involves immediate transmission of data between servers and clients, deviating from the conventional request-response model which relies on client initiation for data retrieval.

- Immediate Data Exchange: Key to real-time data flow is the server's ability to push updates to the client instantly as new data becomes available.

- Two-Way Communication: Many real-time systems enable bi-directional communication, allowing both server and client to send and receive data.

2. Key Design Patterns in Real-Time Data Flow

Effective management of real-time data often utilizes specific design patterns known for their efficacy.

- Publish-Subscribe (Pub-Sub) Model: This pattern allows publishers (data producers) to send data to a channel without knowing the subscribers (data consumers), facilitating scalability and decoupling producers from consumers.

- Observer Pattern: Commonly used in UI development, this pattern enables objects to observe a subject and receive notifications about state changes, ideal for real-time UI updates.

- WebSockets for Continuous Communication: WebSockets support full-duplex communication, allowing simultaneous two-way data flow, crucial for interactive applications such as multiplayer online games or collaborative platforms.

3. Deploying Real-Time Features in Web Applications

Incorporating real-time features into web applications demands strategic architecture and technology choices.

- Protocol Selection: WebSockets and HTTP/2 are foundational for real-time communication, with Server-Sent Events (SSE) being suitable for one-way data flow.

- Efficient Data Handling: Rapid and efficient data serialization and deserialization are critical, usually employing formats like JSON.

- Connection Reliability: Ensuring stable connections, even during drops and reconnections, is vital for uninterrupted data flow.

4. Real-Time Data Management and Storage

Storing and processing data in real-time poses unique challenges, particularly in terms of performance and scalability.

- Stream Data Processing: High-throughput, scalable technologies such as Apache Kafka or Redis Streams are tailored for real-time data stream processing.

- Database Selection: Databases capable of handling frequent and fast operations, such as NoSQL or real-time databases like Firebase, are often preferred.

5. Ensuring Security in Real-Time Interactions

Given the continuous data exchange in real-time applications, implementing stringent security measures is essential.

- Robust Access Controls: Secure channels through authentication and authorization to protect data streams.

- Encrypting Data Transmissions: Employ TLS/SSL encryption to safeguard data in transit, especially for sensitive information.

6. Scaling and Optimizing Performance

Scalability and performance are paramount in handling growing user numbers and data volumes in real-time applications.

- Scalable Architectural Design: Adopt architectures that support horizontal scaling and use load balancers to distribute traffic across multiple servers.

- Data Packet Optimization: Reducing the size of data packets is key to minimizing transmission times and reducing system load.

7. Testing and Monitoring for Reliability

Regular testing and monitoring are crucial in maintaining the efficiency and reliability of real-time systems.

- Proactive System Monitoring: Implement tools to continuously monitor the real-time components for performance and health.

- Conducting Load Testing: Regular load testing is essential to ensure the system's capacity to handle anticipated concurrent connections and data throughput.

8. Prioritizing User Experience

In real-time applications, delivering a smooth and responsive user experience is a primary goal.

- Instant User Interaction Feedback: The UI should reflect immediate responses to user actions, a fundamental expectation in real-time applications.

- Fluid UI State Changes: Managing UI state changes fluidly is important to mirror the instantaneous nature of the application without abrupt shifts.

Conclusion

Design patterns for real-time data flow are integral to developing modern, dynamic applications that respond instantly to user interactions and data changes. By adopting appropriate patterns like Pub-Sub, leveraging WebSockets for continuous data exchange, and choosing suitable data processing solutions, developers can build robust and efficient real-time systems. Considerations for security, scalability, and user experience are also critical in delivering high-quality, real-time applications. As technology evolves, these design patterns remain key in shaping the future of real-time, data-driven application development.

Chapter Five

Advanced Routing Techniques

Dynamic and nested routing in complex applications

In today's web development landscape, dynamic and nested routing are pivotal for crafting sophisticated applications, particularly those that demand a versatile and organized approach to handle numerous views and data displays. These routing methodologies are essential in advanced web frameworks like React, Angular, and Vue.js, allowing the creation of user interfaces that are both intricate and intuitive in navigation.

1. The Essence of Dynamic Routing in Application Development

Dynamic routing stands out for its capacity to define routing paths in real-time, based on user interactions or specific conditions, as opposed to static routing's predetermined paths.

- Dynamic Path Parameters: This approach often utilizes route parameters, which are adaptable parts of URLs changing in response to user actions or data states, as seen in routes like `/users/:userId`.

- Enhanced Flexibility and Scalability: Dynamic routing is key for applications with content or data that varies widely and unpredictably, offering significant scalability and flexibility.

2. Nested Routing for Structured UI

Nested routing enables the development of hierarchically organized views within applications, embedding child routes within parent ones for a more coherent user interface.

- Hierarchical Interface Organization: For applications rich in data with multiple navigation layers, nested routing aids in structuring content into logical hierarchies, simplifying user navigation.

- Component Reusability: It also facilitates the reuse of components, such as a shared layout component across different application sections, with child routes rendering specific content.

3. Implementing Complex Routing Structures

Implementing dynamic and nested routing demands thoughtful planning around the application's architectural needs.

- Using Routing Frameworks: Modern routing libraries (like React Router, Vue Router, or Angular Router) simplify the process of creating complex routing patterns.

- Route Configuration: Routes are configured using path patterns that can include dynamic segments, with parent-child route relationships established in the routing setup.

4. Applications of Dynamic and Nested Routing

Dynamic and nested routing find use in various complex application scenarios.

- E-Commerce Sites: Online stores use dynamic routing for displaying products by categories or IDs and nested routing for organizing products, categories, and user interfaces.

- Enterprise Dashboards: Dashboards with multiple data representations and user roles utilize nested routing to manage different data views and access controls efficiently.

5. State Management in Dynamic Routes

Managing application state is crucial in dynamic routing, especially when data fetching is tied to route changes.

- Fetching Data on Route Change: Changing dynamic route parameters often triggers data fetching to display relevant information.

- Optimizing with Caching and State Persistence: Implementing caching or state persistence strategies can enhance performance and user experience.

6. SEO Optimization in Dynamic Routing

Addressing SEO in dynamically routed applications is critical, especially for indexing dynamically generated content.

- Employing Server-Side Rendering: Server-side rendering ensures dynamically rendered content is indexable by search engines.

471

- Automated Sitemap Updates: Dynamically updating sitemaps with new routes aids in effective content indexing.

7. Security Measures in Routing Systems

Incorporating security measures in dynamic and nested routing is essential to validate route parameters and safeguard certain routes.

- Validating Dynamic Parameters: Ensuring the legitimacy of route parameters is key to preventing unauthorized access.

- Securing Routes: Routes that require user authentication or specific permissions should be adequately protected.

8. Enhancing Performance in Complex Routing

Performance optimization in applications with intricate routing involves techniques like lazy loading and code splitting.

- Implementing Lazy Loading: Lazy loading helps in loading application parts as needed, improving initial loading times.

- Strategic Code Splitting: Dividing the application code into smaller chunks associated with different routes enhances loading efficiency for specific sections.

Conclusion

Dynamic and nested routing play a fundamental role in developing complex, modern web applications. These routing strategies facilitate the management of applications with numerous views and diverse data presentations, offering adaptability and improved user navigation. With thoughtful execution, considering state management, SEO, security, and performance aspects, these routing techniques significantly contribute to structuring and streamlining complex application architectures. As the field of web development evolves, dynamic and nested routing continue to be crucial for tackling the intricacies of advanced navigation and data organization in web applications.

Lazy loading routes for performance gains

In contemporary web development, the technique of lazy loading routes has become a pivotal strategy for enhancing application performance, especially in expansive applications with a variety of routes and components. This method focuses on loading components or specific routes only when they are required, rather than loading all at once during the initial application load. It's particularly effective in extensive single-page applications (SPAs).

1. The Role of Lazy Loading in Web Development

Lazy loading is a technique where specific sections of an application, such as components or scripts, are loaded only when necessary. This differs from traditional methods where all resources are loaded upfront.

- On-Demand Resource Loading: Resources in a lazy loading setup are loaded as needed, triggered by user navigation or certain events.

- Minimizing Initial Load Time: The initial load time is significantly reduced in lazy loading, as only essential resources are loaded at first, enhancing both performance and user experience.

2. Application of Lazy Loading in Modern Frameworks

Frameworks like React, Angular, and Vue.js provide native or integrable solutions for implementing lazy loading.

- Lazy Loading in React: React utilizes the `**React.lazy**` function for component-level lazy loading, alongside `**React.Suspense**` to manage loading states.

- Angular and Lazy Loading Routes: Angular's routing module allows defining routes that are lazy-loaded, improving performance at the route level.

- Vue.js's Asynchronous Components: Vue.js enables lazy loading at the component level through asynchronous components, which load only when required.

3. Advantages of Implementing Lazy Loading

The integration of lazy loading brings numerous performance benefits to web applications.

- Enhanced Initial Loading Speed: By reducing the size of the initial resource bundle, lazy loading quickens page load times, crucial for user experience and search engine optimization.

- Efficient Use of Bandwidth: This technique is particularly advantageous for users with limited bandwidth or slow internet, as it minimizes initial data transfer.

- Optimized Resource Utilization: Lazy loading ensures that browser resources are judiciously used, processing only the necessary scripts and components.

4. Ideal Scenarios for Lazy Loading

Certain types of applications stand to benefit greatly from lazy loading.

- Large Single-Page Applications: SPAs with numerous routes and components can greatly benefit from lazy loading, enhancing responsiveness and user interaction.

- E-commerce Platforms: Websites with a large number of product pages and images can significantly improve the user browsing experience through lazy loading.

5. Challenges and Considerations in Lazy Loading

While beneficial, lazy loading comes with its own set of challenges that need careful management.

- Managing Loading Indicators: Providing user feedback during the loading of components or routes is essential to maintain a smooth user experience.

- Dependencies in Asynchronous Loading: Ensuring that dependencies are properly managed in asynchronously loaded components or routes is crucial.

- SEO Implications: For applications that rely on server-side rendering, ensuring that lazy-loaded content is accessible and indexable by search engines is key.

6. Best Practices for Effective Lazy Loading

To optimize the benefits of lazy loading, certain best practices should be adhered to.

- Prioritize Critical Content: Load essential content, especially above-the-fold content, immediately, while deferring secondary content.

- Anticipatory Preloading: Preloading certain routes or components in anticipation of user actions can further enhance the experience.

- Performance Monitoring: Regular monitoring using tools like Google Lighthouse is important to gauge the impact of lazy loading on overall performance.

Conclusion

Lazy loading routes is an effective performance optimization technique in web application development, particularly valuable in large-scale applications with multiple routes and components. By loading resources strategically on an as-needed basis, it significantly cuts down on initial page load times and optimizes resource utilization, leading to a more responsive and efficient user experience. While implementing lazy loading involves navigating challenges like managing loading states and considering SEO, the performance gains and enhanced user satisfaction make it a crucial strategy in the toolkit of modern web developers. As web technologies advance, lazy loading continues to be a vital practice for developers striving to create fast, efficient, and user-friendly web applications.

Protecting routes and handling authentication

Securing routes and managing authentication effectively are pivotal aspects of contemporary web application development. As applications grow in complexity and feature interconnected systems, robust authentication protocols and secure route management become essential. These security measures are crucial for safeguarding sensitive data and user information, and for upholding a secure and reliable user experience.

1. The Critical Role of Secure Routing and Authentication

Route protection involves limiting access to specific sections of an application based on user credentials. This is particularly important in applications handling personal data, financial information, or administrative functionalities.

- Preserving User Confidentiality: Secure routes ensure private information remains accessible only to authorized users.

- Upholding Application Security: By controlling route access, applications maintain their integrity, preventing unauthorized actions that could compromise service quality.

2. Establishing Robust Authentication Systems

Authentication is the foundational step in application security, typically accomplished through a login process.

- Traditional Username and Password Systems: The most prevalent form of user verification involves credentials like usernames and passwords.

- Token-Based Systems: Modern applications often use tokens (e.g., JSON Web Tokens or JWTs) for authentication, where a token is provided post-login for accessing protected routes.

- Third-Party Authentication Methods: Techniques like OAuth allow for secure third-party access, while social media logins streamline the authentication process for users.

3. Route Security in Various Frameworks

Popular web development frameworks offer tools and libraries for route protection.

- Middleware Applications: Frameworks such as Express.js utilize middleware to validate tokens or session information before granting route access.

- Client-Side Protection in SPAs: SPA frameworks like Angular, React, or Vue.js use specific functionalities, like 'guards', to secure client-side routes.

4. Authorization: A Step Further Than Authentication

Authorization determines if an authenticated user has the necessary permissions to access a particular resource.

- Role-Based Access Systems (RBAC): In RBAC, users are assigned roles with specific permissions, controlling their access to resources.

- Attribute-Based Access Control (ABAC): ABAC offers nuanced access control, based on a combination of user attributes such as role, department, and security level.

5. Handling Authentication Credentials Securely

It's crucial to manage authentication credentials securely to avoid potential security breaches.

- Encrypted Data Transmission: Use HTTPS for secure communication of authentication details.

- Secure Token Storage: Store authentication tokens securely on the client side, using secure storage options.

6. Authentication in Single-Page Applications (SPAs)

SPAs present unique challenges for authentication due to their client-side orientation.

- Session State Management: SPAs need to manage session states client-side, often utilizing JavaScript libraries or browser storage.

- Token Renewal and Expiration: Implement token renewal systems to ensure ongoing session security.

7. User-Friendly Authentication Design

The design of the authentication process should prioritize user experience.

- Simplified Login Procedures: Streamline the login process for ease of use.

- Feedback on Access Restrictions: Provide clear notifications and instructions when users attempt to access restricted areas without adequate permissions.

8. Adhering to Security Best Practices

Incorporating standard security practices is vital for effective authentication and route protection.

- Routine Security Checks: Regularly perform security audits and code reviews.

- Updated Security Patches: Keep all frameworks and dependencies current with the latest security updates.

Conclusion

Route protection and authentication management form the bedrock of secure web application development. These practices ensure that user identities are accurately verified (authentication) and that they have appropriate access rights (authorization). Implementing these security measures is fundamental to protecting sensitive information, maintaining user trust, and ensuring the robustness of the application. As web technologies continue to advance, the methodologies and tools for route protection and authentication will also evolve, remaining integral to the security and functionality of modern web applications.

Chapter Six

Advanced Component Patterns

Compound components and controlled components

In the sphere of modern front-end development, particularly within frameworks like React, two prominent design patterns, compound components and controlled components, have gained significant traction. These patterns are instrumental in crafting interactive and complex user interfaces, each offering unique methods for managing state and behavior in UI components, which is essential for creating modular, scalable, and maintainable applications.

1. Compound Components: Facilitating UI Flexibility and Component Reusability

The compound component pattern in React is a powerful approach for constructing flexible and reusable component architectures. This pattern involves grouping components that share an internal state, allowing developers to build more intricate and customizable UI elements.

- Compositional Approach vs. Inheritance: This pattern focuses on composing components together rather than relying on inheritance, affording greater UI design versatility.

481

- Shared Internal State: Compound components typically share a state managed by a parent component, ensuring cohesive functionality across different parts of the UI.

- Application Scenarios: This pattern is particularly useful in building complex UI structures like navigation menus, dialog boxes, or form controls, where various components need to interact yet remain functionally independent.

2. Controlled Components: Streamlining State Management

Controlled components represent a pattern where the state management of the component is externalized, typically controlled by a parent component. This approach is especially beneficial for form elements or other UI components requiring tight synchronization with the application's state.

- External State Control: In controlled components, the state is managed outside the component, usually passed down as props along with callbacks to modify it, leading to more predictable components.

- Managing Form Elements: This pattern is commonly applied in managing form elements like text inputs and checkboxes, facilitating easy data validation and submission.

- Lifting State Upward: It often involves lifting the state to higher components in the hierarchy, making it accessible to multiple children components.

3. Choosing and Combining Patterns Effectively

Effective implementation of these patterns hinges on understanding their strengths and appropriate usage.

- Pattern Selection: The choice between compound and controlled components depends on the application's specific needs. Compound components are ideal for complex, interrelated UI elements, while controlled components suit scenarios requiring close synchronization with the app's state.

- Integrating Both Patterns: In some cases, integrating both patterns can harness the advantages of each, such as using controlled components within a compound component setup.

4. Advantages in UI Development

Both patterns offer several key benefits in UI development.

- Promoting Reusability and Modularity: They encourage creating reusable and modular components, reducing code redundancy and enhancing maintainability.

- Simplified State Logic: These patterns streamline state management in complex applications, either by centralizing it (controlled components) or sharing it among related components (compound components).

- Flexibility in UI Customization: They empower developers to craft flexible and customizable user interfaces, aligning components as needed.

5. Implementation Best Practices

While implementing these patterns, certain best practices are essential.

- Comprehensive Documentation: Due to the implicit relationships in compound components and external state control in controlled components, thorough documentation is vital.

- Mitigating Prop Drilling Issues: In controlled components, it's important to address the challenge of prop drilling, where data passes through many component layers.

- Performance Optimization: Attention should be paid to performance, especially in controlled components where frequent state updates may impact application performance.

Conclusion

Compound and controlled components stand as two fundamental patterns in contemporary React development. Each provides distinct methods for managing UI component states and behaviors, offering pathways to create flexible, reusable, and modular user interfaces. Understanding and applying these patterns effectively allows developers to build sophisticated, interactive web applications capable of meeting modern user expectations. As the landscape of front-end development evolves, these patterns continue to be integral for developing advanced web applications that are both efficient and user-centric.

Contextual and utility components

In the arena of contemporary web development, especially within the context of React, two significant design patterns have risen to prominence: contextual components and utility components. These patterns serve distinct purposes in the realm of state and logic management, significantly aiding in the creation of maintainable and scalable code structures.

1. Contextual Components: Streamlining State and Logic Across Components

Contextual components in React are adept at passing data and functionality through the component hierarchy in an efficient manner, proving invaluable in scenarios with deep component nesting or where multiple components require access to shared data.

- Utilizing React's Context API: This API enables the distribution of values like user data, themes, or configuration settings across components, bypassing the need to pass props through every level.

- Reducing Complexity: The Context API helps in avoiding the cumbersome practice of prop drilling, where data has to traverse through multiple layers of components, streamlining component structures.

- Ideal Scenarios for Contextual Components: They are particularly useful for handling states that have global relevance within the application, like user preferences, themes, or authentication information.

2. Utility Components: Focused Functionality

Utility components, also known as helper components, are specialized in providing specific functions or encapsulating particular logic. These compact, often stateless components are designed for broad reuse across various application parts.

- Core Functional Units: Acting as foundational elements, utility components are tasked with a single function or a related set of functions, enhancing the building process of an application.

- Common Examples: These include components dedicated to form handling, data formatting, or higher-order components that bestow additional capabilities on other components.

3. Effective Implementation of Contextual and Utility Components

Understanding the unique roles and benefits of these components is key to their effective implementation in application design.

- Judicious Context Usage: The power of the Context API should be balanced with caution to prevent unpredictable component behavior and testing difficulties.

- Designing for Reusability in Utility Components: These components should be modular, focused on a specific task, and designed to be stateless for optimal reusability.

4. Advantages of Employing These Components

The integration of these component patterns brings several developmental benefits.

- Codebase Maintainability: Both patterns encourage cleaner, more maintainable code – contextual components by reducing prop drilling, and utility components by encapsulating functionalities.

- Scalability of Applications: These components contribute to scalable architectures by abstracting common functions and states.

- Development Flexibility: They offer flexibility in state and logic management, allowing for a more dynamic and modular approach to development.

5. Best Practices for Utilization

To fully leverage the strengths of contextual and utility components, certain best practices should be adhered to.

- Context for Broad State, Not Local: The Context API is best suited for states that need widespread application access, not for localized state management.

- Isolating Utility Logic: Keep utility components separate from the business logic, ensuring they are purely functional and easily testable.

- Consistent Application of Utility Components: Maintain a consistent approach in how utility components are implemented across the application to avoid confusion and duplication.

Conclusion

Contextual and utility components have become vital in the toolkit of React developers. Contextual components provide an elegant solution for managing application-wide data, while utility components allow for modular handling of specific functionalities. Properly leveraging these patterns enables developers to construct more effective, maintainable, and scalable web applications. As the field of web development evolves, these patterns underscore the importance of methodologies that can handle modern application complexities, yet maintain simplicity and reusability in the code.

Design systems and component libraries

In the dynamic field of web and application development, design systems and component libraries have established themselves as crucial frameworks for crafting cohesive and scalable user interfaces. These resources are central to developing a unified design language across products, optimizing the design and development workflow, and enhancing collaboration between design and development teams.

1. The Essence of Design Systems

A design system is an extensive collection of guidelines, standards, and design philosophies. It encompasses a range of design elements, such as color palettes, typography, layouts, and interactivity, along with established best practices and foundational design principles.

- Uniformity and Scalability: Design systems aim to provide visual and functional uniformity across applications or a range of products, serving as a singular reference point that enables design scalability.

- Facilitating Team Collaboration: They act as a common language between designers and developers, aligning both groups towards unified design objectives and user experience goals.

2. Component Libraries as UI Fundamentals

Component libraries are assemblies of reusable components that conform to the standards of a design system. These libraries range from basic elements like buttons and text fields to more complex components such as calendars or dialog boxes.

- Streamlining Development Processes: Utilizing a component library accelerates interface development, allowing developers to construct UIs rapidly and uniformly without designing each component from the ground up.

- Framework Compatibility: These libraries are typically designed to integrate with prevalent front-end frameworks, including React, Vue.js, and Angular, enhancing adaptability in various development environments.

3. Interplay Between Design Systems and Component Libraries

Design systems lay out the overarching rules and philosophies, while component libraries translate these guidelines into concrete, deployable elements.

- Actualizing Design Concepts: Component libraries operationalize the abstract ideas of design systems, converting principles and guidelines into ready-to-use code components.

- Upholding Design Integrity: They ensure that the final product remains consistent with the design system's vision, preserving design integrity throughout development.

4. Their Impact in Contemporary Development Practices

In the contemporary development landscape, design systems and component libraries are vital for maintaining consistent branding, upholding design quality, and expediting development workflows.

- Brand Uniformity: These tools are essential in keeping a consistent brand identity across different products and platforms.

- Adhering to Quality and Accessibility: They ensure adherence to high standards of design and accessibility, making products not only visually appealing but also user-centric and inclusive.

5. Developing and Sustaining These Systems

Developing and maintaining these systems necessitates a collaborative and evolutionary approach, with ongoing contributions from both designers and developers.

- Evolving with Needs: Design systems and component libraries should adapt and evolve alongside the product, necessitating regular updates based on user feedback and changing requirements.

- Collaborative Efforts: Their development should involve close cooperation across different teams, ensuring the system meets diverse requirements and expectations.

6. Challenges in Implementation

Implementing design systems and component libraries, while beneficial, comes with its set of challenges.

- Upfront Resource Investment: Establishing these systems initially demands significant time and resources.

- Balancing Standardization and Creativity: Finding a balance between providing clear guidelines and fostering creativity is key. Overly stringent systems can limit creative exploration, while excessive flexibility might lead to inconsistency.

Conclusion

Design systems and component libraries have become fundamental in modern web and application development.

They offer a structured approach to creating consistent and high-quality user interfaces, promote efficient workflows, and support a collaborative environment between design and development teams. As digital platforms continue to expand and diversify, these tools will remain vital for teams aiming to develop unified, user-focused, and scalable products.

Chapter Seven

Full-Stack Development with React

Integrating React with Node.js and Express

Combining React with Node.js and Express has become a standard practice in contemporary web development, creating powerful full-stack solutions. This blend harnesses React's prowess in building engaging user interfaces with the versatile server-side capabilities of Node.js, enhanced by Express's streamlined web application framework.

1. React: Spearheading Frontend Development

React, a brainchild of Facebook, is a JavaScript library renowned for crafting interactive user interfaces. It's celebrated for its component-driven architecture and efficient page rendering techniques.

- Modular Component System: React's component-based approach enables the creation of isolated, reusable UI segments, enhancing code manageability and scalability.

- Optimizing with Virtual DOM: React employs a Virtual DOM to optimize page rendering, ensuring minimal updates to the UI for enhanced performance.

2. Backend Strength with Node.js and Express

Node.js is a powerful JavaScript runtime built on Chrome's V8 engine, allowing for server-side scripting. Express.js, a framework for Node.js, simplifies server-side operations with its minimalist but potent toolkit.

- Unified JavaScript Development: Leveraging JavaScript across both frontend and backend streamlines development processes, allowing for a cohesive full-stack development experience.

- Asynchronous and Scalable Architecture: Node.js's event-driven, non-blocking architecture, complemented by Express.js's features for routing and middleware, makes it ideal for scalable and high-performance backends.

3. Integrating Frontend and Backend

The integration of React with Node.js and Express typically revolves around establishing effective communication channels, often realized through RESTful APIs or GraphQL.

- RESTful API Communication: Building RESTful APIs with Express.js enables the React frontend to interact seamlessly with the Node.js backend, facilitating dynamic content management.

- Server-Side React Rendering: For enhanced SEO, Node.js can be configured to render React components server-side, delivering fully-rendered HTML to the client.

4. Establishing the Development Environment

Initiating a project integrating React, Node.js, and Express involves setting up a supportive development environment.

- Installing Node.js and NPM: Node.js and its package manager, NPM, are fundamental for managing project dependencies.

- React Application Setup: Tools like Create React App can kickstart a new React project with ease.

- Express Server Configuration: Establish an Express server, either within the React project or as a separate entity, based on the desired architecture.

5. Crafting Full-Stack Applications

Developing a full-stack application using this trio involves concurrent frontend and backend development, ensuring cohesive functionality.

- React for UI Development: The frontend is built using React, focusing on creating interactive components and handling user interactions.

- Backend Logic with Express: Develop the server-side logic using Express, creating APIs for tasks like database operations, authentication, and core business logic.

6. Managing Data Interactions

Effective data exchange between the React frontend and Node.js backend is key to application functionality.

- API Integration with React: Use HTTP clients such as Axios in React to connect with Express APIs, enabling data flow between the frontend and backend.

- State Handling in React: Efficiently manage state in the frontend, using libraries like Redux or the Context API for complex state management scenarios.

7. Deploying the Full-Stack Application

Deployment strategies for React, Node.js, and Express applications often differ between frontend and backend.

- Frontend Deployment: The React frontend can be hosted on platforms like Netlify or Vercel, which specialize in static site hosting.

- Backend Deployment: The Node.js server can be deployed on cloud services such as Heroku, AWS, or Google Cloud Platform, accommodating Node.js environments.

Conclusion

The integration of React with Node.js and Express forms a formidable combination for full-stack development, blending React's UI excellence with the server-side efficiency of Node.js and Express. This setup is ideal for developers aiming to create complex, high-performance web applications, taking full advantage of JavaScript's potential across the entire development stack. As the field of web development progresses, this combination continues to be a favored choice for building scalable, maintainable, and feature-rich web applications.

Building RESTful and GraphQL APIs

In today's web development landscape, crafting APIs (Application Programming Interfaces) is a fundamental task. RESTful and GraphQL APIs are two prominent methodologies in API development, each with its distinctive features and benefits. Grasping the intricacies of these approaches is crucial for developers aiming to create robust, scalable, and adaptable web services.

1. RESTful APIs: Core Concepts and Implementation

RESTful APIs, based on the REST architectural style, utilize HTTP protocols for effective communication and have been a long-standing standard in API design.

- Resource-Centric Approach: REST operates on a principle where everything is treated as a resource, identifiable by URIs (Uniform Resource Identifiers). These resources are manipulated using standard HTTP methods like GET, POST, PUT, and DELETE.

- Stateless Interactions: RESTful APIs operate on a stateless basis, meaning every client-server interaction contains all the necessary information to be understood and processed.

- Benefits of Stateless Nature: The statelessness of RESTful APIs aids in their scalability and, combined

497

with their ability to define cacheable responses, enhances performance.

- Consistent Interface: REST APIs provide a uniform interface, easing comprehension and usage.

2. GraphQL APIs: A Modern Query Language

GraphQL, a query language developed by Facebook for APIs, offers a new paradigm in API design, differing significantly from traditional RESTful approaches.

- Client-Driven Query Structure: GraphQL allows clients to define precisely the data they need, which can reduce problems of overfetching and underfetching data.

- Single Consolidated Endpoint: GraphQL APIs usually operate through a single endpoint, processing queries that dictate the structure of the response.

- Subscription Feature for Live Data: GraphQL supports subscriptions for real-time updates, where the server pushes data changes to clients as they happen.

3. Crafting RESTful APIs

Developing RESTful APIs involves several key stages:

- Resource Identification: Pinpoint the resources the API will manage. These should be conceptualized as nouns (e.g., 'users', 'products') and interacted with using HTTP methods.

- Endpoint Design: Craft API endpoints that adhere to REST principles and link them to relevant business logic.

- Implementing CRUD Operations: Ensure the API supports Create, Read, Update, and Delete operations for each resource, aligning with suitable HTTP methods.

- Appropriate Responses and Status Indications: The API should return fitting HTTP status codes and responses that accurately reflect the result of the request.

4. Constructing GraphQL APIs

Building a GraphQL API involves different considerations:

- Schema Definition: Create a schema that describes the types, queries, and mutations available in your API.

- Developing Resolvers: Craft resolvers – functions that fetch data for each field in the schema.

- GraphQL Server Setup: Opt for a GraphQL server solution that aligns with the needs of your application, such as Apollo Server or GraphQL Yoga.

5. Key Considerations in Choosing Between RESTful and GraphQL

Both RESTful and GraphQL APIs present unique advantages, but there are factors to consider:

- Complexity and Resource Demands: GraphQL might introduce more complexity and overhead than REST in simpler applications.

- Caching Mechanisms: While REST benefits from straightforward caching due to its stateless nature, caching with GraphQL can be more intricate due to variable query patterns.

- Learning Requirements: GraphQL generally presents a steeper learning curve than REST, given its departure from traditional HTTP methods and status codes.

Conclusion

RESTful and GraphQL APIs represent two divergent yet effective approaches to API development. RESTful APIs, with their focus on resources and stateless operation, are apt for numerous applications, especially where simplicity and conventional use are key. Conversely, GraphQL offers enhanced flexibility and data retrieval efficiency, suited for scenarios where clients require control over the data they receive. The choice between RESTful and GraphQL APIs hinges on the specific needs and context of the application. In many cases, utilizing both technologies in different segments of an application can be beneficial. As web technology progresses, both RESTful and GraphQL APIs will continue to be essential tools for building responsive, efficient, and user-focused web services.

Managing authentication and authorization

In the realm of web application security, managing authentication and authorization effectively is paramount. These two aspects, while closely related, serve distinct purposes in maintaining security and user access control. Authentication is the process of verifying a user's identity, whereas authorization determines the access rights and privileges of the user within the system. Ensuring robust management of both is crucial for safeguarding sensitive information and providing a secure environment for users.

1. The Role of Authentication in Security

Authentication acts as the initial checkpoint in securing an application, confirming whether users are who they claim to be.

- Authentication Techniques: Common methods include using usernames and passwords, biometric verification, and OTPs. Enhanced security measures like two-factor (2FA) or multifactor authentication (MFA) provide additional security layers.

- Token-Based Systems: Web applications frequently employ tokens (e.g., JWT) for authentication. After successful login, a token is issued for subsequent requests by the client.

- Session Security: Securely managing user sessions is essential for preventing vulnerabilities like session hijacking.

2. Authorization and Access Control

Following authentication, authorization plays a vital role in defining what resources a user can access and their permitted actions.

- Role-Based Access Control (RBAC): A common approach where roles with predefined permissions are assigned to users.

- Attribute-Based Access Control (ABAC): Offers finer control, with decisions based on various attributes, environmental conditions, or resource characteristics.

- Principle of Least Privilege: This principle involves granting users only the necessary access levels to perform their tasks, minimizing unauthorized data access risks.

3. Strategies for Implementing Authentication and Authorization

Developing effective authentication and authorization involves several key strategies and technologies.

- Robust Authentication Processes: Employ secure, proven authentication mechanisms. For web applications, protocols like OAuth 2.0 or OpenID Connect are often used.

- Encryption and Secure Data Handling: Encrypt and securely store passwords and sensitive authentication data. Use secure hashing for password storage.

- Consistent Security Updates: Regularly update and audit security mechanisms to guard against new threats.

4. Balancing Challenges in Authentication and Authorization

Managing these processes involves navigating certain challenges.

- User Experience Versus Security: Achieving a balance between stringent security measures and user convenience is crucial.

- Scalability and Performance Concerns: Ensuring authentication and authorization systems are scalable and do not hinder application performance.

- Compliance with Privacy Regulations: Complying with data privacy laws and regulations in handling user data during these processes is essential.

5. Modern Applications and Security Integration

Today's application frameworks and platforms offer built-in capabilities or integrations for handling user security.

- Utilizing IAM Services: Tools like AWS Cognito, Auth0, or Firebase Authentication provide robust solutions for identity and access management.

- Middleware in Custom Solutions: Middleware can be effectively used in bespoke implementations, especially server-side, for managing security logic.

6. Ongoing Monitoring and Incident Management

Continuously monitoring these security systems is vital for identifying and addressing security incidents.

- Systematic Logging and Observations: Implement and monitor logs for authentication and authorization activities.

- Preparedness for Security Incidents: Establish a thorough incident response strategy for potential security breaches or failures in these systems.

Conclusion

Managing authentication and authorization is a cornerstone in web application security. Authentication verifies user identity, and authorization governs their access and actions within the system. Implementing strong, reliable mechanisms, adhering to security best practices, and ongoing vigilance are necessary to maintain a secure, data-protected environment. As security technologies evolve, the strategies and tools for effective authentication and authorization also need to adapt, requiring developers and security professionals to stay informed and proactive.

Chapter Eight

Scalable CSS for Large Applications

CSS architecture for large-scale projects

In the sphere of web development, particularly for extensive projects, effective CSS (Cascading Style Sheets) architecture is vital. It addresses the challenge of maintaining a clean, efficient, and scalable CSS codebase, which is crucial in ensuring that the styling of large-scale applications remains manageable and consistent.

1. Key Challenges in Large-Scale CSS Management

Handling CSS in large-scale projects can be daunting due to several factors:

- Potential for Redundancy and Increased Load Times: A lack of structured CSS can lead to repetitive code, resulting in bloated stylesheets and slower page loads.

- Risks of Inconsistency and Styling Conflicts: Without a unified approach, different developers might introduce conflicting or inconsistent styles.

- Difficulties in Scalability: As the project expands, so does the complexity of its CSS, posing scalability challenges.

2. Structured Approaches to CSS Organization

Several methodologies have been developed to streamline CSS in large projects, each offering a systematic way to structure styles.

- BEM (Block Element Modifier): This methodology advocates dividing CSS into distinct blocks and elements, facilitating readability and maintainability.

- OOCSS (Object-Oriented CSS): OOCSS encourages treating page components as objects, promoting the reuse of styles.

- SMACSS (Scalable and Modular Architecture for CSS): This system provides guidelines for categorizing CSS rules, aiding in creating a modular and scalable architecture.

3. Leveraging CSS Preprocessors

CSS preprocessors like Sass, LESS, and Stylus add programming capabilities to CSS, providing features like variables and mixins.

- Variables for Unified Theming: Using variables helps maintain consistency in themes.

- Reusable Mixins: Mixins enable the creation of reusable style snippets, aligning with the DRY (Don't Repeat Yourself) principle.

4. Embracing CSS-in-JS for Component-Based Architectures

In frameworks such as React, CSS-in-JS libraries allow CSS to be embedded within JavaScript, offering component-scoped styling.

- Scope and Dynamic Styling: CSS-in-JS ensures styles are contained within components and can adapt based on properties.

- JavaScript Integration in Styling: This approach makes styling more dynamic, leveraging JavaScript's power.

5. Responsive Design Considerations in CSS Architecture

Responsive design is a staple in large-scale projects, requiring a CSS architecture that can adapt to various devices and screen sizes.

- Adopting a Mobile-First Strategy: Starting with mobile styles and scaling up for larger screens often results in cleaner CSS.

- Modularizing Breakpoints: Reusable breakpoints can be defined to maintain consistency across components.

6. Effective File Organization and Naming Conventions

Proper organization of CSS files is key in large-scale projects.

- Breaking Down CSS Files: Segmenting CSS into smaller files based on components or sections aids in manageability.

- Consistent Naming Practices: Employing a uniform naming convention helps in identifying the purpose of different stylesheets quickly.

7. The Importance of Documentation and Style Guides

Documenting CSS styles and maintaining style guides is crucial for collaborative development.

- Comprehensive Style Documentation: A living style guide that details styles, patterns, and components used in the project is essential.

- Tools for Automated Documentation: Utilize tools capable of generating automatic style guides from the CSS codebase.

8. Addressing Performance in CSS

In large-scale projects, the impact of CSS on performance can be significant.

- Strategies for Minimizing Load Times: Employ CSS minification and compression techniques to reduce file sizes.

- Prioritizing Critical CSS: Implement methods to identify and load critical CSS first, while deferring other styles.

9. Ongoing CSS Codebase Refinement

Continual refinement and maintenance are crucial for keeping the CSS architecture efficient.

- Regular CSS Code Reviews: Conducting frequent reviews helps in optimizing the CSS and ensuring adherence to best practices.

- Iterative Refactoring for Enhanced CSS: Continuously refactor CSS for better structure, readability, and performance.

Conclusion

Managing CSS architecture in large-scale projects is about balancing structured methodologies, effective tooling, and best practices. By implementing systems like BEM, OOCSS, or SMACSS, leveraging preprocessors and CSS-in-JS, and maintaining well-organized, documented codebases, development teams can handle the complexities associated with extensive CSS. These practices ensure scalability, maintainability, and optimal performance of the CSS architecture, crucial for the success of large-scale web applications. As web development techniques evolve, a robust CSS architecture continues to be integral to delivering seamless user experiences and streamlined development processes.

Scalable and maintainable styling strategies

In contemporary web development, devising scalable and maintainable styling strategies is essential for the long-term viability and management of large-scale projects. As applications expand in scope and intricacy, adopting a coherent and flexible approach to styling becomes critical.

This includes implementing strategies that ensure ease of management, adaptability to evolving project needs, and scalability across a diverse and extensive codebase.

1. Modular Design as a Cornerstone

A modular design framework is central to maintaining a manageable styling approach. This involves segmenting styles into smaller, reusable units or modules, which can then be combined and utilized across the application.

- Component-Oriented Frameworks: Using frameworks such as React, Vue, or Angular, UI elements are constructed as discrete, reusable components.

- BEM for Clear Structure: The BEM (Block, Element, Modifier) methodology is one way to create modular CSS, enhancing readability and long-term maintainability.

2. The Role of CSS Preprocessors

CSS preprocessors like Sass, LESS, and Stylus add enhanced functionality to CSS, offering features like variables, mixins, and nested selectors.

- Variables for Unified Design: Variables are used for storing and reusing core values like colors and fonts, ensuring design consistency.

- Reusable Mixins: Mixins facilitate the creation of reusable style snippets, aligning with the principle of DRY (Don't Repeat Yourself).

3. Structured CSS Methodologies

Adopting a structured CSS methodology helps in organizing CSS effectively, be it OOCSS (Object-Oriented CSS), SMACSS (Scalable and Modular Architecture for CSS), or Atomic CSS.

- OOCSS for Flexibility: OOCSS promotes the separation of structure and skin, enhancing reusability.

- SMACSS for Modular Organization: SMACSS provides a framework for categorizing CSS rules, aiding in creating a scalable architecture.

- Atomic CSS for Granular Control: Atomic CSS focuses on creating small, single-purpose classes based on visual function.

4. CSS-in-JS for Component-Specific Styles

CSS-in-JS libraries, like styled-components in React, provide scoped styling, where CSS is directly tied to components, enhancing maintainability and reducing conflicts.

- Dynamic Styling Capabilities: This approach allows for styles that adapt based on properties or application state.

- Scoped Styles for Better Management: Styles defined within components are scoped to them, preventing global conflicts.

5. Responsive Design Strategies

Responsive design is crucial for scalable UI development, requiring fluid layouts and adaptable grid systems.

- Mobile-First Approach for Efficiency: Starting with mobile layouts and expanding to larger screens ensures more efficient, performance-oriented styles.

- Reusable Breakpoints: Defining breakpoints modularly allows for consistent responsive design across components.

6. Organized CSS File Management

Efficient organization of CSS files and adherence to clear naming conventions are key in handling large codebases.

- Segmented CSS Files: Break down CSS into smaller files, grouped logically by components or functionalities.

- Standardized Naming for Clarity: Implement a consistent naming convention for classes and IDs to enhance code readability and management.

7. Importance of Documentation

Well-documented styles and comprehensive style guides are crucial, especially for teamwork and maintaining consistency.

- Maintaining a Detailed Style Guide: A style guide that outlines styling conventions and commonly used components is vital.

- Tools for Documentation: Utilize automated tools for generating documentation from the CSS codebase.

8. CSS Performance Optimization

In extensive projects, CSS's impact on performance must be considered, employing techniques for critical CSS extraction and minification.

- Prioritizing Critical CSS: Identify and prioritize above-the-fold styles for quicker load times.

- Optimizing CSS Files: Use tools for CSS minification and optimization to reduce file sizes and enhance loading performance.

9. Regular Refactoring and CSS Maintenance

Ongoing refinement and maintenance are necessary for efficient CSS architecture.

- Routine Code Reviews: Conduct frequent reviews to optimize CSS and ensure adherence to best practices.

- Iterative Improvements: Continually refactor CSS for improved structure, readability, and performance.

Conclusion

Developing scalable and maintainable styling strategies is fundamental in modern web application development. Embracing modular design principles, leveraging preprocessors, adopting CSS methodologies, and maintaining organized and well-documented codebases are key. These practices not only foster better team collaboration but also enhance the overall application's performance and user experience. As web technologies evolve, staying updated with the latest best practices in CSS architecture remains crucial for successful and efficient web development.

Advanced pre-processors and CSS-in-JS techniques

In today's web development arena, advanced CSS pre-processors and CSS-in-JS methodologies stand at the forefront of styling solutions, offering enhanced capabilities beyond traditional CSS. These tools are particularly valuable in complex web applications, where managing standard CSS might be challenging.

1. Enhanced Flexibility with CSS Pre-processors

CSS pre-processors like Sass, LESS, and Stylus augment standard CSS with additional functionalities, bringing in more adaptability and reusability.

- Variables and Mixins for Reusability: These pre-processors introduce variables for common values and mixins for code blocks, promoting consistent styling and reducing code repetition.

- Nested Syntax for Better Readability: They support a nested syntax that aligns more intuitively with HTML structures, enhancing readability and maintainability.

- Dynamic Styling with Functions: Advanced pre-processors include functions and conditional logic, allowing for context-sensitive and dynamic styles.

2. CSS-in-JS: Tying Styles to Components

CSS-in-JS, a paradigm where CSS is integrated into JavaScript, links styles directly with their components, popularized by libraries like styled-components in React.

- Component-Scoped Styles: This technique ensures styles are confined to specific components, minimizing global conflicts and enhancing modularity.

- Responsive Styling Capabilities: CSS-in-JS allows for styles that react dynamically to component states or properties, creating interactive UI elements.

- Theming and Global Styling: These libraries facilitate theming and managing global styles within an application, streamlining theme implementation and basic styling.

3. Implementing Advanced Pre-processors in Development

Incorporating advanced pre-processors into a project involves thoughtful integration and usage.

- Balanced Feature Utilization: Features like nesting and mixins should be used judiciously to avoid overly complex code.

- Build Tool Integration: Pre-processors need to be integrated with build tools since their syntax is not natively understood by browsers.

4. Integrating CSS-in-JS in Applications

Adopting CSS-in-JS requires a shift in styling approach, closely aligning with modern component-based frameworks.

515

- Embracing Component-Level Styling: This approach involves defining styles at the component level, fitting well with component-centric architectures of modern frameworks.

- Managing Global Styles: Utilize the capabilities of CSS-in-JS libraries to handle global styles effectively.

- Performance Awareness: Be aware of the performance implications, especially for server-side rendered applications, as CSS-in-JS can introduce runtime overhead.

5. Synergy Between Pre-processors and CSS-in-JS

Combining pre-processors with CSS-in-JS can harness the strengths of both approaches.

- Base Styling with Pre-processors: Use pre-processors for foundational styles and variables, then apply these within CSS-in-JS for specific component styles.

- Thematic Integration: Create themes using pre-processors and dynamically apply them in components with CSS-in-JS.

6. Scalability in Styling Practices

Regardless of using pre-processors, CSS-in-JS, or both, certain best practices ensure scalability and maintainability.

- Focus on Modular Styles: Aim for modularity and reusability in styling to prevent code duplication and enhance maintainability.

- Consistent Naming Practices: Maintain uniform naming conventions for easier identification and management of styles.

- Documenting Style Approaches: Keep a comprehensive style guide that details the styling architecture and usage protocols.

7. Evolving Styling Techniques in Web Development

As web development evolves, so does the role and application of styling techniques like CSS pre-processors and CSS-in-JS.

- Keeping Up with Evolving Standards: Stay updated with the latest practices and community standards in styling.

- Optimizing for Performance: Continually optimize the performance impact of these styling methodologies, especially critical in large-scale applications.

Conclusion

Advanced CSS pre-processors and CSS-in-JS methods offer robust alternatives to traditional CSS challenges in modern web development. By extending the functionalities of CSS and closely integrating styling with component logic, they empower developers to create dynamic, maintainable, and scalable interfaces. As the landscape of web development continues to shift, these advanced styling techniques will remain integral in defining efficient, modular, and maintainable approaches to web application styling.

Chapter Nine

Performance Optimization and Auditing

Deep analysis of React application performance

Delving into the performance aspects of React applications is a critical task for developers aiming to provide smooth and responsive user experiences. Despite React's reputation for efficiency, certain challenges can arise in complex or large-scale applications. A thorough performance analysis in React necessitates an understanding of typical performance issues, effective utilization of diagnostic tools, and the implementation of strategic optimization practices.

1. Grasping React's Rendering Mechanics

Performance in React is closely tied to how it manages the virtual DOM. React's rendering process, triggered by changes in state or props, can become a source of inefficiency if not handled properly.

- Component Rendering Optimization: Unnecessary rendering of components, especially complex or nested ones, can lead to significant performance degradation.

- Virtual DOM and Reconciliation: A solid grasp of React's virtual DOM and its reconciliation process is vital, as inefficient use can cause performance lags.

2. Tools for Performance Analysis

Various tools are available for profiling React applications, essential in both development and production stages.

- React Developer Tools Profiler: This tool within React Developer Tools aids in pinpointing performance bottlenecks by analyzing component render times.

- Using Chrome's Performance Tab: The Chrome browser's Performance tab offers detailed insights into time spent on scripting, rendering, and painting.

3. Addressing Common Performance Hurdles

Several prevalent issues can affect React application performance:

- Cumbersome Component Trees: Deep component trees can lead to redundant render cycles.

  - *Solution:* Streamline component structures to reduce unnecessary depth.

- State Management Inefficiencies: Excessive or unneeded state updates can trigger multiple re-renders.

  - *Solution:* Enhance state management, use immutable structures, and efficiently utilize state management tools.

- Prop Drilling Issues: Deep prop passing can cause re-rendering and hinder component reusability.

  - *Solution:* Utilize context or state management tools for managing shared state.

4. Optimizing React Applications

Optimizing a React application involves several tactics:

- PureComponent and React.memo Use: These prevent unnecessary re-renders through shallow prop and state comparison.

- Dynamic Code Loading: Code splitting using React.lazy and Suspense or dynamic import() reduces initial loading times.

- Memoization Tactics: Preventing redundant computations in functional components or hooks enhances performance.

- Event Handler Optimization: Defining event handlers outside the render method prevents creating new function instances on each render.

5. Efficiently Rendering Lists and Iterations

Rendering performance can be impacted by how lists and iterations are handled, especially with large datasets.

- Effective Key Usage: Employing unique and stable keys for list items is crucial in optimizing re-render performance.

- Windowing Techniques: Utilizing libraries like react-window or `react-virtualized' can significantly improve the rendering of large lists.

6. Network and Data Fetching Optimization

Network interactions and data fetching are pivotal elements in performance tuning.

- Data Fetching on Demand: Implement lazy data loading strategies, triggered by user actions or component visibility.

- API Call Management: Minimizing the frequency and size of API calls, coupled with caching and data compression, can enhance performance.

7. Regular Monitoring and Iterative Optimization

Ongoing monitoring and enhancement are key components of React performance management.

- Consistent Performance Tracking: Regularly monitor application performance, especially following updates or new feature rollouts.

- Continuous Improvement Cycle: Establish a feedback loop with tools like Lighthouse or WebPageTest for persistent performance optimization.

Conclusion

In-depth analysis and refinement of React application performance encompass understanding React's core mechanisms, adept use of profiling instruments, and applying strategic optimization measures. Developers must concentrate on efficient rendering practices, astute state management, and handling network and data interactions effectively. Embracing these approaches ensures that React applications deliver optimal performance, crucial for a fluid and engaging user experience. Keeping abreast of evolving optimization strategies and tools is integral to maintaining high-performing React applications in the dynamic landscape of web development.

Profiling and auditing tools

Investigating the intricacies of React application performance is a critical endeavor for developers dedicated to crafting responsive, efficient, and robust web applications. React, widely embraced for its user interface development capabilities, can encounter performance hurdles as applications scale up. Tackling these issues necessitates a deep understanding of React's performance nuances, the utilization of precise diagnostic tools, and the deployment of effective optimization strategies.

1. Decoding React's Performance Traits

The core of React's performance revolves around its handling of the DOM and the rendering lifecycle of components. Utilizing a virtual DOM and a sophisticated reconciliation process, React minimizes direct DOM manipulations, a known source of performance degradation.

- Component Render Cycles: React's UI updates involve re-rendering components. Unwarranted re-renders, however, can lead to sluggish performance, particularly in applications with complex component structures.

522

- Virtual DOM Dynamics: Grasping how React compares its virtual DOM with a previous snapshot to identify necessary updates is key to pinpointing performance bottlenecks.

2. Tools for Performance Analysis

Several tools are available to dissect and understand the performance characteristics of React applications, pinpointing areas that need optimization.

- React Developer Tools Profiling: This browser extension is instrumental in assessing the render performance of React components, identifying which components consume the most time to render.

- Detailed Analysis with Chrome DevTools: The Performance tab in Chrome DevTools offers an in-depth view of different activities like scripting, rendering, and painting, providing a comprehensive performance overview.

3. Common Performance Pitfalls

Several typical issues can impede React application performance:

- Frequent Component Rerenders: Over-rendering of components is a frequent source of performance issues.

- Complex Component Hierarchies: Deeply nested components can lead to inefficient render processes.

- State Management Overheads: Suboptimal state management can trigger needless component updates.

- Prop Drilling Challenges: Extensive prop drilling complicates maintenance and can cause superfluous re-renders.

4. Streamlining React Performance

Optimizing a React application involves a blend of strategies:

- Leveraging PureComponent and React.memo: These functionalities prevent unnecessary re-renders through shallow comparison techniques.

- Implementing Code Splitting: Breaking down the code into smaller, manageable chunks using React.lazy, Suspense, or dynamic `import()` can dramatically enhance initial loading performance.

- Effective Memoization: Caching expensive function outputs and render results in functional components can avoid unnecessary recalculations.

- Refining Event Handling: Steering clear of inline arrow functions and repeated function creation in the render method can help in reducing performance costs.

5. Optimizing List Rendering and Iterations

Managing list rendering and iterations is crucial, especially with large data sets.

- Key Utilization in Lists: Employing unique and stable keys for list items aids React in optimizing re-rendering processes.

- Applying Windowing Techniques: Using windowing or virtualization libraries like `react-window` or `react-virtualized` can significantly boost the rendering performance of extensive lists.

6. Network and Data Fetching Efficiency

Network interactions and data fetching are pivotal in optimizing React applications.

- Data Loading Strategies: Implementing lazy loading for data and avoiding unnecessary API calls can enhance application responsiveness.

- API Request Optimization: Reducing the frequency and payload of API requests, coupled with effective caching, can decrease network burden and response times.

7. Persistent Performance Enhancement

Ongoing monitoring and optimization are integral to maintaining React application performance.

- Routine Performance Reviews: Regularly assessing performance using suitable tools and metrics is essential.

- Iterative Enhancement based on Feedback: Utilizing insights from performance analysis to make continuous refinements is crucial in addressing emerging performance issues.

Conclusion

Conducting a thorough performance analysis of React applications is a multi-dimensional task. It encompasses a clear comprehension of React's rendering logic, the adept application of analytical tools, recognition of common performance issues, and the employment of various optimization tactics. By concentrating on rendering efficiency, state management, and mindful network interactions, developers can significantly elevate the performance of React applications. Keeping pace with the evolving landscape of React and performance optimization techniques is indispensable for developing high-performing, responsive, and user-friendly web applications.

Advanced optimization techniques

In the dynamic field of software development, advanced optimization techniques are indispensable for ensuring that applications remain efficient, responsive, and resource-effective, particularly as they increase in complexity. These techniques encompass a wide array of practices, from enhancing code and algorithm efficiency to optimizing system architecture and data handling methods.

1. Streamlining Code and Refactoring Practices

Effective code optimization involves modifying source code to boost its performance while maintaining its functionality. Key strategies include:

- Efficient Code Refactoring: Continual code refactoring is essential to improve code clarity and efficiency, which includes eliminating unnecessary code, optimizing loop structures, and streamlining complex functions.

- Optimal Data Type Usage: Employing the most suitable data types and structures, such as choosing the correct data structures (like hash maps or trees) can significantly enhance memory usage and data processing speed.

- Selective Dependency Importing: Minimizing the use of external dependencies and selectively importing functionalities can decrease loading times and enhance application performance.

2. Enhancing Algorithm Performance

Algorithm optimization is vital for data processing, computation, and problem-solving efficiency.

- Reducing Computational Complexity: Implementing algorithms with lower computational complexity can markedly enhance performance.

- Result Caching Techniques: Utilizing caching, such as memoization, to store previously computed results for reuse can minimize redundant calculations in intensive operations.

3. Utilizing Parallel Computing and Asynchronous Methods

Incorporating parallel processing and asynchronous programming is crucial in enhancing application responsiveness and processing speed.

- Concurrency and Multithreading: Employing techniques like multithreading or concurrent processing for simultaneous operations can significantly boost performance.

- Asynchronous Operations for I/O: Implementing non-blocking I/O operations ensures that the main execution thread remains unobstructed, enhancing throughput and application responsiveness.

4. Database Interaction and Query Efficiency

Optimizing data storage and retrieval is critical in applications involving database operations.

- Strategic Database Design: An efficiently structured database with proper indexing and normalization can accelerate data retrieval and reduce storage requirements.

- Query Optimization: Crafting efficient queries, reducing database interactions, and utilizing stored procedures can substantially improve database performance.

5. Memory Management and Efficient Garbage Collection

Proper memory management is crucial to prevent memory leaks and ensure optimal resource utilization.

- Memory Usage Profiling: Regular monitoring of memory usage and identifying leaks are essential for optimal performance.

- Garbage Collection Optimization: Fine-tuning garbage collection processes, especially in languages with automatic memory management, can help maintain performance efficiency.

6. Network Communication Optimization

In network-reliant or distributed systems, optimizing network interactions is key.

- Data Compression Techniques: Compressing data for network transmission and using efficient protocols can lower latency and reduce bandwidth consumption.

- Effective Load Balancing: Employing load balancing can distribute network traffic evenly across servers to prevent overloading and ensure smooth operation.

7. Adaptive Design for Web and Mobile Applications

Responsive design and resource adaptation are critical in web and mobile app optimization.

- Adaptive UI Design: Crafting UIs that adjust to different screen sizes and device capabilities can lead to better resource management and user experiences.

- Conditional Resource Loading: Dynamically loading resources based on device and network conditions can optimize performance and loading efficiency.

8. Leveraging GPU Acceleration and Hardware Capabilities

Utilizing GPU acceleration and optimizing software for specific hardware capabilities can offer substantial performance benefits.

- GPU Processing for Intensive Tasks: Offloading certain tasks to the GPU, especially in graphics or computation-intensive operations, can drastically improve processing speed.

- Hardware-Specific Optimization: Tailoring software to exploit specific hardware features can lead to considerable performance gains.

9. Routine Performance Monitoring and Testing

Continual monitoring and testing are pivotal for sustaining and enhancing application performance.

- Comprehensive Performance Tracking: Implementing performance monitoring tools to track crucial metrics helps in identifying optimization needs.

- Automated Performance Assessments: Regularly conducting automated performance tests ensures optimizations are effective and do not impact the application adversely.

Conclusion

Mastering advanced optimization techniques is vital for the development of high-performing software applications. These methods span from code and algorithm refinement to system architecture adjustments and resource management. Implementing these techniques demands a deep understanding of the application needs, technology stack, and operating environment. Ongoing evaluation, monitoring, and adaptation are key to achieving and maintaining optimum performance in complex software systems. As technological advancements continue, staying updated with the latest optimization strategies and tools remains essential for developers and engineers dedicated to building efficient, scalable, and robust applications.

Chapter Ten

Security Best Practices

Security challenges in React applications

Securing React applications is a crucial aspect of web development, necessitating vigilance and expertise to safeguard against various cybersecurity threats. React, renowned for its efficacy in building interactive user interfaces, is not immune to security vulnerabilities. Developers must be adept at identifying and addressing these vulnerabilities to ensure the integrity and safety of their applications.

1. Guarding Against Cross-Site Scripting (XSS) Attacks

Cross-Site Scripting (XSS) remains one of the most prevalent security threats in web applications, including those built with React.

- React's Built-In XSS Defenses: By default, React escapes strings in JSX, which is a significant defense mechanism against XSS. Nevertheless, vulnerabilities can emerge through misuse of features like dangerouslySetInnerHTML or improper handling of user input.

- Preventative Measures: To combat XSS risks, limit the use of dangerouslySetInnerHTML and always sanitize the content to strip out malicious scripts if its use is unavoidable.

2. Security Risks in Third-Party Dependencies

React apps often incorporate numerous third-party libraries, which can introduce potential security weaknesses.

- Managing Dependencies Safely: Regularly updating libraries to incorporate security fixes is essential. Tools such as npm audit or Snyk can help identify vulnerabilities.

- Assessing Third-Party Code: Exercise caution when integrating external libraries, scrutinizing their security practices through source code reviews and community feedback.

3. Secure Data and State Management

Handling data securely in React apps, particularly sensitive user information, is of paramount importance.

- Prudent State Management: Refrain from storing sensitive data in the application's state. Use encryption for sensitive information and avoid exposing it on the client side.

- Controlled Data Flow: Ensure all data is thoroughly validated and sanitized. Encrypt data as necessary to maintain security.

4. Avoiding Security Misconfigurations

Incorrect security configurations can leave React apps vulnerable.

- Implementing Security Headers: Use headers like Content Security Policy (CSP) and X-Frame-Options to guard against various attacks.

- Proper Environment Settings: Differentiate and correctly configure development, testing, and production environments with appropriate security measures.

5. Counteracting CSRF Attacks

React applications can be susceptible to Cross-Site Request Forgery (CSRF), where unauthorized commands are executed from a trusted user.

- Utilization of CSRF Tokens: Implement and validate anti-CSRF tokens in forms and requests.

- Selecting Secure Libraries: Choose libraries with inherent CSRF protection features, like Axios, for handling data requests.

6. Strengthening Authentication and Authorization Mechanisms

Effective authentication and authorization are critical for securing React applications.

- Implementing Strong Authentication: Utilize reliable authentication methods and handle authentication logic server-side, using protocols like OAuth or JWT.

- Rigorous Authorization Checks: Conduct stringent authorization verifications server-side and avoid relying on client-side checks for access control.

7. Addressing SSR Security Concerns

Applications using React's server-side rendering (SSR) feature must be mindful of specific security issues.

- Mitigating Injection Risks: Be vigilant against injection threats, including SQL and Command Injection, particularly when client-side data is involved in server-side rendering processes.

- Preventing Data Leaks: Carefully manage the transfer of sensitive data in SSR to prevent unintentional exposure to the client.

Conclusion

Maintaining security in React applications encompasses a broad spectrum of considerations, from protecting against XSS to managing third-party dependencies and securing data transactions. React provides certain inherent security benefits, but developers must proactively implement additional protective measures. This involves staying updated on security practices, regularly conducting security audits, and fostering a security-first mindset throughout the development process. Ultimately, ensuring the security of a React application demands a thorough understanding of potential risks and a commitment to ongoing vigilance and adaptation to emerging security challenges.

Preventing common security vulnerabilities

Securing software applications against prevalent vulnerabilities is a critical aspect of modern software development. As the complexity and interconnectivity of applications increase, the likelihood of security breaches also escalates, potentially compromising user data and system integrity. Developers need to be adept at identifying and mitigating these security risks to ensure robust protection against exploitation.

1. Combating Cross-Site Scripting (XSS)

XSS attacks, where malicious scripts are injected into web pages, pose a significant security risk. These attacks can lead to unauthorized data access and other harmful activities.

- Protection Strategies: Key defenses against XSS include thorough sanitization and validation of user input, and implementing Content Security Policy (CSP) headers to define safe sources for executable scripts.

2. Guarding Against SQL Injection (SQLi)

SQLi is a vulnerability where attackers manipulate SQL queries via user input fields, leading to unauthorized database access.

- Defense Mechanisms: Employ parameterized queries or prepared statements for database interactions, ensuring that user inputs are handled safely. Regularly update and patch databases to close off known vulnerabilities.

3. Preventing Cross-Site Request Forgery (CSRF)

CSRF attacks exploit authenticated sessions, tricking users into submitting malicious requests.

- Mitigation Measures: Use anti-CSRF tokens in web forms and validate them server-side. Configure cookies with the 'SameSite' attribute to prevent cross-site cookie transmission.

4. Strengthening Authentication and Authorization

Weak authentication and authorization can lead to unauthorized system access.

- Robust Authentication Systems: Implement strong, multi-factor authentication. Securely store passwords using advanced hashing techniques. Manage sessions securely with appropriate timeouts and session invalidation mechanisms.

- Comprehensive Authorization Verifications: Regularly check and verify user permissions for actions and data access within the application.

5. Addressing Security Misconfigurations

Inadequate configurations can leave applications exposed to attacks.

- Configurations and Updates: Continuously review and optimize security settings. Remove unnecessary functionalities and services. Keep all software elements up-to-date.

6. Protecting Sensitive Data

Exposure of sensitive data, both stored and in transit, is a common concern.

- Encryption Protocols: Encrypt sensitive data using robust encryption standards. Secure data transmissions with HTTPS. Minimize the exposure of sensitive information to users and in logs.

7. Ensuring Robust Access Control

Faulty access control mechanisms can allow unauthorized data access or modification.

- Enforcing Access Policies: Implement strict access control policies and review them regularly. Restrict user access to only those resources necessary for their roles.

8. Mitigating XML External Entities (XXE) Risks

XXE attacks target XML processors to execute unauthorized actions.

- Prevention Techniques: Disable external entity processing in XML configurations. Prefer simpler data formats like JSON, and ensure regular updates for XML processors.

9. Safeguarding Against Insecure Deserialization

Insecure deserialization can enable various attacks, including remote code execution.

- Safe Deserialization Practices: Avoid deserializing data from untrusted sources. Implement integrity checks like digital signatures on serialized objects. Limit the use of serialization as much as possible.

10. Handling Components with Known Vulnerabilities

Using outdated or vulnerable components can open up various attack vectors.

- Vigilant Component Management: Regularly scan and update libraries and components. Use tools to detect and notify about vulnerabilities in dependencies.

11. Enhancing Logging and Monitoring

Effective logging and monitoring are essential for detecting and addressing security breaches.

- Robust Logging Framework: Develop a comprehensive logging system that records access and errors. Monitor logs for unusual activities and ensure the security of the logging infrastructure.

Conclusion

Addressing common security vulnerabilities in software development involves a comprehensive approach that combines secure coding practices, constant vigilance, and regular security audits. Developers and security professionals must collaborate to identify and address security risks, ensuring that applications are not just functional, but also securely fortified. As new security threats emerge and evolve, so should the strategies to defend against them. Continuous education, awareness, and a proactive approach to security are fundamental in safeguarding software applications against evolving cyber threats.

Secure coding practices and strategies

Incorporating secure coding practices into software development is crucial for creating applications that are resilient to cybersecurity threats. With increasing digital vulnerabilities, embedding robust security measures into code is not just beneficial but imperative. These strategies cover various methodologies and guidelines aimed at reinforcing software from initial development phases through deployment and ongoing maintenance.

1. Grasping Core Security Concepts in Coding

Essential to secure coding is understanding prevalent security risks, as outlined by entities like OWASP (Open Web Application Security Project). Developers should be well-versed in typical vulnerabilities such as SQL injection, XSS (Cross-Site Scripting), and CSRF (Cross-Site Request Forgery) to recognize potential exploits in code.

2. Rigorous Input Verification and Cleansing

Effective defense in secure coding involves thorough checking and cleansing of user inputs. All inputs should be assumed as potentially unsafe and undergo stringent checks to confirm they meet expected criteria. Cleansing data is crucial to remove harmful elements, particularly when inputs are used in browsers or for command execution.

3. Safeguarding Against SQL Injection

To combat SQL injection threats, developers should employ parameterized queries or prepared statements. These techniques ensure that inputs are handled safely, reducing the risk of malicious code execution in databases.

4. Strengthening Authentication and Session Handling

Robust authentication mechanisms are vital. This includes enforcing strict password policies, securely hashing passwords, and considering additional authentication factors. Session management should be executed securely, avoiding vulnerabilities like session fixation and exposure.

5. Enforcing Authorization and Access Controls

Robust access control mechanisms are key to ensuring users only access resources they are permitted to. Applying the principle of least privilege is recommended, providing users with the minimum access needed.

6. Implementing Secure Communication Standards

Employing secure communication methods such as HTTPS is critical to protect data during transit. HTTPS encrypts communication, preventing data from being intercepted or altered.

7. Secure Management of Errors and Logs

Handling errors securely means avoiding revealing sensitive system or application details through error messages. Logs should also be managed securely, ensuring no sensitive data is recorded.

8. Mitigating Cross-Site Scripting (XSS) Risks

To defend against XSS, encode data output, particularly when dealing with user-generated content. Although many web frameworks offer automatic encoding, manual encoding practices should also be understood and applied when necessary.

9. Defending Against Cross-Site Request Forgery (CSRF)

To prevent CSRF, utilize anti-CSRF tokens in web forms and validate these tokens server-side. Modern frameworks often include mechanisms to handle CSRF protection.

10. Managing Third-Party Dependencies

Maintaining security in software projects requires vigilant management of third-party libraries and frameworks. Regular updates and scanning for vulnerabilities in these dependencies are essential.

11. Peer Code Reviews and Automated Analysis

Conducting regular code reviews can identify potential security flaws. Static analysis tools can automate the detection of common security issues, integrating into development workflows for early vulnerability identification.

12. Continuous Security Education

Ongoing education in security is vital for developers. Keeping updated with current security threats and best practices can significantly enhance a software's security standing.

13. Integrating Security in Development and Operations (DevSecOps)

Incorporating security into the DevOps process ensures continuous consideration of security aspects throughout the development cycle. This includes automated security testing in CI/CD pipelines and regular security assessments.

Conclusion

Adopting secure coding practices is a fundamental component of modern software development, necessitating a proactive and knowledgeable approach from developers. By integrating these practices, developers can markedly diminish the susceptibility of applications to cyber threats. As technology and security landscapes evolve, so must the methodologies of secure coding. Ongoing education, vigilance, and embedding security into every phase of software development are key to constructing secure, resilient digital applications.

Chapter Eleven

Internationalization and Localization

Making React applications globally accessible

Ensuring that React applications are accessible to a worldwide audience involves a multifaceted approach that extends beyond technical development to include an appreciation for diverse cultures, languages, and accessibility norms. React, widely recognized for its effectiveness in creating interactive user interfaces, offers a robust platform for this task. However, achieving global accessibility necessitates a blend of localization, adherence to accessibility standards, responsive design, performance optimization, and cultural understanding.

1. Facilitating Multilingual and Regional Adaptation

Key to reaching a global audience is the ability to adapt the application for multiple languages and regional differences, a process known as internationalization and localization.

- Language Support Implementation: Leverage libraries like React Intl or i18next to enable multilingual capabilities. These tools aid in managing translations and formatting data to suit local preferences.

- Adapting to Regional Nuances: Account for regional variations, such as different date formats, currency

543

types, and text direction for right-to-left languages like Arabic and Hebrew, and be sensitive to cultural nuances.

2. Adhering to Accessibility Standards

Making the application accessible to all users, including those with disabilities, is vital. Compliance with guidelines like the Web Content Accessibility Guidelines (WCAG) is essential.

- Using Semantic HTML for Accessibility: Employ semantic HTML for improved screen reader compatibility and keyboard navigation.

- Applying ARIA Labels: Utilize ARIA labels for additional context where HTML semantics fall short.

- Ensuring Keyboard-Friendly Navigation: All interactive elements should be accessible via keyboard, with logical navigation order.

- Color and Contrast Considerations: Ensure text has sufficient contrast and avoid using color as the only means of conveying information.

3. Responsive and Adaptive Design

Global accessibility demands that the application performs seamlessly across various devices and screen sizes.

- Creating Adaptable Layouts: Employ CSS techniques like Flexbox or Grid for layouts that adjust to different screens.

- Device-Specific Styling with Media Queries: Use media queries for tailored styling across mobile phones, tablets, and desktops.

4. Enhancing Application Performance

Performance optimization is crucial, especially given the diverse internet speeds and device capabilities globally.

- Speed Optimization Techniques: Implement code splitting, lazy loading, and optimize assets to reduce loading times.

- Effective Use of Caching: Develop caching strategies to quicken load times during repeated access.

5. Cultural Awareness and Inclusivity

Recognizing and respecting cultural differences plays a significant role in global accessibility.

- Inclusive Content Representation: Use images, icons, and content that reflect cultural diversity responsibly and inclusively.

- Culturally Sensitive UI Design: Consider cultural preferences and norms in UI design, including color usage, symbols, and layout structures.

6. Rigorous Global Accessibility Testing

Thorough testing ensures the application's performance and accessibility across various regions.

- Diverse User Testing: Perform testing with a globally diverse user group to gather comprehensive feedback.

- Utilizing Automated and Manual Testing Tools: Employ automated accessibility tools like axe or Lighthouse, supplemented with manual testing for comprehensive coverage.

7. Commitment to Ongoing Learning and Adaptation

Continuously updating knowledge on global accessibility standards and practices is crucial for maintaining and enhancing application accessibility.

- Keeping Up-to-Date: Stay informed about the latest developments in internationalization and accessibility.

- Seeking Continuous Feedback: Regularly solicit user feedback from around the world to refine and improve the application.

Conclusion

Creating globally accessible React applications is a comprehensive endeavor that transcends simple translation, involving thoughtful internationalization, stringent adherence to accessibility guidelines, responsive design, and cultural sensitivity. By embracing these practices, developers can ensure their React applications meet the needs of a diverse global audience. Staying committed to continuous learning and improvement is key to keeping up with evolving technology and user expectations in the realm of global accessibility.

Implementing internationalization (i18n)

Implementing internationalization, commonly referred to as i18n, is a vital process in the development of globally relevant software applications. It involves designing and crafting software in a way that facilitates easy adaptation to various languages and regional nuances without extensive modifications to the core code. This approach not only enhances user engagement but also broadens the application's global reach and appeal.

1. Comprehensive Scope of Internationalization

Internationalization transcends simple text translation, encompassing aspects like adapting to local date and time formats, currency, text direction, and cultural sensitivities. The objective is to separate all region-specific components from the core functionalities of the software.

2. Architecting for International Adaptability

Initial steps in internationalization include creating a design that inherently supports global adaptation:

- Developing a Locale-Independent Codebase: Constructing a codebase that isn't tied to any specific locale is crucial. All user-facing elements such as texts and culturally dependent items should be externalized.

- Modular Architectural Approach: Adopt a modular structure to seamlessly integrate and update internationalization features.

3. Selecting Suitable Tools and Frameworks

Various tools and libraries are available to aid internationalization across different programming environments. In JavaScript and React applications, for instance, libraries like `react-intl` or `i18next` are popular for managing translations and locale-specific formatting.

4. Efficient Management of Locale-Specific Data

Proper management of locale data is essential:

- Externalization of Texts: Store all user-interface texts in external resource files, avoiding hardcoding them in the application code.

- Accommodating Language Variations: Ensure the chosen i18n tool can handle language-specific rules related to plural forms and gender.

5. Multilingual Support

Incorporating multiple language support entails:

- Utilizing Professional Translation Services: For accuracy and cultural appropriateness, professional translation is recommended over automated translation tools.

- Support for RTL Text: If supporting languages like Arabic or Hebrew, ensure the UI can handle right-to-left text direction.

6. Locale-Specific Formatting

Adapt to regional differences in displaying dates, numbers, and currencies. Internationalization libraries typically offer functions to format these elements based on user locale.

7. Rigorous Internationalization Testing

Testing is a critical component of the internationalization process:

- Testing Across Different Locales: Conduct thorough testing in various locales to ensure text is correctly displayed and formatted.

- Pseudo-localization: This involves testing with a simulated language to identify untranslated strings and layout issues.

8. Ongoing Maintenance and Cultural Awareness

Internationalization requires continuous attention:

- Update Translations Regularly: Keep translations up-to-date with evolving application content.

- Monitoring Cultural Dynamics: Stay informed about cultural and regulatory changes in the regions where the application is available.

9. Emphasizing Cultural Relevance and Sensitivity

It's vital to ensure the application is not only linguistically accurate but also culturally attuned and inclusive.

10. Performance Optimization in Internationalization

Address performance impacts:

- Lazy Loading for Locale Data: Implement lazy loading for language files to load only necessary data.

- Optimized Asset Delivery: For applications with extensive locale-specific assets, optimize their delivery for quick loading.

11. Collaborating with Localization Teams

Work in tandem with localization professionals who have deep insights into the target culture and language to ensure the application resonates well with local users.

Conclusion

Internationalization is a strategic endeavor essential for crafting software applications that are globally accessible and relevant. It involves thoughtful planning, using the right tools, detailed implementation, and ongoing updates. Internationalization significantly contributes to making software adaptable and appealing to a diverse, global audience, highlighting its critical role in the realm of modern software development. As the global market and technology landscapes evolve, the emphasis on proficient internationalization in software development continues to heighten, underscoring its importance in achieving worldwide user engagement and satisfaction.

Challenges and best practices in localization

Localizing software for international markets is a complex yet vital process in today's globalized digital landscape. It involves adapting an application to suit the linguistic, cultural, and regulatory specifics of different regions, extending beyond mere translation to encompass a deep understanding of diverse user bases. Despite its potential to broaden an application's reach, localization poses several challenges that demand strategic approaches to ensure effectiveness and cultural relevance.

1. Navigating Linguistic and Cultural Intricacies

A key challenge in localization lies in accurately translating and culturally adapting the content. Each language and cultural context has its subtleties and expressions, which may be lost or misinterpreted in automated translations.

- Best Practices: Utilize native translators who are well-versed in the target culture and language. Adapt not just the language but also consider cultural elements in images, UI design, and color schemes to ensure cultural fit and sensitivity.

2. Overcoming Technical Hurdles

Localization involves various technical considerations, including supporting different character sets, text directions, and local standards for dates, currencies, and measurements.

- Best Practices: Employ Unicode for diverse character support. Design your application's architecture to accommodate text direction variations and localized formats. Rigorous testing is essential to identify and address layout and format issues.

3. Compliance with Regional Laws and Regulations

Different regions have specific requirements regarding data privacy, content regulation, and digital accessibility.

- Best Practices: Stay abreast of and comply with local regulations, such as data protection laws like GDPR. Ensure that the application meets these legal standards in each locale.

4. Managing Scalability and Content Updates

Maintaining localized content can become increasingly complex, especially with frequent updates and multiple language support.

- Best Practices: Develop a scalable and integrated localization process within your development pipeline. Leverage internationalization frameworks and CMS for easier content updates.

5. Ensuring Quality and Cultural Relevance

Maintaining high-quality standards in localized versions is critical to ensure that they are on par with the original.

- Best Practices: Perform comprehensive quality checks, including linguistic, functional, and UI testing. Local testers can provide valuable insights into the cultural and functional appropriateness of the localized application.

6. Tailoring User Experience for Local Markets

Providing a localized user experience that truly resonates with the target audience requires more than translation; it necessitates an understanding of cultural nuances and user expectations.

- Best Practices: Conduct local market research to grasp user preferences and cultural contexts. Customize content, design, and user interactions to meet local expectations and norms.

7. Efficient Resource Utilization and Cost Management

Localization can be resource-intensive, posing challenges, particularly for smaller organizations.

- Best Practices: Focus on key markets aligned with business objectives. Consider efficient localization methods, such as community-driven translations, for certain aspects.

8. Collaborative Efforts Across Teams

Successful localization requires effective collaboration among developers, translators, and stakeholders.

- Best Practices: Establish clear communication channels and collaborative workflows. Utilize tools that facilitate easy sharing and updating of localized content.

9. Adapting to Local Market Dynamics

Keeping up with evolving trends and preferences in different regions is essential for the continued relevance of localized versions.

- Best Practices: Continuously gather user feedback and market intelligence. Be agile in making adjustments based on evolving local trends.

10. Extending Localization to Marketing and Support

Effective localization also encompasses marketing materials, user documentation, and customer support.

- Best Practices: Localize all user-facing materials and ensure customer support is available in the local language, providing a holistic user experience.

Conclusion

Addressing the challenges of localization requires a multifaceted strategy, blending linguistic accuracy with cultural empathy, technical adaptability, and legal compliance. By tackling these aspects, developers can ensure their applications are not only functionally robust but also culturally resonant in diverse markets. As the demand for localized digital experiences grows, the role of strategic localization in software development becomes increasingly integral to engaging and expanding global user communities.

Chapter Twelve

Advanced React Patterns

Higher-order components, render props, and hooks in-depth

In the realm of React development, Higher-order Components (HOCs), Render Props, and Hooks stand as pivotal constructs that empower developers to craft reusable, efficient, and elegant code. These elements are central to enhancing functionality and composition within React applications, each offering unique approaches to common development challenges.

1. Higher-Order Components (HOCs)

HOCs are a pattern in React that allows for component logic reuse. Essentially, they are functions that take a component and return a new component with augmented functionalities.

- Usage and Advantages: HOCs are typically used for repetitive tasks like data fetching, context handling, or conditional rendering. They facilitate the modularization of common functionalities, enhancing code reusability and separation of concerns.

- Example in Practice: Redux's `connect` function is a classic example, linking a React component to the Redux store.

- Potential Complications: Despite their utility, HOCs can introduce complexity, particularly in debugging, and may lead to issues like prop name clashes.

2. Render Props Pattern

Render Props refer to a technique in React where a component's children are a function. This function as a child pattern allows components to share logic and state in a flexible manner.

- Usage and Advantages: This approach is highly useful in scenarios where the rendering of a component needs to be decoupled from its behavioral logic. It offers significant flexibility in component rendering.

- Typical Example: A data-fetching component that passes its data to children via a render prop is a common implementation.

- Considerations: Render Props can lead to nested and potentially less readable component structures.

3. Hooks in React

With React 16.8, Hooks have revolutionized functional component development, allowing state and other React features to be used in these components.

- State Management via `useState`: This Hook introduces state handling capability to functional components.

- Handling Side Effects with `useEffect`: Used for executing side effects in functional components, this Hook has become integral in modern React apps.

- Crafting Custom Hooks: Developers can create their own Hooks for encapsulating stateful logic, promoting logic reuse and component simplicity.

Advantages of Using Hooks:

- Code Simplification: Hooks simplify the process of managing state and lifecycle features in class components.

- Better Reusability and Composition: Custom Hooks are a boon for reusing stateful logic across multiple components.

- Ease of Testing and Organization: Hooks enhance the testability and isolation of components and logic.

4. Selecting the Appropriate Construct

When choosing among HOCs, Render Props, and Hooks, the decision should be based on the application's specific requirements:

- HOCs for Broad Abstractions: Ideal for enhancing components with added data or functionality.

- Render Props for Rendering Control: Best when the focus is on separating a component's rendering from its logic.

- Hooks for State Management and Effects: The preferred choice for managing state and lifecycle features in functional components.

Conclusion

Higher-order Components, Render Props, and Hooks each offer significant benefits for managing state, side effects, and logic sharing in React applications. While HOCs are suited for adding extra features to components, Render Props provide greater control over component rendering, and Hooks bring a more intuitive approach to state management and lifecycle methods. Understanding the appropriate usage of these constructs is crucial for building effective, clean, and maintainable React applications. As React continues to mature, these concepts remain integral to its ecosystem, underscoring the library's commitment to versatile and composable user interface development.

Context API for complex state management

In the sphere of React development, adeptly managing complex state is essential for crafting applications that are both scalable and easy to maintain. The introduction of the Context API in React 16.3 has been a game-changer in this regard, offering a streamlined approach to state management that is particularly useful in avoiding the pitfalls of prop drilling.

1. The Essence of the Context API

The Context API in React serves as a means to transmit state across the component tree in a more direct and efficient manner. This method allows for the sharing of states like user settings, themes, or authentication data across various component levels, bypassing the need for prop drilling.

2. Operational Mechanics of the Context API

Utilizing the Context API involves several steps:

- Context Creation: Through `**React.createContext()**`, a Context object is established, comprising both a Provider and a Consumer component.

- Provider Role: The Provider component wraps around the root component, holding the state that needs to be shared, and can pass it down through the component tree.

- Consumer Usage: The Consumer component, or the `**useContext**` hook in functional components, is used to access the state from the nearest Provider.

3. Addressing the Prop Drilling Challenge

Prop drilling, the process of passing props through various component layers, often complicates code and leads to inefficient re-rendering. The Context API offers a centralized approach to managing shared state, simplifying this process.

4. Practical Applications of the Context API

Ideal use cases for the Context API include scenarios where certain states or functionalities are needed across many components, such as user authentication data, theme settings, or language preferences.

5. Implementing the Context API

To effectively implement the Context API:

- Define the Context: Establish a new Context for the specific state you want to distribute.

- Setting Up the Provider: Encase your component hierarchy with the Context Provider, passing along the state to be shared.

- Accessing the Context: Either use the Context Consumer or the `useContext` hook in functional components to tap into the shared state.

6. Context API Usage Guidelines

While powerful, the Context API should be used judiciously:

- Limit Usage: Utilize the Context API sparingly to avoid complications in component reuse and refactoring. Keep the Context close to its consumers.

- Encapsulating State Logic: Centralize state logic within the Provider for a cleaner and simpler Consumer interface.

- Optimize for Performance: Be aware of re-rendering issues and optimize as necessary.

7. Comparing Context API with Other State Management Libraries

The emergence of the Context API has led to comparisons with other state management libraries:

- State Management Libraries Like Redux: These remain relevant for managing more intricate application states, offering robust features like debugging tools and middleware support.

- Context API's Niche: The Context API is particularly effective for simpler state management requirements where ease of use is a priority.

8. Amplifying with Hooks

The advent of Hooks in React has further enhanced the capabilities of the Context API. The `useContext` hook simplifies accessing context values in functional components, leading to more concise and readable code.

Conclusion

The Context API has marked a significant stride in React's state management capabilities, particularly for scenarios where traditional prop drilling is inefficient. It fosters easier state sharing across components, enhancing the maintainability and scalability of the codebase. While not a complete substitute for more comprehensive state management solutions in all scenarios, the Context API, especially when combined with React Hooks, provides a streamlined and effective option for managing shared state in web applications. Its role in React's evolution underscores the library's commitment to offering developers powerful tools for creating dynamic and user-friendly interfaces.

Reconciliation and virtual DOM deep dive

Reconciliation and the Virtual DOM are pivotal concepts in React, playing a crucial role in how modern web applications are constructed and managed. These key concepts are instrumental in optimizing the way user interfaces are updated, making React highly efficient and performant.

1. Delving into the Virtual DOM

The Virtual DOM is essentially a lightweight representation of the actual Document Object Model (DOM). It exists as an abstraction layer in memory, managed by React, and is used to optimize interactions with the actual DOM, traditionally known for being resource-heavy and slow for direct manipulations.

2. The Functionality of the Virtual DOM

The Virtual DOM's primary function is to enhance application performance. By reducing the number of direct DOM manipulations, React ensures a more efficient and smoother update process.

- Consolidated Updates: React accumulates changes in the Virtual DOM before applying them, minimizing the frequency of direct DOM interactions.

- Efficient Comparison Mechanism: A diffing algorithm in the Virtual DOM identifies necessary updates, comparing the new virtual tree with the previous one to determine the exact changes needed in the actual DOM.

3. The Reconciliation Mechanism

Reconciliation is React's method of syncing the Virtual DOM with the actual DOM, ensuring the UI reflects the current application state.

- Change Detection: Upon state or props alteration in a component, React constructs a new Virtual DOM tree and compares it with the preceding version.

- Selective DOM Updates: The diffing algorithm pinpoints the minimal updates required, enhancing performance and user experience.

- Actual DOM Synchronization: React then applies these determined changes to the real DOM, maintaining UI consistency.

4. Insights into the Diffing Algorithm

React's diffing algorithm optimizes the reconciliation process using heuristic techniques:

- Handling Element Type Alterations: A change in element types (like `<div>` to `<p>`) leads to a complete rebuild of that element's subtree.

- Key Utilization in Lists: React leverages keys in lists to efficiently track item modifications, insertions, or deletions.

- Comparisons at the Component Level: The algorithm assumes different component types will produce distinct trees, avoiding cross-type comparisons.

5. Challenges Associated with the Virtual DOM

While the Virtual DOM and reconciliation process offer significant advantages, they also present certain challenges:

- Memory Overhead: The Virtual DOM can be resource-intensive, particularly in large-scale applications.

- Algorithmic Limitations: The diffing algorithm, while efficient, may not always yield the most optimal change set due to its heuristic nature.

6. Optimal Performance Practices

To leverage the Virtual DOM and reconciliation effectively:

- Strategic Use of Keys: Employ stable and unique keys for list items to facilitate accurate and efficient item re-rendering.

- Minimizing Unnecessary Rerenders: Utilize mechanisms like **`shouldComponentUpdate`**, **`React.memo`**, or **`useMemo`** to control component updates and avoid needless rerendering.

- Embracing Immutable Data: Immutable data structures can assist React in quickly identifying state changes, streamlining the reconciliation process.

Conclusion

The concepts of the Virtual DOM and reconciliation are fundamental to the efficiency of React in rendering user interfaces. These mechanisms allow for sophisticated management of UI updates, ensuring React applications are dynamic, responsive, and performant. Understanding and effectively applying these concepts is crucial for developers to fully harness the power of React in web application development. As React continues to evolve, the Virtual DOM and reconciliation remain central to its success and popularity in the developer community for creating cutting-edge web applications.

Chapter Thirteen

React in Monorepos

Managing large-scale projects with Monorepos

Monorepos, a strategy for managing extensive and interconnected projects within a single repository, have emerged as a practical approach in large-scale software development. This methodology, which consolidates multiple codebases into one repository, stands in contrast to traditional multi-repo approaches where each project or module is maintained separately. The adoption of monorepos brings distinct advantages as well as challenges that necessitate strategic management and tooling.

1. Monorepo Fundamentals

A monorepo (monolithic repository) is a strategy in software development where a single repository houses the code for several projects. This can range from small libraries to entire applications, offering a centralized version control system for a diverse range of projects.

2. Advantages of Adopting Monorepos

- Streamlined Dependency Handling: Monorepos simplify the management of dependencies across projects, allowing immediate application of changes to shared resources and ensuring consistency.

- Consolidated Version Control: A single repository for multiple projects simplifies the tracking of changes and version history, aiding in comprehensive change management and audits.

- Enhanced Collaboration and Reusability: Monorepos foster an environment where code reuse and team collaboration are more straightforward, as developers have access to shared components and utilities.

- Unified CI/CD Processes: Implementing CI/CD for multiple projects within a monorepo can lead to more uniform and efficient build and deployment practices.

3. Challenges in Monorepo Environments

Despite their benefits, monorepos present specific challenges that require careful navigation:

- Handling Repository Size: As the repository grows, performance issues such as longer times for cloning or pulling can arise.

- Complex Build Configurations: Managing builds for multiple projects within a monorepo can get complicated, demanding advanced build tools and setup.

- Access Control Complexity: Implementing detailed access controls in a monorepo, especially in multi-team scenarios, can be more challenging compared to separate repositories for each project.

4. Effective Monorepo Management Practices

To effectively manage monorepos, certain practices and tools are recommended:

- Tool Selection: Opt for tools specifically tailored for monorepos, such as Bazel, Lerna, or Yarn Workspaces, to manage dependencies and testing efficiently.

- Modular Organization: Keep the codebase modular, clearly demarcating different projects or packages while allowing shared dependency management.

- Optimized CI/CD Setup: Configure CI/CD pipelines to selectively build and test projects based on the scope of changes, preventing unnecessary processes.

- Code Ownership and Access Rules: Establish clear rules for code ownership and access, ensuring code integrity and security, particularly in environments with multiple development teams.

5. Monorepos in Practical Scenarios

Monorepos are especially useful in settings where:

- Projects Share Common Dependencies: Efficiently manage shared libraries or services across multiple projects within the same repository.

- Large Teams Work on Related Projects: Encourage collaboration and code sharing among large teams working on interconnected parts of larger projects.

- Rapid Iteration Across Projects Is Needed: Facilitate quick, cross-project modifications without juggling multiple repositories.

6. Industry Adoption of Monorepos

Notable tech giants like Google, Facebook, and Twitter utilize monorepos to handle their expansive codebases, showcasing the approach's scalability and efficiency in managing large-scale projects.

Conclusion

Monorepos present a viable option for handling large-scale, complex projects, offering streamlined dependency management, improved collaboration, and unified version control. However, their successful implementation hinges on thoughtful consideration of the tools, infrastructure, and practices necessary to manage the challenges unique to this approach. For organizations with multiple, interdependent projects and large development teams, monorepos can significantly enhance operational efficiency and development speed. The decision to adopt a monorepo strategy should be based on a careful evaluation of its advantages and drawbacks in the context of the organization's specific project requirements and team structures.

Tools like Lerna and Yarn Workspaces

In contemporary software development, particularly in handling monorepos, tools such as Lerna and Yarn

Workspaces have become critical. These tools facilitate the management of projects with multiple interrelated packages, significantly easing the development process in expansive and intricate projects. A deeper understanding of how these tools operate and their unique advantages is crucial for developers aiming to enhance their productivity in multifaceted development environments.

1. Lerna: Enhancing Monorepo Workflows

Lerna stands out as a tool specifically tailored to improve the management of monorepos, which contain multiple npm packages. It simplifies several key aspects such as versioning, dependency management, and the publishing process.

- Principal Features and Capabilities:

  - Versioning Automation: Lerna automates version control for packages, identifying which ones need updates based on recent changes, thus streamlining the release cycle.

  - Dependency Symlinking: It creates links for interdependent packages within a monorepo, allowing immediate reflection of changes across all reliant packages.

  - Efficiency with Large Repositories: Lerna is adept at managing large repositories containing multiple packages, aiding in handling complex project structures.

- Typical Scenarios for Use:

  - Multi-package Publishing: Lerna eases the process of releasing multiple packages to npm, addressing the intricacies of versioning and interdependencies.

  - Unified Project Management: It enables centralized handling of issues, version control, and collaborative elements, promoting consistency and collaboration.

2. Yarn Workspaces: Streamlining Dependency Handling

Yarn Workspaces, part of the Yarn package manager, is integral for efficient dependency management in monorepos. It is known for its effectiveness in managing package dependencies within large-scale projects.

- Core Features and Functions:

  - Consolidated Node Modules: Yarn Workspaces enable sharing of a single node_modules directory amongst various packages, enhancing installation speed and reducing disk space usage.

  - Dependency Management Efficiency: It ensures a unified version of a package is installed across all workspace packages, solving version conflicts and decreasing redundancy.

  - Integration with Yarn's Ecosystem: As an element of Yarn, it benefits from Yarn's performance strengths, such as accelerated package installation and resolution.

- Ideal Usage Scenarios:

  - Projects with Shared Dependencies: Yarn Workspaces is highly effective in environments where numerous packages share a substantial amount of dependencies.

  - Simplifying Complex Project Structures: It reduces the complexity involved in setting up and maintaining large-scale projects by optimizing dependency management.

3. Combining Lerna and Yarn Workspaces

Lerna and Yarn Workspaces are often used together to harness the strengths of both. While Yarn Workspaces deals with dependency installation and linkage, Lerna manages versioning and package publishing.

- Synergistic Functionality: The combined use of Yarn Workspaces for efficient dependency management and Lerna for versioning and publishing provides a comprehensive toolset for managing extensive monorepo projects.

- Enhanced Workflow Efficiency: This integration significantly streamlines the development process, automating many routine tasks associated with multi-package management.

4. Optimizing Usage of Lerna and Yarn Workspaces

For optimal use of Lerna and Yarn Workspaces:

- Structured Repository Organization: Maintain a clear separation between individual packages while allowing shared configurations and dependencies where suitable.

- Keeping Tools Updated: Regularly update both Lerna and Yarn to leverage the latest features and enhancements.

- Integrating with CI/CD Processes: Embed these tools into your CI/CD pipelines to automate testing, building, and deploying processes within the monorepo.

Conclusion

Lerna and Yarn Workspaces have markedly simplified the challenges associated with managing monorepos. By offering effective solutions for multi-package management within a single repository, they empower developers to efficiently maintain large-scale, complex projects. The combination of Lerna's versioning and publishing focus with Yarn Workspaces' dependency management prowess makes them an invaluable pair in modern software development practices. As software development continues to evolve, the significance of tools that can adeptly manage elaborate project structures grows, placing Lerna and Yarn Workspaces at the forefront of this developmental shift.

Best practices for code sharing and dependency management

In the dynamic field of software development, adept code sharing and meticulous dependency management are pivotal for crafting robust, scalable applications. Implementing best practices in these realms not only streamlines the development workflow but also minimizes the likelihood of bugs and incompatibility issues, particularly in complex, collaborative projects.

1. Effective Practices for Code Sharing

Code sharing, the practice of reusing code in various parts of an application or across multiple projects, is crucial for ensuring code consistency and reducing redundancies.

- Embracing Modular Architecture: Adopt a modular approach in your codebase. Design functions, classes, and components to be independent and reusable.

- Package Manager Utilization: Employ package managers such as npm or Yarn in JavaScript environments to facilitate code sharing. Develop and maintain internal libraries or packages for use across various projects.

- Unified Coding Standards: Establish and maintain consistent coding standards across your team to guarantee that shared code remains accessible and maintainable for everyone.

- Comprehensive Documentation: Keep detailed documentation for shared code segments to aid other

574

developers in understanding and using these modules effectively.

2. Strategies for Efficient Dependency Management

Managing external libraries or packages that a project relies on is a key aspect of dependency management.

- Judicious Dependency Selection: Carefully assess the need and stability of external dependencies. Opt for libraries that are well-documented, actively maintained, and backed by a strong community.

- Regular Dependency Updates: Consistently update your dependencies to incorporate security patches, bug fixes, and performance enhancements, ensuring thorough testing for compatibility.

- Semantic Versioning Adherence: Stick to semantic versioning principles when upgrading dependencies to prevent issues arising from incompatibilities.

- Lockfile Implementation: Use lockfiles like `**package-lock.json**` or `**yarn.lock**` to ensure uniform dependency installations across different environments.

- Security Audits of Dependencies: Periodically conduct security checks on your dependencies using tools like npm audit or Snyk to identify and address vulnerabilities.

3. Integrating Monorepos in Multi-package Projects

For projects encompassing multiple interdependent packages, a monorepo approach can be beneficial. Tools such as Lerna and Yarn Workspaces can efficiently manage such setups.

- Business Logic Segregation: Separate core business logic into distinct services or modules to streamline both code sharing and dependency management.

- Workflow Automation: Employ automation for updating and auditing dependencies, utilizing Continuous Integration (CI) tools to manage these tasks effectively.

- Code Review and Quality Assurance Processes: Enforce rigorous code reviews and quality checks for shared code and updates in dependencies to ensure overall code integrity and stability.

4. Leveraging CI/CD for Code and Dependency Management

CI/CD pipelines are integral in maintaining effective code sharing and dependency management, facilitating automated testing and deployment.

- Automated Testing Integration: Configure CI/CD pipelines to automatically test shared code and new dependency integrations, ensuring seamless functionality.

- Streamlined Automated Deployment: Ensure that automated deployment processes are in place for correctly deploying and integrating shared packages across various projects or services.

Conclusion

Adhering to best practices in code sharing and dependency management is crucial for developing high-quality, efficient software, especially in team-based and large-scale project settings. By implementing modular design, prudent dependency management, consistent coding standards, and leveraging automation and CI/CD tools, development teams can ensure a more efficient and risk-averse workflow. As software development complexities continue to evolve, the importance of effective code sharing and dependency management grows, directly influencing the success and quality of software projects.

Chapter Fourteen

React with Microservices and Micro-

frontends

Architecture patterns for microservices

In today's software architecture landscape, microservices have become a dominant framework, especially for businesses aiming to boost their agility, scalability, and continuous deployment for complex, large-scale applications. Microservices architecture divides applications into smaller, self-sufficient services, each functioning in its own process and communicating typically via HTTP-based APIs. For organizations to fully utilize microservices, it's essential to implement effective architecture patterns.

1. Decentralized Control and Data Management

The microservices approach is built on the foundation of decentralized control, granting teams the autonomy to select the most suitable technologies and design patterns for their specific service needs. This independence fosters innovation and expedites development.

- Data Independence: Each microservice manages its own data and state, steering clear of complex shared data structures. This approach typically involves a database per service, promoting loose coupling and independent scaling.

- Polyglot Approaches: Microservices can utilize varied database systems (polyglot persistence) and programming languages (polyglot programming), tailoring their choices to their specific functionalities.

2. Utilizing API Gateways

An API gateway serves as the primary entry point into the system for client requests. It directs requests to the appropriate microservice and addresses broad concerns such as authentication, SSL termination, and rate limiting.

- Streamlining Service Communication: The API gateway can effectively translate between web-friendly and internal communication protocols.

- Unified Response Handling: It can also combine responses from various microservices, delivering a cohesive response to the client.

3. Service Discovery Approaches

Microservices necessitate dynamic discovery and interaction among themselves, which can be achieved through two principal patterns:

- Client-Side Discovery: Here, clients consult a service registry, which tracks all active service instances and their locations, and then directly communicate with the needed services.

- Server-Side Discovery: In this approach, clients send requests to a router that queries the service registry and forwards the request to an available service.

4. Circuit Breaker Mechanism

The circuit breaker pattern is vital in a microservices framework to prevent failures in one network or service from impacting others. When calls to a microservice fail repeatedly, the circuit breaker trips, diverting calls to a fallback mechanism to maintain system stability.

5. Communication Strategies

Microservices can communicate synchronously (through protocols like HTTP, REST, gRPC) or asynchronously (via messaging queues like RabbitMQ or Kafka). Asynchronous communication, known for its loose coupling and resilience, is often preferred.

- Event-Driven Structures: Many microservice architectures adopt an event-driven approach, where services communicate via events instead of direct requests, enhancing scalability and responsiveness.

6. Embracing Containerization and Management

Microservices are often deployed in containers, which provide streamlined, consistent environments for their execution.

- Docker for Containerization: Docker is commonly used to containerize microservices, encapsulating them for consistent development.

- Kubernetes for Orchestration: Kubernetes is employed for automating the deployment, scaling, and operation of containerized applications, essential for managing microservices efficiently.

7. Monitoring and Observability

In the distributed setup of microservices, effective monitoring and observability are crucial.

- Centralized Logging and Tracing: Implementing centralized logging and distributed tracing is key for tracking transactions and diagnosing issues across multiple services.

- Monitoring Tools: Tools like Prometheus, Grafana, or the ELK Stack are employed for monitoring the health and performance of microservices.

8. Integrating DevOps and Continuous Processes

Microservices align closely with DevOps, particularly in continuous integration and continuous delivery (CI/CD), automating the testing and deployment of individual services.

- Independent Service Deployment: Microservices enable updates to be deployed independently, without the need to redeploy the entire application, facilitating continuous delivery.

9. Security Strategies

In a microservices setup, security must be enforced at each service level.

- Secure Inter-Service Communication: Implement protocols like OAuth, JWT (JSON Web Tokens), or mutual TLS for secure communication between services.

- Fortifying the API Gateway: Secure the gateway with mechanisms such as API keys, rate limiting, and IP whitelisting.

Conclusion

Adopting a microservices architecture goes beyond merely breaking down an application into smaller components. It requires a holistic approach that includes decentralized governance, resilient communication patterns, and advanced containerization and orchestration strategies, coupled with robust monitoring and security measures. While microservices offer significant advantages in flexibility and scalability, they also bring complexities that must be expertly managed. Understanding and implementing appropriate architectural patterns is key to effectively leveraging microservices for developing modern, scalable, and robust applications.

Building and integrating micro-frontends

Micro-frontends, a concept borrowed from the microservices architecture in backend development, involve segmenting a front-end application into smaller, independently manageable units. This approach enables distinct parts of a web application to be crafted, tested, and deployed autonomously, greatly benefiting scalability, adaptability, and the pace of development.

1. The Essence of Micro-Frontends

Micro-frontends are a design strategy where a web application is segmented into numerous "micro-apps." Each of these functions as a semi-independent entity within the larger application, allowing for independent development, testing, and deployment. This methodology is particularly advantageous in extensive projects with several development teams.

2. Advantages of Micro-Frontends

- Team Independence: Teams gain the autonomy to work on distinct sections of the application, reducing inter-team dependencies and accelerating development.

- Scalable Architecture: Individual micro-frontends can scale independently, optimizing resource use and performance.

- Technological Flexibility: Teams have the liberty to select the most suitable technologies for their segment of the application, fostering innovation.

- Simplified Maintenance and Updates: Smaller and more focused codebases are inherently easier to manage and update.

3. Architectural Approaches in Micro-Frontends

Various architectural models exist for implementing micro-frontends:

- Build-Time Integration: This model compiles micro-frontends into a unified bundle during the build phase, enhancing performance but limiting independent deployments.

- Server-Side Composition: Servers dynamically assemble pages from different micro-frontends, which is beneficial for SEO and initial load times.

- Client-Side Composition: Micro-frontends are loaded and merged in the browser, maximizing team autonomy and allowing for separate deployments.

4. Effective Integration of Micro-Frontends

Integrating micro-frontends demands strategic planning, particularly in their communication and data sharing methods:

- Seamless Interoperability: Ensure that micro-frontends can communicate effectively, especially in browser-based compositions, possibly through shared state management or messaging systems.

- Managing Shared Dependencies: Handle common dependencies efficiently to prevent redundancy and conflicts, ensuring shared libraries are loaded singularly for all micro-frontends.

- Versioning and Backward Compatibility: Employ consistent version control and maintain backward compatibility to avoid issues during independent updates of micro-frontends.

5. Challenges and Key Considerations

Micro-frontends offer numerous benefits but also pose certain challenges:

- Performance Concerns: The architecture can lead to performance issues due to additional network requests and JavaScript execution.

- Complex Team Coordination: Coordinating between multiple teams becomes intricate, necessitating well-defined communication channels and planning.

- Unified User Experience: Achieving a cohesive user experience across diverse micro-frontends demands shared design systems and style consistency.

6. Best Practices for Micro-Frontend Development

Adopt these best practices to maximize the effectiveness of micro-frontends:

- Consistent Design System: Implement a unified design system for consistent UI across all micro-frontends.

- Coherent State Management: Develop a clear strategy for managing state and data flow across the micro-frontends.

- Focus on Performance Optimization: Continuously monitor and optimize performance, particularly by minimizing bundle sizes and improving load strategies.

- Comprehensive Testing and Deployment Pipelines: Set up thorough testing and CI/CD processes to handle the complexities of multiple deployable segments.

7. Supporting Frameworks and Tools

A range of tools and frameworks can aid in developing and integrating micro-frontends:

- Webpack 5's Module Federation: A feature in Webpack 5 that allows real-time sharing of modules, useful in a micro-frontends setup.

- Single-SPA Framework: A JavaScript framework that enables different front-end frameworks to coexist smoothly on a single page.

- Tailor Library: A tool for server-side integration of micro-frontends.

Conclusion

Micro-frontends mark a significant shift in front-end development, providing a scalable and efficient way to manage and evolve sizeable web applications. By enabling teams to independently develop, select technology stacks, and deploy their segments, micro-frontends can considerably enhance development agility and efficiency. Nonetheless, this strategy demands thoughtful consideration of integration, resource sharing, overall application performance, and user experience consistency. As with any architectural model, the decision to implement micro-frontends should be based on the specific needs and context of each project.

Orchestrating services in large applications

Orchestrating services in extensive applications is a critical component of contemporary software architecture. This practice involves coordinating the interactions and dependencies of diverse services within an application, particularly in settings like microservices architectures. Proper orchestration is vital for ensuring these services collaborate effectively, which is key to achieving robustness, scalability, and maintainability in applications.

1. Importance of Service Orchestration

In complex applications, such as those using microservices, multiple services must communicate and function together efficiently. Service orchestration is about managing these services and their interactions in an organized way. It is crucial for ensuring operational efficiency, reliability, and scalability.

2. Service Orchestration Strategies

There are various methods to orchestrate services in large applications:

- Centralized Orchestration: Involves a central orchestrator or engine that oversees service interactions. This central entity initiates and controls service processes and manages the request flow and dependencies.

- Decentralized Orchestration: Here, the orchestration logic is distributed across the services themselves. Each service independently manages its interactions and workflows, resulting in more autonomous operations.

587

3. Challenges in Orchestrating Services

Orchestrating services in large applications presents specific challenges:

- Complexity of Management: Coordinating a growing number of services increases complexity.

- Handling Service Dependencies: Managing the dependencies among services, particularly in a microservices setup, can be difficult.

- Resilience and Recovery: It's crucial for the system to be resilient to failures and capable of recovering from them.

4. Best Practices for Orchestrating Services

To effectively orchestrate services in large applications, certain best practices are essential:

- Design for Loose Coupling: Aim for services that are loosely coupled but functionally cohesive to simplify orchestration.

- Automation of Workflows: Automate regular tasks to minimize manual errors and improve efficiency.

- Use Scalable Tools: Employ orchestration tools like Kubernetes or Docker Swarm for containerized services, which provide powerful mechanisms for deploying, scaling, and managing applications.

- Implement Monitoring and Logging: Set up thorough monitoring and logging to track service interactions and performance.

- Plan for Failures: Develop systems that handle failures gracefully, using strategies like circuit breakers and fallbacks to maintain stability.

5. Orchestrating Microservices

In a microservices architecture, orchestrating services is particularly crucial:

- Dynamic Service Discovery: Use service discovery mechanisms for services to locate and interact with each other.

- API Gateway Implementation: Utilize API gateways for routing service requests to the appropriate microservices.

- Effective Load Balancing: Implement load balancing to distribute requests across services, optimizing resource use and avoiding service strain.

6. Integration with CI/CD

Integrating service orchestration with CI/CD processes can enhance automation and streamline the integration and deployment of services:

- Automate Service Deployment: Incorporate service deployment into CI/CD pipelines for quicker and error-free deployments.

- Automated Rollbacks: Set up mechanisms for automatic rollbacks in case of deployment issues.

7. Security in Service Orchestration

Maintaining security is a key aspect of orchestrating services:

- Secure Service Communication: Ensure secure communication channels between services, using encryption and secure protocols.

- Robust Access Controls: Establish strong access controls to regulate service access and protect sensitive data.

Conclusion

Orchestrating services in large-scale applications is a complex yet indispensable task that ensures the coordinated functioning of various services. By adhering to best practices in service design, leveraging powerful orchestration tools, and integrating with CI/CD pipelines, organizations can manage their service ecosystems effectively. In microservices architectures, this orchestration is essential to balance the independence of individual services with the overall application's efficiency and coherence. As software systems continue to expand in scope and complexity, proficient service orchestration remains crucial in developing responsive, scalable, and resilient applications.

Chapter Fifteen

Future Trends and Technologies

Upcoming features in React and ecosystem

React, a prominent JavaScript library for crafting user interfaces, is on a continuous trajectory of innovation and enhancement. For developers and organizations vested in creating cutting-edge web applications, keeping up with the latest developments in React and its surrounding ecosystem is essential. These advancements generally aim to boost performance, refine the development experience, and expand the functional scope of the library.

1. Concurrent Mode on the Horizon

A major feature in the pipeline for React is Concurrent Mode. This mode is poised to transform the way React renders and updates the UI, enabling the library to handle multiple tasks in parallel.

- Interruptible Rendering: Concurrent Mode will permit React to pause a rendering process to prioritize more pressing updates, such as user interactions, enhancing responsiveness.

- Enhanced Resource Utilization: This mode is designed to optimize CPU usage by managing the priority of updates, which is particularly beneficial for complex applications with intensive rendering demands.

2. Expanding Suspense to Data Fetching

React's Suspense, currently utilized for code splitting, is anticipated to extend to encompass data fetching. This extension is set to revolutionize the handling of asynchronous operations in React apps.

- Simplified Asynchronous Data Handling: Suspense for data fetching is expected to streamline managing loading states and asynchronous data within React components.

- Integration with Data-Fetching Libraries: The feature is designed to work seamlessly with prominent data-fetching libraries, offering a more cohesive approach to asynchronous data management.

3. Server Components Introduction

React Server Components, an upcoming innovation, aims to refine how components are rendered and delivered. Rendered on the server, these components are sent to the client as minimal, interactive UI elements.

- Client-Side JavaScript Reduction: Server Components can significantly decrease the JavaScript footprint on the client side, improving loading times and overall performance.

- Fluid Integration with Client-Side Components: Designed for smooth integration with client-side components, these server components provide a versatile architecture for dynamic applications.

4. Advancements in the Hooks API

Since its introduction in React 16.8, the Hooks API has been transformative, and further enhancements to this API are on the horizon.

- Introduction of New Hooks: Future releases may include new hooks to address additional use cases and simplify common functional component tasks.

- Optimization of Existing Hooks: Continued improvements to existing hooks, such as `useState` and `useEffect`, are anticipated to focus on performance and ease of use.

5. Progress in React Native

React Native, used for building native mobile apps using React, is also slated for significant updates.

- Fabric: A New Architecture: This new architecture, known as Fabric, is directed at boosting performance and responsiveness in React Native apps.

- TurboModules for Enhanced Efficiency: This feature is expected to improve the interaction between JavaScript and native modules, providing more robust native functionalities.

6. Enhanced Developer Tools and Ecosystem

- Elevated Development Experience: Upcoming versions of React are likely to emphasize an improved experience for developers, with more intuitive tools and enhanced error handling.

- Deeper Integration with Development Environments: Expect better integration with popular development tools and IDEs, offering improved debugging and testing capabilities.

7. Augmented TypeScript Support

With the rising adoption of TypeScript, future versions of React are poised to offer enhanced support, facilitating the development of strongly-typed applications and components.

8. Expansion of the React Ecosystem

The React ecosystem, encompassing state management libraries, routing solutions, and UI component frameworks, is expected to evolve further, with libraries like Redux, React Router, and Material-UI introducing new functionalities and optimizations.

9. Focus on Accessibility Features

A key area of focus is accessibility, with future releases aiming to introduce additional features and improvements to make React applications more accessible.

Conclusion

The outlook for React and its ecosystem remains bright, with a focus on boosting performance, refining the developer experience, and broadening capabilities. Upcoming features like Concurrent Mode, Suspense for Data Fetching, Server Components, and enhancements in React Native are set to provide developers with advanced tools for building dynamic and high-performance applications. As React continues its evolutionary path, it retains its status as an essential asset for developers and organizations striving to remain at the cutting edge of web and mobile application development.

Exploring experimental features and RFCs

Investigating experimental features and RFCs (Request for Comments) is a pivotal element in staying updated with the fast-paced advancements in the software development field. This practice involves examining and experimenting with new technologies and proposals that are currently under development or discussion. For developers, product strategists, and technology companies, this engagement is crucial for gaining insights into emerging trends, contributing to community-driven development, and fostering innovation in their own projects.

1. Significance of Experimental Features and RFCs

Experimental features and RFCs are at the forefront of technological advancements. They provide a window into possible future developments in programming languages, frameworks, and tools. By exploring these areas, professionals can:

- Anticipate and Adapt to Future Developments: Understanding experimental features enables foresight into the technological landscape's evolution, allowing for early adoption and strategic planning.

- Shape Technological Progress: Active participation in RFC discussions can influence the maturation and finalization of new features or standards.

- Maintain a Competitive Edge: Implementing experimental features in projects can lead to innovative solutions and a competitive advantage.

2. Delving into Experimental Features

Programming languages and frameworks often introduce experimental features, labeled as such due to their preliminary development stage.

- Trial and Feedback Contribution: Experimenting with these features and offering feedback to their developers is crucial for their refinement and standardization.

- Risk Consideration: While experimental features can offer unique capabilities, they also come with risks such as lack of long-term support or potential changes in future versions.

3. Understanding the RFC Process

RFCs are documents that suggest and elaborate on new features or modifications. They are a fundamental aspect of open-source software development, promoting community engagement and collective decision-making.

- Community Engagement: Participating in RFC discussions, commonly hosted on platforms like GitHub, offers valuable insights and the chance to impact technological advancements.

- Drafting RFCs: Developers can also propose new ideas or improvements through RFCs, contributing to the technological evolution.

4. Approaches to Exploring Experimental Features and RFCs

To effectively engage with experimental features and RFCs, it is advisable to:

- Stay Updated: Regularly monitor relevant repositories, forums, and community channels for announcements on new experimental features and active RFCs.

- Evaluate Impact: Assess how an experimental feature or RFC could potentially affect or enhance your work or projects.

- Team Collaboration: Discuss within your team the prospects of experimenting with new features and collectively provide feedback.

- Innovate Responsibly: Innovation is essential but should be balanced with the stability and dependability of your projects.

5. Navigating Challenges with Experimental Features

Engaging with experimental features can present challenges, including:

- Potential Instability and Bugs: Being in the development stage, these features might be unstable or contain bugs.

- Limited Documentation and Support: There may be scarce documentation or community support for experimental features.

- Complex Integration Processes: Incorporating experimental features into established systems can be complicated and involves certain risks.

Conclusion

Engaging with experimental features and RFCs is critical for software professionals aiming to stay ahead in the technology curve. This proactive approach not only offers insights into what the future of technology might hold but also provides an avenue to contribute to its development. While such explorations entail risks and challenges, they are essential for driving innovation and ensuring that one's skills and strategies remain relevant and advanced in the continually evolving technology sector.

Preparing for the future of front-end development

Staying ahead in the field of front-end development is vital for developers, businesses, and tech leaders in an increasingly digitalized world. The swift evolution of technology and changing user needs call for a forward-thinking stance in front-end development. Adaptation to emerging technologies, adherence to best practices, and continuous education are fundamental to mastering this dynamic domain.

1. Adoption of Contemporary Frameworks and Libraries

Front-end development is heavily influenced by modern frameworks and libraries such as React, Angular, Vue.js, and Svelte. Keeping pace with these technologies is essential:

- Deep Diving into Modern Frameworks: Acquiring proficiency in at least one modern framework is imperative, given their robust capabilities for building intricate user interfaces.

- Embracing Component-Based Design: Adopting the component-based design paradigm advocated by these frameworks enhances code reusability and maintainability.

2. Focus on Responsive and Adaptive Design

The diversity of device screen sizes and resolutions necessitates a strong emphasis on responsive and adaptive design:

- Advanced CSS and Layout Skills: Proficiency in advanced CSS, Flexbox, and Grid is crucial for crafting responsive designs.

- Mobile-First Design Approach: Prioritizing mobile-first design, which starts with designing for smaller screens, is becoming increasingly important.

3. Enhancing User Experience and Performance

User experience, greatly influenced by an application's performance, remains a core focus in front-end development:

- Performance Optimization Techniques: Learning methods to enhance website performance, including image optimization and efficient script loading, is key.

- Commitment to Accessibility: Upholding web accessibility standards is crucial for creating inclusive and universally accessible applications.

4. Effective State Management in Complex Applications

Proper state management is pivotal in managing the complexity of front-end applications:

- Exploring State Management Solutions: Familiarize yourself with tools like Redux, MobX, or React's Context API for more efficient state management in large applications.

- Distinguishing Local and Global State: Understanding when to employ local versus global state is important for optimal performance and maintainability.

5. Embracing SSR and SSG Technologies

Server-Side Rendering (SSR) and Static Site Generation (SSG), popularized by frameworks like Next.js and Nuxt.js, are becoming crucial for performance and SEO:

- Utilization of SSR and SSG: Grasping when to use SSR and SSG can significantly enhance load times and search engine visibility.

- Exploration of JAMstack: Delve into the JAMstack architecture, which combines modern web development practices with headless CMSs for more efficient and secure applications.

6. Progressive Web Apps (PWAs) Development

PWAs are increasingly vital for delivering an experience akin to native apps:

- Mastering PWA Fundamentals: Understand the core principles of PWAs, including the implementation of service workers and offline functionality.

- Developing Installable and Offline-Functional Applications: Focus on making web applications installable and functional offline.

7. Staying Current with JavaScript Developments

JavaScript continues to be the backbone of front-end development and is constantly evolving:

- Keeping Up with ECMAScript Updates: Stay informed about the latest ECMAScript standards and advancements.

- Incorporating Modern JavaScript Features: Adopt modern JavaScript features for more concise and effective coding.

8. The Rising Relevance of TypeScript

TypeScript is gaining traction for its ability to add strong typing to JavaScript:

- Learning TypeScript: Acquire skills in TypeScript to enhance code quality and maintainability, especially beneficial for larger projects.

9. Leveraging Development Tools and DevOps

Effective utilization of development tools and DevOps methodologies can greatly enhance development processes:

- Proficiency in Git: Develop expertise in version control with Git for collaborative codebase management.

- Implementing CI/CD: Learn to create continuous integration and continuous deployment pipelines for automated testing and deployment.

10. Anticipating Future Trends

The future might introduce yet-to-be-mainstream technologies and practices. Remain inquisitive and adaptable:

- Commitment to Lifelong Learning: Stay updated with the latest trends and forecasts in front-end development.

- Experimentation and Prototyping: Actively experiment with nascent technologies and frameworks as they emerge.

Conclusion

The trajectory of front-end development promises continued dynamism and innovation, driven by technological advancements and evolving practices. Developers who are proactive in learning and adapting to new technologies, and who embrace modern development methodologies, will be well-prepared for the future challenges and opportunities in front-end development. Prioritizing user experience, optimizing performance, and maintaining flexibility in the face of emerging trends are key to success in the ever-changing world of front-end development.

Conclusion

Summarizing the journey to pro-level React development

Advancing to a professional level in React development encompasses a trajectory of consistent learning, application of knowledge, and adaptation to the ever-changing realm of front-end technology. React, renowned for its capability to construct dynamic user interfaces, requires a deep understanding of its core concepts, advanced methodologies, and its expansive ecosystem. This journey is characterized by a foundational grasp of React, exploration of more sophisticated concepts, and keeping up-to-date with ongoing advancements.

1. Solidifying Core React Principles

The bedrock of becoming adept in React involves a thorough comprehension of its fundamental concepts:

- Grasping JSX: Mastery of JSX, React's syntax extension, is vital as it seamlessly integrates HTML with JavaScript.

- Component Development and Props Utilization: Skill in crafting reusable components and efficiently employing props to transmit data and handle events.

- State Management Proficiency: Profound understanding of managing component state using React's useState and the lifecycle of React components.

- Event Handling Mastery: Competence in managing user interactions within React components.

2. Exploring Advanced React Concepts

Progressing further entails delving into React's more complex functionalities:

- Leveraging Hooks and Functional Components: Utilizing hooks such as useEffect and creating custom hooks for side effects and state management in functional components.

- Context API for Global State: Employing the Context API to manage global application state and reduce prop drilling.

- Advanced Component Patterns: Implementing higher-order components and render props for logic sharing and reusability.

3. External State Management with Redux or MobX

Intricate applications call for an understanding of external state management systems like Redux or MobX:

- Redux Essentials: Acquiring knowledge of actions, reducers, store, and middleware for asynchronous operations.

- MobX for Reactive State Management: Investigating MobX for a more dynamic approach to state management.

4. Navigational Elements in React

Managing transitions between different views and states in applications:

- Utilizing React Router: Grasping React Router for handling SPA (Single Page Application) navigation and managing route parameters.

5. Proficiency in Testing and Debugging

Skills in testing and debugging are crucial for ensuring the reliability of React applications:

- Test Creation: Applying testing frameworks such as Jest and React Testing Library for unit and integration tests.

- Effective Debugging Techniques: Developing strategies for debugging React applications with tools like React Developer Tools.

6. Harnessing the React Ecosystem

The React ecosystem is vast, offering a range of tools and libraries:

- Implementing UI Libraries: Using UI libraries like Material-UI or Ant Design for standardized components.

- Patterns for Data Fetching: Understanding effective data fetching methods using hooks or libraries such as Axios or SWR.

7. Server-Side Rendering and Static Site Generation Techniques

Knowledge of SSR (Server-Side Rendering) and SSG (Static Site Generation), especially with frameworks like Next.js, is vital for optimizing performance and enhancing SEO.

8. Backend Integration Skills

Integration with backend services is a frequent requirement for React developers:

- Handling RESTful Services: Communicating with REST APIs via fetch or Axios.

- GraphQL Usage: Employing tools like Apollo Client or Relay for GraphQL services interaction.

9. Focusing on Performance Optimization

Expert React developers prioritize application performance enhancement:

- Implementing Code Splitting and Lazy Loading: Utilizing code splitting and lazy loading to reduce initial loading times.

- Applying Memoization and Optimization Strategies: Utilizing React.memo, useCallback, and useMemo for rendering performance optimization.

10. Staying Updated with React and Community Trends

Continuous learning and community involvement are crucial:

- React Updates Monitoring: Keeping track of the latest developments and features in React.

- Active Community Participation: Engaging in community forums, contributing to open-source projects, and attending relevant conferences.

11. Real-World Application of React Skills

Practical application of React skills in real-world projects is the true test of theoretical knowledge:

- Developing Personal or Open-Source Projects: Building personal projects or contributing to open-source initiatives to refine and expand React skills.

Conclusion

Reaching professional proficiency in React development is a journey marked by foundational knowledge, advanced technical skills, practical application, and continuous updates in the field. It involves mastering React's fundamental principles, venturing into its advanced aspects, and staying aligned with its ecosystem and the broader community's best practices. By committing to this pathway, developers can create interactive, efficient, and scalable web applications, positioning themselves at the forefront of modern web development.

Continuous learning and adapting to new trends

In today's swiftly evolving tech landscape, the commitment to ongoing education and keeping pace with emerging trends is critical for professionals to stay relevant and competitive. The technology sector is characterized by its rapid progress and continuous emergence of new tools and methodologies. This dynamic environment necessitates that those in the field remain well-informed, flexible, and proactive in their educational pursuits.

1. Imperative of Ongoing Education

The tech industry is defined by its rapid advancements and continual innovations. Staying updated with these developments is crucial for several reasons:

- Maintaining Skill Relevance: With the swift obsolescence of current technologies, continuous education is vital to ensure one's skills and knowledge stay pertinent and in demand.

- Fostering Innovation: Being knowledgeable about the latest technologies and trends enables professionals to introduce novel ideas and solutions in their work.

- Career Progression: Professionals dedicated to lifelong learning and skill enhancement are more likely to advance in their careers and seize new opportunities.

2. Embracing New Technological Trends

With the rise of technologies like AI, machine learning, cloud computing, and others transforming the industry, adapting to these trends is key and involves:

- Fundamental Understanding of Novel Technologies: Acquiring a basic grasp of new technologies, even those outside one's primary expertise, can offer a wider perspective on the industry's future.

- Real-World Application: Practically applying new technologies in projects or experiments aids in solidifying understanding and skillsets.

- Community Participation and Networking: Involvement in technology communities and events connects professionals with industry leaders and current trends.

3. Approaches to Lifelong Learning

Developing a lifelong learning strategy is crucial for effectively keeping up with the industry. This includes:

- Defining Learning Objectives: Set clear, realistic learning goals that align with personal interests and industry developments.

- Utilizing Digital Learning Platforms: Take advantage of online resources, courses, and tutorials, many of which are accessible at little to no cost, providing a flexible learning avenue.

- Learning Through Projects: Hands-on projects or contributions to open-source initiatives offer practical ways to apply and deepen new knowledge.

4. Overcoming Learning Challenges

Continuous learning, while essential, comes with challenges:

- Balancing Time: Managing learning alongside professional and personal commitments can be challenging.

- Navigating Information Abundance: The sheer volume of available information can be overwhelming. It's important to prioritize quality learning materials.

- Sustaining Motivation: Keeping up the motivation for self-directed learning can be tough. Setting small, achievable goals can help keep the learning momentum.

5. Employer's Role in Encouraging Education

Employers have a significant part in cultivating a culture of continuous learning:

- Access to Educational Resources: Providing employees with learning materials, training, and certification opportunities.

- Promoting Knowledge Exchange: Foster an environment that values and rewards sharing knowledge and collective learning.

- Support for Professional Growth: Employers that invest in their employees' professional development benefit from a more skilled and engaged workforce.

6. Adapting to Industry Shifts

Adapting to industry shifts involves not just learning about new trends but also understanding their practical applications:

- Exploratory Projects: Testing new technologies in a controlled setting can provide insights into their potential applications and limitations.

- Participation in Industry Events: Attending conferences and workshops is invaluable for gaining insights into how new trends are being applied in the industry.

7. Cultivating a Growth Mindset

A growth mindset is a cornerstone in the journey of continuous learning:

- Welcoming Challenges as Learning Opportunities: View challenges as chances to learn and grow rather than as barriers.

- Seeking Feedback and Self-Reflection: Regular feedback and reflection on learning experiences are crucial for identifying improvement areas.

Conclusion

In the technology field, continuous learning and adapting to emerging trends are indispensable for maintaining relevance, inspiring innovation, and advancing careers. By establishing defined learning objectives, leveraging a variety of educational resources, engaging in community interactions, and fostering a growth mindset, professionals can confidently navigate the ever-changing technological landscape. Additionally, employers play a significant role in supporting and promoting a culture of continuous learning and adaptability.

Contributing to the React community and beyond

Engaging with the React community, and contributing to open-source initiatives in general, is a fulfilling activity that not only enhances one's own skills but also benefits the broader development ecosystem. With React's status as a highly favored JavaScript library for interface development, its community is dynamic and extensive. Involvement in this community can vary, encompassing everything from direct code contributions to educational resource development, and offers immense value both to individual developers and the collective group.

1. The Value of Community Involvement

Participating in the React community is a meaningful way to contribute. It aids in:

- Enhancing the Framework: Contributions from the community aid in refining and expanding React, bolstering its capabilities and flexibility.

- Dissemination of Knowledge: Sharing insights through tutorials, articles, or presentations helps spread valuable information and practices.

- Professional Networking: Community interaction opens doors to connections with fellow developers and industry professionals.

2. Diverse Forms of React Community Contributions

There are several ways to contribute to the React community:

- Code Contributions: Enhancing the React codebase or its related projects (such as Redux, React Router) by resolving bugs, developing new features, or improving documentation.

- Developing Educational Material: Producing and sharing educational content like tutorials, articles, or conducting workshops and talks.

- Mentorship and Support: Active participation in discussion forums and channels, offering guidance and support to fellow React developers.

3. Contributions to Open Source React Projects

Contributions to open-source projects within the React ecosystem include:

- Adhering to Contribution Standards: Most projects have specific guidelines for contributors that are important to follow.

- Starting Small: Initial contributions can be minor, like rectifying documentation errors or simple bugs, before progressing to more significant contributions.

- Community Interaction: Engage with the project's community through discussions, issue tracking, and pull requests.

4. Organizing and Engaging in Community Events

Being involved in or organizing community events, such as meetups or conferences, is a significant way to contribute:

- Experience Sharing: Offering insights and experiences in talks or workshops can be motivational and educational for others.

- Building Connections: These events are prime opportunities for networking and forming connections within the React community.

5. Blogging and Creating React Content

Content creation, such as blogging or video production, plays a key role in knowledge sharing:

- Guides and Experience Sharing: Writing instructional content or sharing project case studies can assist others in learning from your experiences.

- Updates and Trends: Providing regular updates and insights on the latest in React and associated technologies.

6. Challenges in Community Participation

There are challenges associated with community involvement:

- Time Allocation: Balancing contributions with personal and professional responsibilities can be challenging.

- Handling Critique: Contributions, especially public ones, can sometimes draw criticism, necessitating resilience and a constructive approach.

7. Reputation Building within the Community

Steady contributions can lead to a notable reputation:

- Emphasis on Contribution Quality: The quality of contributions is more impactful than their frequency.

- Consistent Engagement: Regular, albeit small, contributions can help in establishing a recognizable presence in the community.

8. Advantages of Contributing

There are several benefits to contributing to the React community:

- Skill Development: Tackling various projects and challenges enhances technical skills.

- Career Advancement: Contributions can lead to professional recognition and advancement.

- Personal Fulfillment: Contributing to the community offers personal gratification and the joy of seeing one's work benefit others.

Conclusion

Engaging in the React community is a rewarding venture that fosters both personal development and communal advancement. It's a journey of continuous learning, sharing, and both personal and professional growth. Whether through coding, content creation, or active participation in discussions and events, each contribution is valuable. As the React ecosystem continues to evolve, the contributions of its community members play a crucial role in shaping its trajectory.